P³

Look, Mom, I'm on TV!
Winter X Games at Snow Summit, 1997.

ISBN 0-06-076179-2

P³

↓   ↓   ↓

PIPES, PARKS, AND POWDER

TODD RICHARDS*

*WORLD CHAMPION SNOWBOARDER
Weltmeister Snowboarder
Campeón Snowboarder Del Mundo
Champion Snowboarder Du Monde

_WITH
ERIC BLEHM

10 ReganBooks
Celebrating Ten Bestselling Years
An Imprint of HarperCollinsPublishers

Page 239 constitutes a continuation of this copyright page.

A hardcover edition of this book was published in 2003 by ReganBooks, an imprint of HarperCollins Publishers.

First paperback edition published 2004.

Designed by Nancy Singer and Richard Ljoenes

The Library of Congress has cataloged the hardcover edition as follows:

Richards, Todd, 1969–
  P3 : pipes, parks, and powder / Todd Richards with Eric Blehm.—1st ed.
    287 p. : ill. (some col.); 23 cm.
  ISBN 0-06-056040-1 (alk. paper)
      Richards, Todd, 1969–Snowboarders—United States—Biography.
  GV857.S57R53 2003
  796.939 / 092 B 22   2003056706

  ISBN 0-06-076179-2 (pbk.)

04 05 06 07 08 ❖/RRD 10 9 8 7 6 5 4 3 2 1

This book is dedicated to three souls who
lived their lives to the fullest in the pipes,
parks, powder, and beyond:

CRAIG KELLY
JEFF ANDERSON
TRISTAN PICOT

R.I.P.

CONTENTS

P_THREE /

INTRODUCTION/ Everyone's Dream / ix

1 PUNK RUNT/ Dropping Into Life / 1
2 TOO COLD TO SKATE/ 32 Degrees and Riding / 27
3 THE RIDE NOT TAKEN/ Career Daze / 45
4 ONE-TRACK MIND/ My Boarderline Obsession / 63
5 SHRED AND DESTROY/ Snowskaters on Ice / 75
6 TEAM MOM, DAD, AND SIMS/ Emotional Rollercoaster / 103
7 SNOW JOB: OBJECTIVE/ To Be the World's Best Snowboarder / 117
8 SNOWBOARDING/ The International Language / 135
9 PIPE DRAGON/ Tricks of Fury / 147
10 RIP, SPIN, AND WIN/ Getting My Game On / 161
11 RAMEN NOT REQUIRED/ The Salad Days of Snowboarding / 181
12 THE OLYMPIC HYPE MACHINE/ The Longest Winter / 191
13 JIBBERS AND JUMPERS/ There's No Style Like Slopestyle / 217
14 THE THREE S's/ Surf, Skate, Snow / 235
15 OVERALL GUY/ Pipes, Parks, and Rails / 245
16 LOVE, AMERICAN STYLE/ Don't Choke the Chicken / 249
17 BOARD OF THE RINGS/ The Sequel / 257
18 FULL CIRCLE/ Life, Death, and Rebirth / 269

EPILOGUE/ Life Goes On / 283
ACKNOWLEDGMENTS / 285
PHOTOGRAPHY CREDITS / 289

Unleashing the Wet Cat at the Westbeach Classic in 1998.

_TODD RICHARDS /
LOCATION: Breckenridge, CO
PHOTO: Rob Gracie

Gearing up for the '98 Olympics at
Breck's Peak 9 pipe, December 1997.

EVERYONE'S DREAM

Then we entered the Olympic stadium in Nagano, Japan.

Nothing could have prepared me for that moment. I was totally screwing around, not taking anything seriously, but when I walked into that arena, it just gripped me in so many ways. I was overwhelmed with American pride. I saw the flag at the front of the line of the American team, and the crowd was roaring like nothing I'd ever heard. Every nationality and every country I've ever heard of was there—we felt like we were all one big team. The camaraderie got me right in the throat. Borders and politics melted away. North Korea and South Korea walked out together. I forgot about who was warring with whom. I forgot about all the bad in the world.

Then the speeches began, first in Japanese and then French and English. I hung on to every single word, even the ones I didn't understand. A hypnotic numbness set in: I realized I was on the inside of the Olympics, not on the outside looking in. Then, as it went on, I forgot about my nationality. I forgot about the competition and that I was a favorite to win the halfpipe event for the first American Olympic Snowboard team. I even forgot that I was a snowboarder. For a few minutes, I was just a human being and part of something so much bigger.

_The calm before the storm: me in 1970.

PUNK RUNT/
DROPPING INTO LIFE

I was conceived when my parents, Ken and Patricia Richards, got busy on a weekend ski trip to Wildcat Mountain, New Hampshire, during the spring of 1969. I entered the world nine months later on December 28, 1969—the exact due date the doctor had calculated. According to my mom, that was the last predictable thing I ever did.

My parents were living in the tiny house in Worcester, Massachusetts, that my mom bought when she was seventeen. She was a modern woman and way ahead of her time for the sixties, mainly because of her mother, an entrepreneur who owned a hair salon where my mom started working when she was still in high school. By the time she graduated, she was pulling long hours and doing all the crazy beehive hair-dos. That's how she qualified for the mortgage.

My mom met my dad, a leather-goods salesman, on a blind date, and they got married in 1966 when she was nineteen and he was twenty-three. They moved into her house, and two years after the marriage they took that trip to Wildcat Mountain. Spring was in the air. They named me Brandt Todd Richards, Brandt after mom's mom's maiden name. The only person to ever call me by my first name was my third-grade teacher, Mrs. LaPearle.

The house where I was born
in Worcester, Massachusetts.

Both driven professionals, my parents found out quickly enough that juggling work and family life was a full-time job—plus overtime. In order to give me the attention they thought I deserved, they decided I wouldn't be having any brothers or sisters. Way ahead of her time once again, my mom volunteered to "get that taken care of," which was absolutely fine by my father, who didn't like the idea of anybody messing around down around his family jewels with a sharp scalpel.

As an only child, I had to be creative in order to entertain myself. My imagination was out of control. It wasn't enough to play with plastic dinosaurs; I had to go out in the woods and become a T-rex. I was obsessed with dinosaurs, and then I discovered Godzilla and G.I. Joe, both of which became obsessions of mine. Halloween was my favorite holiday because I could dress up as scary as possible and rampage the neighborhood behind the guise of something I definitely wasn't: Early on that was monsters, then ninjas, and then the cat burglar look. In reality I was a runt, and I was young for my grade. I started kindergarten when I was four and was a bit immature in social situations.

In 1974, we moved from the city to a suburban town called Paxton. Our new place was a New England–style farmhouse built in the twenties, and my parents converted the entire back of the house into a beauty salon named Hair Unlimited. It was a thriving business with three or four hairdressers, and women would drive for hours for appointments with my mom and her staff. She was the shit as far as hairdressers went. The only downside to the business was that our house constantly smelled like perm solution, chemicals, and hair products. It stunk.

Mom and Dad getting hitched in 1966.

My aunt or grandparents used to watch me after school when I was really little. Once Hair Unlimited got rolling and I'd been in grammar school for a while, my mom felt confident enough to leave me on my own until she closed up the shop or my dad came home from work. I'd get off the bus and wave at her while she put curlers in some lady's hair. Then I'd make a high-energy, sugar-based afterschool snack and wreak havoc on my room, the house, or the nearby woods. I was just a step above a latchkey kid.

Around 1975 Hollywood was cooking up two things that would have a major impact on my life: Some guy named George Lucas started writing a science fiction story called Star Wars, which would eventually lead to one of the most embarrassing moments of my life, and Peter Benchley teamed up with Steven Spielberg to bring *Jaws* to the big screen. I begged my parents to let me see *Jaws,* but they refused, pulling the usual, "You're too young." *Whatever,* I thought. I was six.

By the time I was eight, my parents had become familiar with my imagination but weren't yet willing to accept that I wasn't like other kids. My mom thought it was cute that I liked Halloween better than Christmas, but she had no idea I was a closet monster-movie fanatic. I'd sneak downstairs late at night to watch horror movies, and then torment my parents by crawling into bed with them. After repeated occurrences of my chronic nightmare syndrome, they figured out that I loved to scare myself. So, it was probably a good idea, considering how much they liked the beach, that they pulled rank on the whole *Jaws* thing.

In the summer of 1978, we took one of our annual pilgrimages to the Cape with

My monster phase.   Increasing my toy collection. It was great being an only child at Christmas.

At the Cape, before *Jaws* ruined the beach for me.

my cousins. I was a short, underweight eight-year-old kid who made up for a lack of physique by making believe I was Godzilla, stomping through the shore break like a 500-foot-tall radioactive lizard. Sometimes, I'd turn into the six-million-dollar runt, running through the shallow water, bending seaweed as if it were steel, and hucking the cooler all over the beach—all in super slow motion with lots of sound effects. In deeper water, I got a little edgy. I still hadn't seen *Jaws*, but I could sense the quiet before an attack. I knew it was coming. It always did. The big kids would get bored and they'd eventually need something to play with. Me. I was the most convenient "thing" available, my size was conducive to the feared head dunking accompanied by an inhalation of salt water. I'd come up coughing and barfing just in time for the biggest wave of the day to knock me off my feet and roll me along the bottom, pounding my micro-body toward shore until I could crawl out onto the sand.

In the late seventies, there weren't a half-dozen Blockbuster Video stores in every town. Both Beta and VHS home movie machines were cutting edge, and if you had one, you were living large. It took a couple years for movies to make it from the big screen to living rooms, and when I heard one of my friend's parents owned *Jaws*, I made immediate plans to visit that weekend. My love of horror overruled my phobia of water. Actually, I didn't really put the two together. Shark. Water. I never was very good at math. I was nine years old and had grown up on a steady diet of imaginary things with big teeth, but not realistic animals that actually exist. Fate almost saved me when my friend broke the news that we couldn't watch the movie because there were boobs in it. Full-frontal nudity meant nothing to me, but the challenge of out-smarting his parents only strengthened my resolve to commando downstairs late that night and traumatize myself for life. I watched the entire thing, and by the time it was over, drowning seemed pretty mellow. Getting eaten by a submarine with teeth was my new horror.

In 1977, my mom took me to see *Star Wars*. Even though Darth Vader scared the hell out of most kids, I thought he was just misunderstood. Laser blasters, light sabers, and good battling evil in outer space captivated me. If a recruiter from the Rebel Alliance had knocked on my door, I would have signed up without hesitation. In fact, I dreamed of such a moment. Anything and everything *Star Wars* became an obsession. I organized make-believe battles in my bedroom, in my backyard, in the backseat of the car during road trips. Though dinosaurs, Godzilla, and army men still held a special place in my heart, I began to clear space on the shelves in my room for a Wookie family of my own.

Not far from our house, in Princeton, there was a local "mountain" called Mount Wachusett, which is where my parents went to get in shape for the real ski trips to Vermont. That puny hill was the place I first slid on snow when I was three by standing in front of my dad on his skis. As I got older, my skiing got better—meaning faster—but I was still more into eating french fries in the lodge. My version of skiing, or schussing (what the traditional East Coast skiers called skiing), consisted of going as fast as I possibly could without turning. The only reason I turned was to avoid hitting schuss mogul men (what I called skiers). I rarely schussed alone—I almost always had a couple *Star Wars* action figures in my jacket pocket.

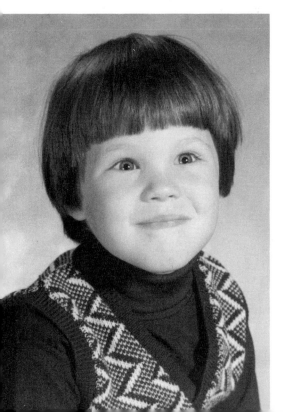

Second grade (nice East Coast sweater).

The three years following the release of *Star Wars* dragged by painfully slow. Finally, in May 1980, *The Empire Strikes Back* hit theaters. I was eleven years old and Boba Fett, the bounty hunter, was my hero. As I approached eighth grade, I began to realize how cool it was to have the kind of freedom I had around my house. Most of my friend's moms stayed at home. We didn't have a sit-down-for-dinner-together family, and I liked it that way. It's not that we didn't love and appreciate one another. On the contrary, we were just comfortable with our lives. My dad sold leather goods, my mom made people beautiful, and I was being groomed for future accomplishments like Little League All-Star, All-State hockey goalie, football quarterback, and prom king.

Yeah right. I was the kid who got picked last for any team sport, was a liability in football, and made a better hockey puck than player. My dad practically had to drag me to the fields to play Little League, where I'd sit down in the outfield and daydream. I hated it so much, he eventually gave up.

By the time I hit eighth grade, Mount Wachusett became more of a hangout than a place to go skiing. Since my dad couldn't get me to play organized sports, he became a chaperone for the Paxton Middle School weekend ski trips. We'd take buses from the school parking lot and I'd bring my skis, but I wouldn't get any serious schussing in. I'd do the mandatory lift ride up with my dad, then ditch him and head straight to the lodge with my friends Matt Swanson and Darryl Clark. We'd hang out, eat french fries, and look at girls who didn't like us.

Dad used to dress me up in goalie gear and practice slap shots at me in the basement.

Darryl Clark, my childhood
Star Wars pal.

Matt had been my friend since we were in grammar school. We clicked because he was also into *Star Wars,* monster movies, and the British science fiction show *Doctor Who*. We always ended up out in the woods with our blowguns or throwing stars—aspiring ninjas, the closest thing to a Jedi Knight I could imagine. We even had the black outfits and split-toe booties.

Darryl was my primary *Star Wars* friend. We'd known each other since sixth grade and used to build elaborate bases for our *Star Wars* figures out of dirt, sticks, and tree bark. We constructed tunnels, bunkers, and booby traps for unsuspecting Storm Troopers. So when Matt, Darryl, and I got together over fries and hot chocolate in the Wachusett lodge, our conversations usually centered around *Star Wars* trivia. Skiing was more a pitiful, geeky social calling than a sport.

One Sunday afternoon in January 1983, I was over at Matt Swanson's house when my mom called unexpectedly. I thought she was going to ask me to come home early. It was way worse. "There was a really bad accident this morning," she told me in a shaky voice. "Your friend Darryl was killed."

My grandfather had died when I was in sixth grade, but "losing" a friend when I was twelve years old seemed even worse. I'd been playing with Darryl only days

Trying to increase my height in eighth grade.

before, and that made it even stranger and sadder. After my mom's call, I just wanted to go home, and that was where I learned the details: Darryl had been hit by a car while he was delivering newspapers. The death dealt a huge blow to the community and, being a small town, a lot of parents came together to support Darryl's folks. It was heavy, and I went to school the next day not knowing what to expect.

When I got there, it was obvious everybody knew. All these girls were crying, and it made me angry because they were the same girls who made fun of Darryl and me. They never gave him the time of day. I felt like lashing out, "What right do you have to cry? You didn't even know him. You didn't even want to know him." But instead I kept my mouth shut, didn't shed a tear, and stewed about it. I was very analytical and tried to dissect why they were crying. I'd watch them and doodle and wonder if they were just crying to fit in because it was the right thing to do. I eventually concluded that they were just trying to be cool. It never occurred to me that they might have been crying because they felt bad that they had made fun of him. I was bitter and couldn't believe that they were as bummed as I was, or that their sorrow was genuine.

I attended the wake, and what had been heavy got heavier. It was an open casket, and it was harsh. I don't think it's right to see someone like that, especially someone so young. But it was closure. It showed me what death was. It made me pull my emotions inward, because all I did during the entire wake was try to maintain.

After the funeral, I went home and kicked it with my toys. About a week later, my dad showed up in the middle of the day, right after I got out of school, and he broke down and told me how much he loved me. I hugged him and he started crying. I was this puny little kid patting my dad on the back, telling him, "I love you too, Dad." I was a rock. The way I dealt with death was simple: I didn't deal with it.

Darryl's parents became friends with my parents and, years later, after I started snowboarding competitively, they followed my career. They even took up snowboarding. Sometimes I wonder if this was because they knew Darryl would have gotten into snowboarding also. He was so young when he died, but it is really, really cool to know that these people have a connection with me that I think kind of keeps the spirit of their son alive.

The rest of my eighth-grade year was all about waiting for *Return of the Jedi* to premiere. Life was mostly back to normal when it finally hit theaters in May. All *Star Wars* enthusiasts were excited about the movie, but what separated the fans from the fanatics, i.e. nerds, was the sheer magnitude of the occasion. In my opinion, opening day should have been declared a national holiday.

Around that same time, I also discovered the gore magazine *Fangoria*, which alternated with karate and ninja magazines as my favorite literature. My toy collection continued to expand with doubles of almost every action figure and most of the vehicles—two Millennium Falcons, two Tie-Fighters, two X-Wing fighters, you name it. I alternated between playing with G.I. Joe and *Star Wars*, and concentrating on my ninja training. I took one karate class—the master was like the "sweep the leg, Johnny" guy from *Karate Kid*, psycho dojo from hell—and was over it. Instead, I stalked imaginary bad guys in the woods, assassinated numerous trees with blow darts, and honed my lethal aim with an impressive collection of throwing stars. As summer approached, I made a new friend in my grade named Mark Finneran. He was a supersmart kid from a supersmart family, and he got me hooked on Dungeons and Dragons. His older brother and sister dressed differently—à la a Flock of Seagulls—

and listened to The Clash, The Misfits, Dead Kennedys, and Black Flag. I liked their year-round Halloween attire and drew everything I saw on their album covers on my book covers and notebooks. My mom wasn't too pleased when she noticed that I'd drawn in black magic marker "Suicidal Tendencies" with a skull and upside-down cross, but she brushed it off as a phase. My dad tried to ignore it because it aggravated him too much. We didn't really fight or anything, but we weren't on the same page. He certainly couldn't understand me. I couldn't even really understand myself. I was just a weird kid trying to figure out life.

Toddler

Wachusett High was a big high school in the Worcester area. It was a conglomerate of four rural middle schools whose students merged together as a cluster of hormones with new friendships to forge and identities to establish. I was the kid who must have gotten on the wrong bus. I was five foot zero and looked like I was still in sixth or seventh grade. I scurried from class to class, and at lunchtime I found my friends—safety in numbers. Matt and Mark, like most of the student population, had undergone a transformation over the summer. Deeper voices, taller, bigger: Everything that hadn't happened to me.

Soon enough, I discovered that Wachusett High was divided into two distinctive groups: You were a jock and into Van Halen, or you were a hippie and listened to the Doors and Grateful Dead. There were subcategories, like the band or drama kids, and the sub-subcategories consisting of punkers or nerds. Below that, the lowest of the low, the no-category kids. I was somewhere between the no-category and nerd category, a flyweight looking for a place to land.

I'd had it pretty wired at my old school and, well, it's weird how you're in eighth grade and it's perfectly acceptable to play with toys, then you have one summer to wean yourself off all that shit, and—bam!—you're a high school freshman. Nobody told me that playing with toys was unacceptable behavior for a high schooler.

One day in October 1983, my freshman year, I'd gotten home from school, grabbed my toys, and gone into the woods behind my house to re-create the battle of Endor. I had a bunch of Ewoks, Imperial Walkers, Storm Troopers, Han Solo, Princess Leah, Imperial Speeder Bikes—the whole entourage from *Return of the Jedi*. I was out there crawling around in the dirt and leaves, doing my best to infiltrate the secret Imperial base—you know, blowing up Ewoks, knocking over Walkers, hucking Storm Troopers in the air—when I realized that three pretty girls from my grade were watching me from the trail that ran behind my house. They were laughing. For a brief

Freshman year (no, seriously).

instant, I thought they were stoked on my collection or maybe laughing with me, not at me. But I got the picture real fast, and it got back to the entire school.

It was horrible. I was razzed almost immediately. From the minute I jumped on the bus the next morning, I heard, "There's baby Todd." "Did you bring your toys for show and tell?" "Toys are for toddlers." Crap like that. By the end of the day, it had mutated from Baby Todd to Baby Toddler to just Toddler—the worst nickname in the world for a freshman. After school that day, the realization hit me that I wasn't a kid anymore and that I had to grow up. I came down with a cold that night and faked it for three days so I wouldn't have to face anybody. When I got back to school, they were already on to the next victim. My razzing, which had been my fifteen minutes of fame, was over.

Excalibur, Only with Wheels

My friends and I naturally grew apart: Matt started getting heavily into military stuff. Mark was into being weird, and he started going Goth and freaking the freaks out. Mark and his siblings had made an impression on me with their punk rock attitudes about life.

Too scared to drop in.

They were all confident in themselves, something I aspired to, but I wasn't there yet. School wasn't fun. I just wanted each day to end so I could go home and play—in private.

Then something magical happened my freshman year. I'd been hanging out with another freshman living near me who soon became my geek counterpart. Joey Nanigan was into the stuff I liked, and he had no problem secretly playing with toys, plus he was an acclaimed roller skater who won competitions at the local skating rink. Jay, his alter-ego cousin, was our age and was the stereotypical bad kid. Jay owned a rifle that shot bullets and a motorcycle. He was punk rock and smoked cigarettes. He was a no-bullshit kid who either liked you or didn't. He was straight-up Kelly from the Bad News Bears.

During Christmas break, Joey and I went to Jay's house so he could roller skate around the basement while I hung out and attempted to be cool. It was freezing outside, so Jay had built a little banked ramp against a wall and was doing kick turns on a skateboard. Joey laced up his skates and roller-moon-walked around the basement. I sat there and flipped through one of Jay's *Playboy*s. After a while, Jay threw a copy of *Thrasher* magazine at me, and that introduced me to the world of skateboarding.

At school, Jay was way more popular than Joey and I, and he was the coolest person I knew, so it wasn't long before I began emulating him. The first step would be getting a skateboard. A good skateboard was an expensive investment, like seventy dollars, and I knew that my parents would require that I prove I was really into skateboarding before they bought one. I figured that to prove this, I actually had to try skateboarding.

I remembered seeing one of my neighbors, a nineteen-year-old kid named Dave Carlson, skateboarding in his driveway during the summer. He had graduated from high school the year before, and I thought maybe he'd gotten sick of skateboarding and tossed it in his closet. It was snowing outside, and I walked over to his house, knocked on his door, and asked him, "Hey Dave, whatever happened to that skateboard you used to have?"

"I threw it away," he answered, and my heart sank. Then he said, "It's in one of the woodpiles."

The Carlsons were famous for the woodpiles they kept in their backyard. I looked out across their property, and the piles seemed like small white mountains—enormous piles of assorted lumber, firewood, discarded furniture—with all sorts of things poking out through a foot of snow, along with brush and god knows what else. "Can I have it if I can find it?" and Dave said, "Fuck, I don't care. Sure."

I trudged through the snow, picked one of the mountains, climbed up, and dug in. I cannot emphasize enough how much crap there was in those woodpiles. After fifteen minutes of searching, I knew the effort was futile, but I gave myself five more minutes anyway. I moved a few sticks and an old chair, shook some snow off a tree branch, and underneath was a fricking skateboard! The wheels were caught on something down deep, but I eventually yanked it out and held it up in the air like Excalibur.

The skateboard was a filthy old Kryptonics deck, weathered and delaminating, with greasy Independent Trucks and muddy OJ wheels. I was happier than a pig in shit, mainly because I knew Independent Trucks were the best to have. At home, I discovered the wheels barely rolled, but that didn't matter. I brushed off some of the grime, put some motor oil on the wheels, and I had a skateboard.

Jay's basement was the venue for a comedy on wheels. I would push straight ahead until I ran into a wall, stop, turn around, set the skateboard down, and hit the next wall. I wasn't confident having wheels under my feet, but I managed to survive without breaking anything.

Eventually Joey toned down his roller-skating habit, probably because of Jay's relentless ridicule that climaxed when he threatened to label Joey a pussy if he didn't start skateboarding. Joey showed up at the basement the following week with a shiny new skateboard and no roller skates. Thus was born my dysfunctional skateboarding posse.

When he wasn't skating, Jay listened to punk rock, ripped perfectly good clothes, and wrote on his jeans with magic markers. Behind Jay's back, Joey and I logged in a great deal of Dungeons and Dragons, but eventually I matured and started ripping my clothes, too. I returned to school after Christmas break my freshman year with a new outlook on life. I felt like I was part of something. With that new sense of belonging came spiky hair, safety pins in place of buttons, and *Thrasher* magazine stickers on my punk-deco three-ring binders. Combine that with my "Toddler" stature, and you get a bad strategy for blending in.

Soon after I'd discovered the punk rock world, I began to experiment with my hair. No mohawks or anything like that, just a more subdued version of whatever Jay was running. One time Jay and I sneaked into my mom's salon and did a suicide-mix with her chemicals to turn his hair purple. My mom wasn't stoked, but she softened up the second she realized I was into "doing my hair." She was all over that.

Hair Unlimited became my laboratory, and my mom was my mentor. She taught me the right techniques and correct mixtures, and then she pretty much left me alone to experiment with the best chemicals available. Jay had previously bleached his hair Billy Idol white. I waited a couple weeks so it didn't seem like I was copying him, then gave myself about twenty-five applications of bleach. That's how many it took to fry my dark-brown hair to an appropriate shade of nuclear white. In doing so, I melted my scalp. Second-degree burns, scabs, and a month of blizzard dandruff were not worth the image. Being that punk was too painful.

In late February 1984, Jay built a quarterpipe in his garage that became our new hangout and first skate spot. My tendency to be obsessive fueled my skateboarding progression, and soon I was skating full speed toward the quarterpipe and riding high onto the wall of the ramp. After a few falls, I began doing kick turns, just like Jay, and riding back down into the garage without hurting myself. When Joey and I both mastered this simple trick, we thought we were pretty cool. We memorized *Thrasher* magazines cover to cover and considered ourselves a tiny extension of the glamorous world of professional skateboarding portrayed in those pages. Being the default "king of the dipshits," Jay knew a lot of older skaters and introduced us to a whole new scene.

Tom "Twistah" Putnam was a local hero who had a halfpipe in his backyard. He had graduated high school and, by all accounts, was the coolest person in Paxton. Skateboarders in the Worcester area gauged themselves against Twistah. In addition to his skills, he was connected and knew all the East Coast heavies: Metal Man, Fred Smith, Sean McClean, Jeff Thompson, and Jake Phelps, who were the famous skaters during that period on the East Coast. They were as big as Tony Hawk and Steve Caballero were on the West Coast, so we felt like we were rubbing elbows with celebrities. Still, skating was an underground derelict hobby. It wasn't huge like it is today, but that didn't make them any less famous in our eyes. They were sponsored, and their photos were in *Thrasher* magazine, which gave them instant credibility. It was testament to Twistah's ramp-building skills that these guys regularly converged at his backyard ramp, which is where I first saw them all skate during the spring of my freshman year.

We showed up at Twistah's one afternoon and were in awe of the skills we witnessed. Even Jay was out of his league: He could talk the talk, but he waited until the ramp was empty to hop in and start pumping the walls, throwing in kick turns every once in a while. I waited until everybody had gone home—even Jay and Joey—and then I skated the ramp fakie (without dropping in) after Twistah had gone inside. I started in the flat bottom of the ramp and pumped back and forth to get up on the walls. Going back and forth on that ramp for the first time felt like I was flying. I didn't want to stop.

Although the older skaters tormented us, our crew became a fixture at the ramp. Of course Jay was the first one with balls enough to drop in from the top. Joey did it next. I was too scared. For weeks I couldn't meet the challenge, and to add insult to injury, everyone laughed at my gear, too. I was still skating on the piece of shit board from the woodpile. That board became my crutch, my excuse, and my savior, all balled up into one.

My parents have always been neat freaks; my dad kept his car notoriously clean. This didn't bode well for my skateboard's future. It was disintegrating and just plain gross, leaving behind wood sludge and grease residue everywhere it went. I insisted on hauling it with me everywhere. I'd practice in the parking lot if my mom went into the grocery store, or at the ice rink where my dad would sometimes drag me when he played hockey on weekends. Eventually, I talked my parents into buying me a new skateboard. I'd proved skateboarding wasn't just a temporary thing and, truth be told, my dad couldn't stomach having my filthy board in his car anymore. Not even in the trunk.

By this point, I was pretty well tied in to my group of friends, so any time my parents could actually get me to grace them with my presence for more than a couple hours was cause for celebration. It was like a family vacation when the three of us drove down to Beacon Hill Skates in Boston for the big purchase. I had memorized a list of exactly what I wanted: Kryptonics deck with OJ wheels and Independent Trucks. We walked up to the counter and my mom said to me, "Tell the man what you want." The "man," who was probably a high schooler himself, listened to my dream list. "Okay," he said, "we can order that and it'll be here in about two weeks."

This was fine with my parents. After all, that meant another field trip to the city. I, on the other hand, was like, "What? Order it? I can't get it right now?!" In a panic, I glanced around the shop, pointed at a pre-assembled skateboard hanging on the wall, and said, "Okay, then, I'll take that." The Sure Grip High Voltage board was complete with trucks, wheels, griptape, big beefy plastic rails, and a tail guard. I had no idea it was a pre-fab P.O.S. (piece of shit) beginner board. My parents added a helmet and knee and elbow pads to the purchase, and I showed up the next day at Twistah's ramp with my new setup. Everybody laughed, but I didn't care. So I had the crappiest setup in the world—at least it was a brand-new crappiest setup in the world.

During sessions in Twistah's backyard, skateboarding magazines were always being passed around. An older kid I thought was really good brought a copy of *TransWorld SKATEboarding* over to me—I thought he was going to show me a cool picture or something. Instead, he pointed out that Sure Grip had a two-inch-by-two-inch black-and-white advertisement in the back of the magazine, whereas Schmitt Stix, Powell, Kryptonics, and all the other "cool" brands had spreads or full-page color ads. *Thanks for pointing that out,* I thought and kept on skating.

I went as much as possible, oftentimes alone so I could practice at my own pace. At the end of my freshman year of high school, I still hadn't dropped into a ramp from the top. I always started at the bottom and s-l-o-w-l-y worked my way up. It would take forever for me to get to the top, so I was a target for incessant heckling like, "Learn to drop in!" or "Drop in or go home!" or the ever-popular "Pussy!"

Hanging out at Twistah's ramp introduced me to a world I hadn't known existed. I respected the guys who skated there and despite their heckling, had the feeling they respected me, too. Between the insults to and comments about the "little guy," I'd receive an occasional compliment. Those pats on the back were what I lived for. They're what got me pulling basic tricks—frontside airs, backside airs, and shaky handplants—all of which I learned from watching the older kids and studying the magazines.

The first *TransWorld SKATEboarding* magazine I ever bought was an issue with Kevin Staab on the cover doing a tuck-knee frontside air at some ramp in Arizona. My parents had become fully aware of what they thought was my newest "fad." To show their support, my mom took that issue to one of those screen-print T-shirt shops and had the guy airbrush the cover onto a T-shirt with the words TRANSWORLD SKATEBOARDER stenciled underneath, which was just beat. I was like, "Ahhh, Mom?" but I wore it. Hell yeah, I wore it. All the time.

Putting My Mind to Something

Early in the summer of 1984, at the end of my freshman year, Twistah put together a contest in his backyard. Jay and I showed up at Twistah's house, and there were cars parked everywhere with license plates as far away as New York and New Jersey. Walking into the scene, we hooked up with Rob LaVigne, who was also fourteen and a guy I'd known forever. Rob was a diplomat: His friendships crossed all different borders. He was an athlete and hung with the jocks, but he was also a good skateboarder who slummed it with us. He was a walking contradiction in that he looked like a conserva-

Showing off at a family BBQ, junior year.

tive East Coast prep but carried a skateboard. He kept an open mind and had a vision of things to come (as I would soon learn).

The tricks being pulled on Twistah's ramp didn't seem possible. Rob, Jay, and I were the youngest ones there, but we'd all been semi-accepted into some of the older skaters' circles because we tried hard, and they liked watching us get worked. Most of those guys were upcoming high school seniors on a steady weed-and-beer diet. When the bong-brothers saw me milling around in the crowd with my skateboard, they gave me a rundown of the rules for the weekend, the most relevant being, "You can only skate the ramp if you drop in."

For those of you who haven't had the privilege of dropping into a nine-foot-high vert ramp, let me try and explain the anxiety of your first time. It's kind of like jumping out of an airplane—a leap of faith, where you have to rely solely on your own skills, not a parachute, to see you through to safety. You hear comments like, "You're wearing pads. Just go for it." No. No. No. Let me explain. Climb on top of a nine-foot-tall ladder, making sure you're wearing a helmet and kneepads. Now do a belly flop or, better yet, a swan dive onto a piece of plywood. No problem, right? Suck it up, tough guy.

Well, I had absolutely no intention of skateboarding the weekend of Twistah's competition. Then I saw her in the crowd. The cute red-haired girl from school whom I'd had a crush on all year but never talked to. In fact, a lot of chicks had shown up for this backyard skate party, mostly girls who were sick of their jock boyfriends and wanted to rebel by hanging out with derelict skateboarders. I locked my tractor beam on her and got close, really close, danger close. She locked eyes with me and I had a momentary fourteen-year-old fantasy: Me impressing her with my skateboarding skills; her saying, "Wanna make out?" Back in reality, she glanced down at my Sure Grip High Voltage board and smiled. The horror. Now I had to deliver.

What happened next was a pheromone-induced bout of insanity. It was like one of those near-death experiences in which you see yourself lying on the operating table before the doctors bring you back to life . . . only I wasn't on an operating table. I was watching myself climb the ladder to the top of the vert ramp. I adjusted my pads, tightened the strap on my helmet, and, with completely unprecedented confidence, set down my skateboard tail on the coping, just like I'd watched all the good skaters do a thousand times. With a single glance to make sure the girl was watching, I leaned forward—and nearly killed myself.

Not really understanding the process, I leaned too far forward over my board and free-fell to the bottom of the ramp. Even with a helmet on, I think I got a concussion. Everybody laughed and I was crushed, but I was also pissed. I made a pact with myself then that I wasn't going to get picked on anymore. I was determined to be better than all of them. That was the first time I ever put my mind to anything.

That night I had a serious adult-to-adult conversation with my parents. I explained to them my future career plan to become a professional skateboarder so I could get free T-shirts and stickers. I stressed that I needed the best possible equipment in order to fully capitalize on this goal. I backed up my claims by showing them success stories in the magazines, and then I dazzled them with a well-researched request for a start-up kit on this path to success: "Mom, Dad, I need a Zorlac Pusshead deck with G&S YoYo wheels, and Indy trucks."

My parents had often explained to me the difference between the words "need" and "want." In this case they threw me a curve ball and asked, "What's wrong with the other one we just got you?" Even though they understood the importance of top-of-the-line ski equipment, a skateboard was just a skateboard, and if it still rolled and wasn't broken in two, it was fine.

I proceeded to skate that board into the ground for more than two months. I would skate down hills and grind the shit out of the tail in an attempt to kill it, but the damn thing refused to die. Before the summer was over, however, my parents relented to the purchase of the Zorlac, in part because I'd displayed that I knew the value of a dollar by being a paper boy and selling the hell out of both the morning and evening editions of the *Worcester Telegram* and *Gazette* newspapers. We ordered the deck from Skates On Haight, a shop in San Francisco that had run an advertisement in *Thrasher.* The fact that the board came from California—the mecca of skateboarding—was extra rad. I sat on my front lawn for a week straight waiting for the Brown Santa (aka, UPS truck). When it finally arrived, it was titty city and I was the mayor.

Sophomore Year: Eye of the Toddler

Matt Finkle, a kid my age who went to a private school, lived a short skate from my house. He had constructed an eight-foot-tall quarterpipe in his driveway during the summer. I'd been threatening to drop into that quarterpipe, and I was livid because I still hadn't done it. I was determined to drop in before I turned fifteen in December, but I suffered vivid flashbacks of Twistah's ramp, when I'd knocked myself silly in front of the little red-haired girl. Mind games, I learned, were the hardest obstacles to overcome in skating. But on this day, I was ready.

Two months into my sophomore year, I skated over to Matt's and padded up like a micro-version of the Road Warrior. "Today's the day," I told him, but he'd heard it before—many times. We skated all day, but I couldn't bring myself to drop in. It kept getting darker and finally, Matt had to go inside to eat dinner. I was getting pissed at myself and refused the invitation to join him. Yet again, I went through the motions: I

My early handplant fetish in Paxton.

climbed the ladder, set the board down, looked down at the foot of vert and the curve of the transition, tightened the Velcro on my wrist guards, stood on the board, and did nothing. I have to emphasize that this was an eight-foot-tall quarterpipe with a foot of vert—straight to asphalt.

I was busy mentally bludgeoning myself for being a pussy—how stupid was it that I could pull all the tricks I knew and not drop in?—when three things happened in quick succession: "Eye of the Tiger" came on the radio; I leaned forward to look at the ramp; I lost my balance and accidentally dropped in. Holy shit! I was rolling across the driveway with no broken bones. I should have shadowboxed for a second or raised my arms or something to mark the moment, but I was so shocked that I climbed back up and did it again to make sure I wasn't dreaming.

I never had the chance to redeem myself on Twistah's ramp, because it was torn down when Twistah moved shortly after my fifteenth birthday. He relocated to a suburb outside of Boston that had more of an active skate scene, which was sad for Paxton, but our scene persevered. Breaking that mental barrier of dropping into a vert ramp was the turning point for learning more and more tricks; it coincided with the beginning of the golden age of vert ramps in and around Paxton.

A junior at my school named Matt Jones built an eight-foot-wide, eight-foot-tall vert ramp in his backyard in the center of Paxton. By modern vert-ramp standards, these dimensions presented a serious hazard along the lines of, say, an aircraft carrier with runways that are way too narrow. There was no margin for error, which was typical for the East Coast. Twelve feet of width would have been a luxury.

Compared to Twistah's place, the Jones Ramp was a much friendlier environment. We all sucked, so we could go there and suck together as a unit, but it was the first *real* ramp I ever dropped in on. To get there, I had to skate seven miles uphill on Route 122, a major thoroughfare through Paxton. Sometimes, I'd get a note from my parents so I could take a different school bus and get dropped off in town, but regardless of how I got there, I always had to get home. That meant braving the "Hill."

By the time I'd finish skating, it was always late, pitch-black, and sketchy. I'm not talking a hundred yards with a run-out at the bottom. I'm talking miles of blacktop that produced treacherous wheel wobbles. On top of that, there was speeding traffic inches away. I'd use the vehicles' headlights to see where I was going. Full-sized Ford and Chevy trucks would swerve like they were pretending to hit me, while half-empty Budweiser grenades flew out their windows. I'd hang on and pray that I didn't hit a rock. Miraculously, the only time I did have to bail, I timed it between wolf packs of traffic and ran it out across the highway without getting nailed.

Matt Jones's parents eventually got sick of having 300 kids at their house every day and scheduled the ramp for execution. Word of the injustice spread, and skaters milled about like hapless town folk hoping for a miracle. The day came, and the adults donned hockey masks and sawed the ramp into three pieces with chainsaws. Then, just as they were about to turn the three pieces into firewood, a flatbed truck rolled up and Matt Finkle's parents saved the day.

The Finkles lived far enough from the center of town that they probably figured the vermin wouldn't brave the "Hill" to get to their place. They were cool enough to sacrifice their yard for a while, just like the Joneses had done, thus giving the structure a new lease on life, and all the skaters lived happily ever after. Especially me, since I practically lived next door to the Finkles. The ramp was reassembled, and life was good.

I was a sophomore in high school, and skateboarding was my life. I had a few friends who were as obsessed with it as I was, but most of them also played team sports. I ended up skating that ramp a lot, and usually alone, especially when Matt Finkle started losing interest. After school and every weekend, I logged hours and hours on that ramp, a small boom box cranking out some sort of punk rock music. I loved to skate solo so I could get new tricks wired, then unveil them for my friends. I loved hearing, "Holy shit! When did you learn that?"

Fight! Fight! Fight!

The first and only fight I've ever gotten into happened early that school year. The confrontation stemmed, not from being a skater, but because I was a runt. There was a group of jock kids who liked to talk shit and use me as a punching bag. On this morning, I was with a few of my friends in the corridor where freshmen had their lockers, and the mouth was a freshman jock who was obviously trying to make a name for himself. For some reason, I felt like I deserved more respect that day, or maybe it was my group of friends razzing me with, "Don't take that horse shit."

Adrenaline was flowing, and I squared off in front of this stocky kid who was a little bit taller than me. It was the classic "Fight! Fight!" scenario, with his jock friends behind him egging him on, and my pseudo-punk/skater nerds behind me doing the same thing. He must have felt pretty secure having his meathead friends around because he said something like, "What are ya gonna do, baby Toddler?" I popped him right on the nose. A second later he was bleeding, the bell rang, and a teacher came out and broke it up before the kid had time to kick my ass.

I don't recommend fighting. It's stupid and, despite the pats on the back I got, I felt pretty crummy. But then, as I sat in class first period and reflected, I have to admit, I felt a certain amount of satisfaction for standing up for myself, all five foot one of me.

Three periods later, I still hadn't been called to the principal's office and I began to relax, sure that I'd avoided getting busted by the man. I had gym right before lunch period and it was there, in the locker room, that I made the fatal mistake: I took my time changing clothes.

I tied my shoes, then looked up to see the freshman kid I had popped with an entourage of redneck jocks from the nearby town of Rutland. There were four of them—future farmers of America, destined for careers as gas station attendants from day one—and they were bent on saving face. They pushed me around, shoved me to the ground, and took turns punching me. Nothing too serious physically, they just wanted to scare me, and it worked. After they were through, they picked me up and stuffed me inside a locker—and locked it.

For forty-five minutes, I kicked the shit out of that locker, trying to escape. I screamed and banged on the door with my fists, trying to get someone's attention. Finally, I heard a woman's voice: "What is going on in here?!" It was the school nurse, whose office was down the hall. I looked at her through the grate, my foot hanging out of the corner of the locker door I'd bent outward. She left. A few minutes later, she returned with a janitor who liberated me from the sweatbox. Prepared for sympathy, I stood upright. What I got was a severe verbal beat-down.

The nurse was infuriated that she'd had to enter the boys' locker room, and the janitor was pissed that I'd ruined the locker. Because I wasn't willing to reveal the names of my captors, they thought I'd locked myself in the locker for fun. I ended up in the principal's office and got suspended a day for skipping class—I'd missed lunch period—and for vandalism and destruction of school property. Had I turned in the redneck mob, I could have possibly gotten off, but I didn't want six weeks in intensive care. My parents weren't very happy about how the school handled it, but they were mellow with me and didn't make a big deal out of it.

Weeks later, after another stimulating day of education, I took the bus home, walked over to my ramp (occupation is half the law of ownership, right?), and found a mob of people. I eyed them suspiciously from a safe distance but realized they knew how to skate and weren't driving tractors—definitely not the redneck mob come to lynch me.

Word had spread about the ramp's new location, and my private training center had been breached. Come to find out, they were all kids from Worcester. They went to my school's rival, Doherty High, which apparently had a lot more skateboarders than my high school did. These skaters ranged from eighth graders to seniors, and they had driven to Paxton in a couple of packed vehicles. The fact that our schools were rivals meant absolutely nothing to me. The session was fun, and we vowed to meet again the next day and the day after that.

Meeting the Doherty skaters was a lucky occurrence because a bunch of vert ramps popped up around the same time, and the skaters were transportation. Jeff Simons and Rob LaVigne, who lived on the other side of Paxton, built an even more screwed-up ramp than Finkle's, with six-foot trannies, a foot of vert with cracked-up pool coping on top, and that sketchy East Coast width of eight feet. Not long after that, John Weston, a kid who lived in Holden near my high school, built the first real ramp in the area: sixteen feet wide with big decks and pool coping. Then another kid named Mike Lambert put a ramp in his backyard. So there were four ramps to choose from. Our skateboarding scene had entered the Golden Age.

I had two different crews of skateboarding friends. My high school friends living mostly in Holden and my new Doherty High friends who had cars and came from the big city—Worcester, five miles away. My parents weren't entirely confident in my friends' driving abilities and limited my rides with them to daylight hours, with a perimeter lockdown not to extend beyond Holden or Worcester.

Too Drunk to Fuck

One Saturday, I told my parents I was going skating in Holden, and a few of us drove an hour to go down into Boston in search of skate spots. The older kids I was with knew all the seedy skate spots and music stores, and I found a Dead Kennedy's T-shirt that I couldn't live without: black with TOO DRUNK TO FUCK on the chest. The next day, my parents and I were going to a Sunday Rotary Club pancake breakfast at our town hall. My dad, a Rotarian, dressed up for the occasion, as did my mom. We were running late, so things were a little frantic when I asked my mom, "Is it cool if I wear my new shirt to the pancake breakfast?" She glanced at me and said, "Yeah, sure."

We got to the place and were walking through the parking lot when my mom finally saw that I was announcing to the world that I was too drunk to fuck. A huge blowout followed this discovery. We were already late to the breakfast and there wasn't anything else for me to wear, and my dad was yelling about my lack of judgment and respect. The situation Band-Aid was to turn the shirt inside out. We mingled and ate our pancakes behind the facade of a proper East Coast family, but all the while, my dad showed his disappointment by throwing me the Darth Vader chokehold when nobody was looking.

Back home, my mom cut the word "fuck" out of my shirt and sewed a blank piece of black material in its place, so it read TOO DRUNK TO. I told my friends the story and I became the "Too Drunk to Blank" guy. I loved that shirt.

That was one of the few times in my life that there was a bit of a rift in my family, more so with my dad and me. My mom was like (sweet voice), "Oh, Todd." And

My mom and me, junior year.

my dad was like (deep voice), "You gotta shape up. Learn some responsibility." He wanted me to be like other kids, but I was a "punk rock kid" who didn't get good grades, skateboarded, hung out with the fast crowd, and wasn't going anywhere in a traditional sense. Occasionally, he threatened me with the prospect of a forty-hour-a-week job since I wasn't taking school seriously.

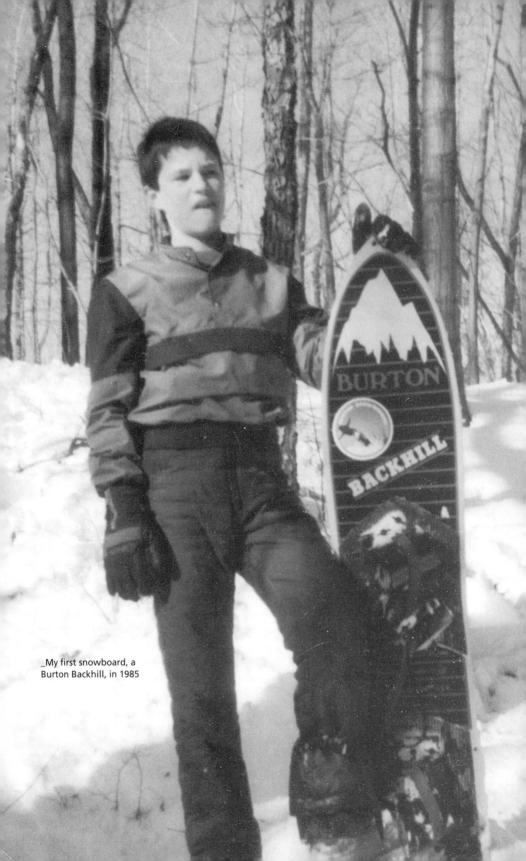

_My first snowboard, a
Burton Backhill, in 1985

TOO COLD TO SKATE/
32 DEGREES AND RIDING

During the fall of my sophomore year, most of the skaters were dreading the coming snows that would bury the ramps. Rob LaVigne, on the other hand, was getting fired up to go snowboarding.

At the time, snowboarding was akin to stand-up sledding. Sherman Poppen started Snurfing way back in 1965, but the "modern" snowboard had been on the market for only a few years. The majority of ski resorts didn't allow it in 1984, and those that did required you to exhibit a certain level of skills before they let you on the mountain. They would actually test you, which usually meant you had to hike up the bunny slope and ride down exhibiting left and right turns, and the ever-important ability to stop. Once you passed this test, the mountain would give you a card that you had to show to get on the lifts. This was probably a good idea considering the rudimentary equipment. No steel edges for control, no brakes to stop a runaway board from decapitating a downhill skier, and no bungee cord or rubber waterski bindings to keep you attached (temporarily) to the board. I'd seen a few advertisements for snowboards in the back of the skate mags, but it didn't appeal to me. There was no such thing as a snowboarding magazine, and for me winter was nothing more than a dismal, depressing, nonskateboarding season. Likewise, skiing had lost any appeal it had ever had. I only went skiing with my mom and dad once or twice a winter because I knew it would break their hearts if I didn't join them.

We fought Old Man Winter valiantly to preserve our skateboarding grounds. Around New Year's Day, 1985, the plywood ramps really started to freeze and get snowed on. We did everything possible to deter the deep freeze. We shoveled the ramps, chiseled away the ice, and dried out slippery trouble spots by pouring gasoline on them then lighting them on fire just long enough to evaporate the water. Then, we skated the slightly charred ramps until the snows got too deep.

That winter, after I'd turned fifteen and hadn't been able to skate for a few weeks, was the first time I'd ever experienced true depression. There were no indoor skateboarding parks to keep me stoked and, as a result, my endorphins went into hibernation. I needed skateboarding bad. The magazines didn't help; they just reminded me that the kids on the West Coast were learning new tricks while my progression was stagnating like a frozen mud puddle. To make matters worse, my parents began to let on that they didn't like some of the kids I ran with because they assumed (correctly) that they were pot-smoking, beer-drinking losers.

Rob LaVigne was the exception. He had become a sort of ringleader for our Holden pack because he had a ramp in his backyard and, just as important, everybody—including parents—liked him. My parents liked Rob's haircut, clothes, and sincere, outgoing personality. To avoid losing my sanity, I convinced them to buy me a snowboard because (a) Rob had one, (b) Rob's parents and my parents were friends, and (c) it might rekindle my interest in skiing (not a chance).

They took me to Strands Ski Shop in Worcester and bought me the cheapest board on the rack, an all-wood Burton Backhill with rubber waterski bindings and no steel edges. It was the same old story. I had to prove that the board wasn't going to end up in the closet before my parents would agree to buy the top of the line, which at Strands was a Burton Elite with steel edges and a P-tex bottom.

Rob LaVigne, the guy who showed me that winter wasn't so bad after all.

My first air on a snowboard on a hill near my house in Paxton.

I put on my ski bibs and snow boots and went to a sledding hill behind my house. I gave it four miserable runs, and I hated it. The bindings made my feet feel claustrophobic compared to a skateboard, but were loose and sloppy compared to ski boots—the worst of both worlds. Plus, I was soaking wet and cold. After falling on my ass repeatedly, I dragged the board home and chucked it in a snowbank.

The Last Great Lange Bang

My parents worked really hard and loved our annual family ski trips. These holidays were set aside for quality time. When it came to ski equipment, they didn't pinch pennies. Serious coin was dropped for skis and boots, but despite my top-of-the-line Lange ski boots, my feet killed me. On the East Coast, it can get so cold that your toes freeze up like popsicles. Then they bang painfully against the front of your ski boots. A "performance fit" meant "downsize and deal with the pain."

Once I got a snowboard, we had to find a mountain that would let me in. Loon Mountain, about a three-hour drive from Paxton, was one of the first ski areas in New Hampshire to allow snowboarding and it was the first real mountain I snowboarded at.

We showed up in February and the snow was typical East Coast polished blue ice—and my Burton Backhill had no edges. The rudimentary board didn't have high-back bindings (a new technology that securely locked your feet onto a board, and greatly improved turning and stopping control) either, because the Backhill wasn't intended for ski resorts. It was made for wide-open backhills, golf courses, and powder snow. Without edges or highbacks my board had zero control, like ice skating without ice skates. Heelside turns were impossible, toeside turns were laughable, but I managed to make it up and down the mountain a few times without running down any men, women, children, or trees. Getting off the lift was almost sketchier than going down the trail. My ass was permanently bruised, however, and the next day, much to the relief of my mom and dad who had spent the previous day waiting for me to flail down the mountain, I opted to ski.

Toward the end of the next day, I saw another snowboarder working the edges of the runs where skiers had scraped the ice into a pathetic version of New Hampshire powder. He made a few turns off the top of a pile of "powder," and it looked a bit like a kick turn on a skateboard. This intrigued me enough to trade in my skis for one more shot on the board.

I got off the lift, headed straight for the softer snow on the edges of the run, and managed to swivel my way down the mountain for long stretches without falling. I found I could actually turn left and right in succession, and the feeling was like carving a skateboard with loose trucks. Still, it took me a half hour to finish a run I could ski in three minutes. It was at once humbling and frustrating, two key elements that I would find to be necessary to maintain focus and revive excitement throughout my life. Before that run, the mountains bored me. Then all of a sudden, I had something new to learn. It ignited a fire in me that changed my entire outlook on winter.

When we got home, I put my skis and boots in the closet knowing I'd probably never use them again. I later sold the equipment to some high school kid, using the money for candy, soda, and various punk-rock necessities like albums, more T-shirts I couldn't wear to pancake breakfasts, and stickers. When my parents found out about the sale after the fact, my dad didn't seem to equate my salesmanship with following in his footsteps. I don't know if he wanted a better life for me, or if he just didn't want such an embarrassing child. I didn't fit the all-American kid mold, and I think he was disappointed about that. He grounded me, which probably overlapped with one or another grounding. I was constantly grounded.

Spring 1985 rolled around, and my parents allowed me to sell my shitty backhill board so I could buy a hand-me-down snowboard with steel edges from Rob, the first snowboarder I ever knew who was sponsored. Flite Snowboards had been giving him boards for cost (around 50 percent off) because he was one of the better East Coast riders at the time. He sold me the last year's model, a swallowtail Flite Comp Rocket at a really good price, like fifty dollars.

There was still snow on the ground, and my parents and I took a late-season trip to Magic Mountain, a little resort four hours away in Vermont that eventually closed down in the early nineties. That was a breakthrough day. The board didn't have high-back bindings, but the steel edges on The Rocket made all the difference in control. The springtime slush was perfect ego snow. I was skateboarding—albeit with speed wobbles and minus the wheels.

That summer was a breakthrough for my skateboarding, too. I had grown a couple inches to five-foot-two, gained five pounds, and started to get better than the other kids on the vert ramps. Some skaters started wanting to hang out with me, but others thought I was cocky if I got excited about pulling off a difficult trick. Maybe I was kind of a "claimer," but it was the first time I had ever been good at something besides making messes. I didn't get it. You're bummed because you're a misfit, so you try really hard and you get good at something, and then, when you're finally happy with yourself and having a good time, you have to downplay it. Otherwise you're not humble enough or something. It was confusing. It's hard being a kid.

Sometimes my parents would watch me skate a ramp or in the driveway, but they didn't have much time for it because they both worked. I think they also believed that I'd grow out of it. Instead, skateboarding consumed me more and more. I also dressed weirder and weirder, but it wasn't to rebel against my parents because they were too strict, and it wasn't for attention. I just liked it. I had a lot of freedom. My parents didn't keep me on a short leash. I'd go out and skate, and as long as I was home when I said I would be home, it was cool by them.

When my junior year of high school began, my parents decided I needed a job to learn the value of a dollar and have some responsibility. My grades had sucked the year before, and I was spending a lot of their money on magazines and skateboard stuff, all of which was supporting a lifestyle I apparently wasn't growing out of. They were thinking college, and that maybe if I had a low-paying job, I'd realize that I would someday want a career. So I took a job as a shrimp peeler and dishwasher at a family-owned

My second board, the Flite Comp Rocket (check out those steel edges!).

restaurant in the center of Paxton. I would sneak into the freezer and do whip-its and eat Bon Bons until I was sick. I hung in there for a week or two before I quit.

But I told my parents that I was still working. This really freed up my afternoons and evenings for skateboarding. Some time later, my mom went to the restaurant when I was supposed to be at work and my ex-boss told her he hadn't seen me in six weeks. That night when I came home from skateboarding, I faced the Richards Inquisition. They seemed to think I'd been out doing those things parents always worry about—you know, drugs, unprotected sex, pornography—but all I did every single day and night was skate. Since I hadn't been making any money from the job, I was forced to sell some of my possessions (the skis, a radio, cameras, a Walkman) and some of my parents' stuff, too, like my dad's old bicycle.

At the time, I rationalized that it was stuff that sat around and never got used. Occasionally they'd realize something was missing and ask me, "What happened to blah blah?" And I'd look confused and say, "Blah blah? I don't know. Gotta go to work . . . bye." Granted, it was a bad thing to do, but I wasn't using it to buy drugs or anything like that. It was just that my parents were borderline packrats. They held on to everything—old shoes, broken tennis rackets, you name it. My father had this weird obsession with pocket change. He didn't spend it. Instead, he'd fill up socks with it and store them in his closet—presumably for a rainy day. Some of those suckers looked like penny pythons; others were round and as big as soccer balls. I didn't touch those change socks, but everything else was fair game.

My parents were pretty good at holding me accountable for my actions, but they were a little clueless about following through with my punishment. They were livid when they found out I'd been lying about working, and on fire when they realized I'd been selling their belongings.

"What were you doing when you were supposed to be at work?" my mother asked me.

"I was skateboarding," I answered.

"Where's your skateboard?"

"In my room."

So upstairs went my dad, and he returned with my old Sure Grip board in his hand. "No skateboarding for eternity," he said. He was bent.

My parents didn't pay enough attention to realize that I hadn't skated that board for about a year, and I didn't say a damn thing. I immediately hid my good skateboard under my bed and moped around for the rest of the night acting as depressed as I possibly could. Next day after school—in fact, every day after school—I did a lot of "studying" at friends' houses and learned a bunch of new tricks on my real skateboard.

I don't think they realized what a problem-solver, maybe even lifesaver, skate-

I was addicted to street plants during my senior year.

boarding was for me. In addition to my fairly harmless skateboard friends, I started hanging out with a bunch of bored youths who were essentially hoodlums. For fun they did drugs, stole car stereos, keyed cars, broke windows, and pillaged freight cars at the Worcester railway yards. These weren't the kids I'd bring home for dinner, but I associated with them, and they'd invite me to join them in their escapades. I was too into skateboarding to have any interest in breaking the law, so I always declined. The fast kids respected me for this. And even though I was smaller than all of them, I could hold my own as long as a skateboard was involved.

Mobile

My high school guidance counselor junior year was a short man with a Napoleon complex. He hated everybody, especially me because at five foot three, I could look him straight in the eye. He moonlighted as the driver's ed teacher and made us watch all the bad movies—*The Blood Flows Red on the Highway* and *Black Ice*—scare tactics regurgitated from the sixties. "Use your turn signal OR YOU WILL DIE!"

Driver's ed required fifteen hours of behind-the-wheel time, but I drove with Mr. Napoleon only once, which amounted to about an hour. When the class ended, I went to his office to see what I had to do to make up the missing fourteen hours, and he was locked in battle with a girl who was trying to put together a schedule of college prep classes for the next three semesters. Holding my behind-the-wheel sign-in sheet, I hung back and waited my turn. The girl finished with the college stuff and handed him a piece of paper, saying, "Oh, by the way, Mr. Napoleon. Can you please sign this?"

"Okay, give me that," he said and scribbled his signature. Then he looked at me and said, "What? You have one of those, too?" and signed me off for the entire fifteen hours.

I got my learner's permit and was the sketchiest driver in the world. I narrowly missed catastrophe dozens of times, pulling out in front of cars, stalling while turning left into oncoming traffic, rolling through pedestrian-occupied crosswalks. If my parents needed something from the store and I was driving, they'd rock, paper, scissors to see who had to go with me. So for good reason, I was forbidden to get my license until I could prove myself behind the wheel. It wasn't so much for my own personal safety. It was for the world at large.

Finally, four months later, my dad took me out for an intense day of pre-driver's test training. Got my three-point-turn wired, parallel parked, and passed the real test no problem. A week later I had my first opportunity to solo when my mom ordered a pizza and dangled the keys in front of me. As soon as I was faced with pulling out onto busy Route 122 by myself, I seized up. Ten minutes passed before I got the balls to pull out into traffic. I would later grow into a fast and calculating German-automobile-driving connoisseur. Some people might call me an Audi snob.

Contests, Kisses, and Chemicals

In high school, I wasn't much of a ladies' man, probably because I looked like everybody's little brother. But one girl saw something in me after I turned sixteen. I thought she was cool, too, because she was a full-on weird-punk-rock-skate-betty. Her name was Lauren, and we went on a mall date. We window-shopped, ate pizza, and went to see the first re-release of *Star Wars*. She knew I was shy, so she'd mess with me by getting really close, face to face, almost taunting me to kiss her.

Inside the dark theater it happened, completely by accident. I was probably mouthing the script, which I knew by heart—"Help us Obi Wan Kenobi, you're our only hope"—when I thought Lauren said something. I turned to say, "What?" and she turned at the same second, and we locked jaws and ended up making out for the entire movie. I think I walked out holding her hand. I had a sore tongue and was thinking, "So, that's what making out is all about?"

That spring, I caught wind of a skate contest in Rhode Island, run by some guy named Peter Pan. I convinced my parents to let me drive to it with the skaters from Doherty High School that I'd been hanging out with. It was a super-skate expedition as far as I was concerned, but they were less than thrilled. Rhode Island? Are you kidding me? It was like going to another country.

My pals, Tom and Raff, and I got to the spot in Providence and found a parking lot with a street course set-up, but not the kind of street courses you see in today's summer X Games. This was a rudimentary collection of street obstacles that included a curb, a small jump ramp, a tire, and a bigger jump ramp—plenty to stoke everybody there. Kids were doing nutty crap, like big judo airs, really cranking methods. We got a big dose of, "Okay, so this is what other skateboarders besides us are into." We were such a small-town scene, we weren't exposed to much live-action stuff outside of the skating we witnessed in the occasional Powell video.

I signed up in the fifteen- to eighteen-year-old advanced, non-sponsored category. The launch-ramp era of skating was in full swing, and I couldn't compete with the airs but I was really good at street plants, hohos, and all that crap. A hoho is when you go up handplant, put both hands on the ground, and then reach up egg, and come back in eggplant. I could start egg and do things like walk on my hands, funny stuff like that. I could do every fricking variation of the hoho that ever existed. I did some meager jumps on the launch ramps and then held my breath and put on my street-plant show. Just as my routine was ending, I had Tom and Raff run out of the crowd and lie side by side on the ground. I ollied them and the crowd went nuts, all eight people.

Winning my division earned me a skate deck, a pair of Life's a Beach shorts, and a hat. The deck was a Vision Gator, and I was bummed because even though Mark "Gator" Ragowski was a ripping skater from Southern California, I hated Vision (it was nerdy), which is funny, because eventually I'd get sponsored by them.

Senior Citizen

Senior year—1986/1987—would probably be considered the dark era of vert skating in Paxton. Only one problem: Vert skating never truly came into the light; it was always in the shadows, just on the fringe.

All the ramps had been torn down except for Mike Lambert's, and his was in sorry shape. He'd gotten "vert-rampitis," a commonplace disease that is caught when people build ramps in their backyards. They start out super-stoked, skating it all the time, but as the infection spreads the skating stoke disappears, and before they know it, they have no desire to skateboard at all anymore.

The only real treatment for this terrible disease is to remove the tumor (the ramp), a procedure usually performed by a parent. Rehabilitation, if any desire to skate even remains, consists of skating other people's ramps in small doses or, in severe cases, experimenting with street skating, though this can lead to chronic-launch-ramp syndrome.

Transporting a launch ramp to my house proved nearly fatal when a friend I'll call John Smith helped me move the ramp from his house to mine. We decided to do it one day without recruiting our parents or any mechanized transport. Thus, we negotiated the "Hill" by using spare skateboards for wheels to carry the substantial weight and girth of John's four-foot-tall, eight-foot-wide beast. We dragged it from his driveway and muscled it onto two skateboards (one on either end), and then for the sake of speed, we opted to skate alongside instead of walking. Big mistake. Midway down the hill, it was too late to undo our fatal error. Objects in motion will stay in motion, until, perhaps, a parked car stops said object. After a quick inspection of the vehicle, which had a few dents in it already, and confirmation that nobody had seen us, we lifted the ramp back onto the two skateboards with Incredible Hulk strength and vacated the scene of my first hit and run. A half hour later, the ramp was safely delivered to my driveway.

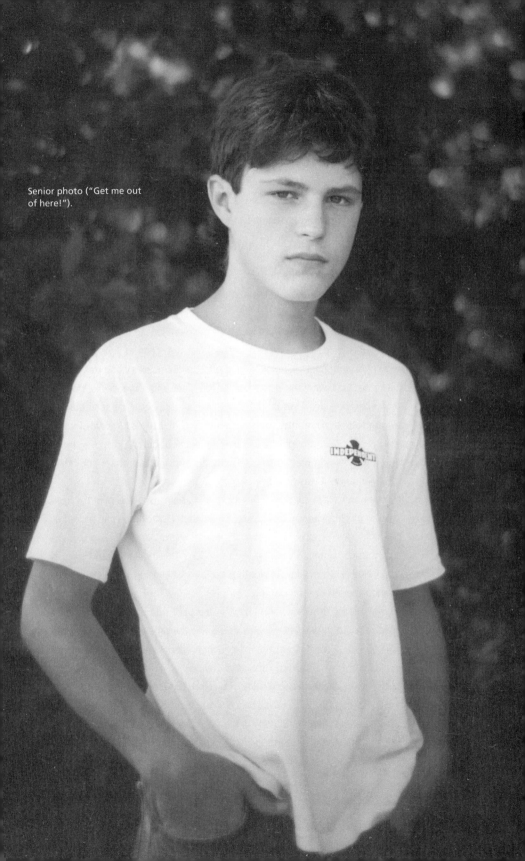

Senior photo ("Get me out of here!").

After weeks of repetitive launching off the ramp and multiple rolled ankles upon landing, I yearned for a vert ramp. My body had almost forgotten how it felt to truly bludgeon itself against a rock-hard surface.

Word on the street was that the town of Canton had the best ramp in Massachusetts. This was a problem, considering it was pretty far away and I'd been having some recent parental-parole violations in regards to driving outside the county. I think some of the kids who drove me were actually afraid to get caught by *my* parents, simply because my dad's temper was legendary.

My old pal Jay, however, was immune to any and all forms of punishment, and tongue lashings by parents were par for the course as far as he was concerned. He lived life for the moment and was more than happy to ditch school for the most insignificant of reasons. He was the perfect partner in crime, because, honestly, I felt safe with him. My dad had always told me that the Boston area was sketchy and dangerous. All my skating pals had always told me that Boston area skaters were the best on the East Coast, which was true. When we finally got directions to the Canton ramp in October, it was colonized by East Coast heavies, like the scene at Twistah's ramp times two, with photographers taking pictures and fast girls smoking cigarettes on the sidelines. The ramp itself was ridiculous: twenty-four feet wide, big decks, perfect transitions. For a baseball kid, it would probably have been the equivalent of playing in a perfectly groomed stadium after years of sandlot ball. I weaseled my way into as many runs on the ramp as I thought I could manage without getting run over. I was stoked because I was skating pretty well and getting compliments from all the heavies. They probably thought I was twelve.

On the drive home, Jay's car died in Framingham, about forty-five minutes from my house. The car was hopeless and I had to call my parents, who came and picked us up at ten that night at a gas station. I got in a shatload of trouble for driving to Canton without permission, but I still didn't learn my lesson. A few weeks later, I was off on another seek-and-skate mission to another ramp in Chelmsford, Massachusetts, which was even farther away than Canton.

That Saturday, some other kids and I piled in the back of a pickup truck owned by a kid named A-Bomb. It was late November, and by the time we got to the ramp an hour and a half later, I was frozen stiff and couldn't feel my feet. All the big names were there, including Fred Smith and this one guy named Mark Connahan—nickname, Max Concave—who was doing a lot of artwork for *Thrasher* magazine. Max was pulling big airs to axle, and it was so cold out that the plastic copers on his Tracker trucks shattered when he hit coping. I jumped around to get the blood flowing and skated a heated snake session, which is when skaters drop into a ramp the instant the person skating falls. There is no line-up or orderly method so everybody gets a turn. It's a free-for-all—in wild west terms, "You're either quick, or you're dead." I could not get a run in. I'd set my board down, and people would snake me. I finally got about four runs in after everybody else was packing it in because it was too dark to see. Those runs were enough for me to be completely soaked with sweat. Then it started snowing—puking snow.

We climbed into the back of A-Bomb's truck for the drive home. It was dark and icy so we had to drive slow, and my parents thought I'd been skating in Paxton, which was impossible since a major storm had covered Paxton under a foot of snow earlier that day. The hour-and-a-half drive turned into a three-hour drive. I was seriously thinking, "I'm dead," not only from my parents (although they expected me home five hours before), but because I was hypothermic, huddling with the other skate rats like mice in a burrow. We were all wet with sweat and only wearing shorts and T-shirts. The lucky ones had on sweatshirts, too.

When we pulled up to my house around 9 P.M., I could barely climb out of the truck. I had blue lips, a gray nose, and was frozen solid. I still tried to commando in the front door, but my parents ambushed me with both barrels.

"Where in the fricking hell have you been?" said my dad. My mom was so worried, she was nearly in tears and could only manage, "You don't call?" Though the whole situation sucked, it was still really, really fun to discover this new ramp, and I hadn't lost any fingers or toes. Without knowing it, my parents were teaching me valuable life skills—weighing out positives versus negatives and living with the consequences. I was grounded for a month. Totally acceptable repercussions.

When winter snows turned everything white my senior year, depression set in black as ever. In addition to chipping ice off ramps and lighting them on fire, we'd spend hours sweeping a parking lot just to "street" skate, which was catching on more and more. I never understood why we'd get kicked out. I thought we were performing a public service, sweeping and shoveling sidewalks and parking lots. We were always polite and kept our skateboards away from pedestrians, no different than kids at the park tossing around a football or Frisbee.

Despite the grounding, my mom and dad didn't mind me accompanying them on their ski trips, and they even bought me a new snowboard, another swallowtail, a Sims 1500 FE Pro with high-back bindings. The board was a step up from the Flite, and I hunted down little jumps all over the mountain. Every snowboarder on the hill sucked, but I sucked just a little less.

I started dating this girl named Michelle that winter. She was the first popular girl I met who saw something in me, and because she seemed normal, my parents didn't mind me seeing her while I was grounded. Girls had not been a priority in my life, but I'd be lying if I didn't admit that Michelle was my first love. I was pretty serious with

Senior Prom with Michelle (I had a little accident in the car later that night).

her. She would show up at a ramp and have fun fakieing around. I respected her for that because most girls at ramps were just lurkers or girlfriends, and they seldom actually skateboarded. Michelle also had a car, drove me everywhere, and even fooled around with me under a local vert ramp.

Out of nowhere, one of my friends, Mike Emond, built a perfect ramp in Holden. This development was not good for my already downward-spiraling attendance record at school. For me, school was a nuisance. What I needed was to practice so I could learn all the tricks on *Bones Brigade Video Show* and *Future Primitive*.

I got in the habit of picking a trick or two for the day and doing only that over and over and over again until I could practically do it with my eyes closed. My drive was insane. If I started trying a trick in the morning, I would not leave the ramp until I nailed it. If the vert tricks started to get boring, I'd switch things up, find a fun street spot in Worcester, and camp out all day. I had no problem being alone because my mind was constantly occupied. It was me versus the trick, and it pissed me off to no end if a trick got the best of me. It never occurred to me that it wasn't me versus the trick, it was me versus myself. This self-competition made me feel alive. I'd never been this passionate about anything, except maybe candy.

Todd Squad

End of senior year, my dad went to the dealership to trade in his truck for a new one. He came home and said, "Found you a nice Chevette today, Todd." And I was shits and giggles. "Are you kidding me? A car?" So I drove with him to the lot and, booyah, there it was, a semi-shiny red Chevette.

I was still dating Michelle, who had driven me everywhere up to that point, and I was dying to pick her up with my own wheels. But first I had to customize the vehicle. Ever since I saw *Thrashin'*, I'd been saving stickers for years in anticipation of making my car look like the one in the movie. Within ten minutes of getting my Chevette home, I had stickered the shit out of the entire back end. My dad brought my mom out to show off his purchase, and he lost his marbles. "Gawd-dammit, Todd," he bellowed. "You have no respect for your belongings." But my mom cut in with her sweet, soft voice of reason: "It's his car, Kenny, he can do what he wants with it." So my dad grumbled something or other and went back inside to watch the Stanley Cup finals.

A few months after I got my wheels, my folks loosened the parental-wrench and accepted the fact that I was going to occasionally leave city limits. I had begun to collect a posse of younger skaters who were totally into skateboarding, so I was the one who drove to the Canton ramp after school. The kids pitched in change for gas. One day we rolled up with no fewer than five kids packed into the Chevette, and this guy Kevin Day, one of the better skaters at the time, said, "There's Todd and his squad." That mutated to "Todd Squad" and then turned into "Squad." That became my name: "Squad." I thought it was a pretty damn cool nickname. I drew my own Squad logo on my skateboard in the old *Thrasher* Skate & Destroy–style lettering.

My new squad of skate friends were into street skating too, so we balanced out our time between vert ramps, launch ramps, and any piece of concrete we could find around the county. O'Neil's Bike Shop in Worcester was one of the better skate shops around, and they had no problem letting skaters loiter in and around the parking lot. The store advertised an upcoming street contest (all local skate contests were street, not vert) in which the winner would become the star of O'Neil's next local television commercial. During the contest I unveiled the mute 360s I'd been practicing, and I won a pretty rad prize package. I got a skate deck, a pair of custom Vans that showed up—literally—five months later, some pads, stickers, T-shirts, and a spot on the O'Neil Team, which was like a 10 percent discount for any products the shop sold. My mom and dad were impressed, too. They told all their Rotary friends to watch for me on television. I did a hoho street plant for that commercial. In the grass. You couldn't even see a street. My scene was so stupid and so fast—0.99 second of fame—if you blinked, you missed me.

At the end of my senior year, Michelle and I went to the prom together, which made my mom really proud. This hint of normalcy lasted almost twenty-four hours. I barfed all over the car that night and spent the next morning scrubbing down the interior to get rid of the smell.

I Got a Scholarship?

When I was a freshman, one of my teachers told my mom that I was really smart because I did just enough in school to pass my classes—nothing more, nothing less. I followed through with that strategy until graduation in 1987. School was something I dealt with to keep my parents off my back. I always did well in my English and art classes. Outside of that, I've always had a knack for retaining totally useless information, like *Star Wars* trivia (to this day, I'll challenge anybody to a standoff), *Godzilla* movies (in order, including their original Japanese titles), and *Thrasher* magazine covers (name of the skateboarder *and* trick). If I was interested in something, I had a photographic memory.

The day of my graduation ceremony at the high school gymnasium, I went to find my name on the seating chart. My name wasn't in the section with the rest of the

Graduation ("No, really, *get me out of here!*").

Rs, and I kind of freaked. Considering my absences, there was a distinct possibility that I wasn't going to graduate. I scoured the list and finally found my name in a section up front, so I immediately thought I was sitting with the short-bus kids or something. Having no choice, I sauntered up front and sat down with a bunch of people I didn't know, figuring there must be a mistake.

The ceremony began with the principal calling off the names of kids who had received scholarships, which oddly enough were the people in my section. *Definitely a mistake,* I thought, and slouched in my chair. "Brandt Todd Richards," the principal called out, "Graphic Arts scholarship, New Hampshire Vocational Technical College."

I stood up tentatively and shook the hand of the principal, who looked almost as shocked as I felt. Apparently, my parents had gathered up my transcripts, swiped some of my artwork samples, and applied for the school and the scholarship months earlier. They said that they told me about the scholarship before the ceremony, but I had no recollection. At that point in my life, I brushed off anything my parents told me as unimportant. Sometimes I just ignored them. I wasn't trying to be a jerk to them; I was just in my own world.

_Grunting up a double-handed handplant at Tenney Mountain, 1988 (note the refined style).

THE RIDE NOT TAKEN/
CAREER DAZE

Before I headed off to college in 1987, my girlfriend, Michelle, called and gave me the classic "maybe we should see other people" line. I was so wrapped up in skateboarding that it didn't even phase me. I told her "okay," and that was the last I heard from her.

In August, I packed up the Chevette and followed my parents the two hours to Laconia, New Hampshire. My mom and dad found out that a kid who graduated with me named Dave LaRue was going to the same college, so they and Dave's parents found us an apartment, stocked the fridge, and got us settled. They left me with an ATM card, an ever-abused "emergency" credit card, and a reminder: "Have fun, but don't forget that you're here to get an education." They left. I was seventeen, a respectable height of five foot nine inches, and on my own.

Dave and I were from the same town, but that was the only thing we had in common. He was a jock. I was a skateboarder. We became friends, but we were definitely an odd couple. I'd go and skate, and he'd go play hockey. I was still a punk, but I'd scaled it down for college and grown a dreadlock mullet. Believe it or not, mullets were totally acceptable back then, and I had four big moldylocks hanging down my neck.

Classes started, and it took about three days for me to realize that I had nothing in common with *any* of the students. Everybody seemed like they were stereotypical East Coast preps—khaki pants, sweaters, and collared Oxford shirts were the norm. Everybody was nice enough, but there was a general lack of individuality, and rather than stand out, I tended to try and blend in myself. I couldn't find a single skater or snowboarder to slap me out of my funk and help me maintain my dignity. It was unsettling, but what disturbed me the most about college was that everybody seemed to be there to get an education. Then one day, after a couple of depressing weeks of class, I drove around Laconia to find something fun to skate and saw a couple skateboarders sessioning a parking lot: high school sophomores Scott and Peter. I showed off a bit with my skateboarding circus act, walked on my hands and shit, and they seemed impressed. I dropped Scott off at his house in a nearby neighborhood, and he said we should meet there the next day because all the Laconia skate locals would be there. Finding some of my own kind put me in a great mood. I went back to my apartment and actually studied that night. No wait, I didn't. But I contemplated it.

I went back the next day and found Scott, Peter, and another high school sophomore named Joel Muzzey dorking around in the driveway. Joel and I hit it off, and from that day forward I'd pick him and his little crew of skateboarders up after school, and we'd go skate. Joel had a naturally quick wit, and he noticed that the way I wrote "Squad" on my skateboard looked like "Penos" when read upside down. Whenever I fell or did something stupid, he'd give me shit and call me Penos. Mutual degradation was a key ingredient for friendship. I can't emphasize enough how important meeting Muzzey and those kids was for me. I was excited about being away from home and living on my own, but I'd also been bored because I wasn't into partying and sucking down beer bongs. Connecting with the local skate rats who knew the skate spots around town was the saving grace of my college years.

We kept our ears open for new spots, and one day Joel heard a rumor from some derelict about an insane ramp at a mansion on the Connecticut coast. We devoted a weekend in October to locating what became known as the Mansion Ramp, and when we did find it, we were stunned. To the side of this hotel-sized house was a perfect halfpipe on a big green lawn with a kid skating it all by himself. It was surreal: this serene scene, the ocean breeze blowing in, and Jimi Hendrix blasting on an insane outdoor sound system. At the time, we scoffed anything that wasn't punk, but looking back, I realize that kid was on his shit. He welcomed us to his ramp, and at the end of a long day we still couldn't believe we'd actually experienced something that cool.

The next road trip was spurred on by talk that the University of Vermont had a vert ramp on its campus. I took the skate rats four hours away to Burlington to check it out. The drive was long and we were jonzing to skate, but when we found the ramp, it was chained up: i.e., closed for the weekend. Just as we were about to turn around and drive back, another pack of skate rats rolled up. One of the younger kids, fourteen-year-old Jeff Brushie, invited us to session his backyard ramp, so we followed him and his friends, Kris Swierz and Josh Bromley, to Hinesburg, Vermont, a half hour away.

It was one of those chance meetings that makes skateboarding such a rad thing to do. The ramp was fun, and they were all decent skaters. There were no bad vibes, just instant camaraderie based on nothing more than a common interest. The only competitive energy was with yourself, trying to skate clean for a new audience. On the flip side, we were always looking to learn new tricks. The best way to stay on top

Joel Muzzey, my savior in college, in fine form at a Laconia high school.

of that, outside the magazines and videos, was to travel, hit contests, and keep your eyes and mind open.

I called my friend from Paxton, Rob LaVigne (who was going to college in Burlington), that night about hooking up with these guys. He knew Brushie and his friends as the Boarding House crew. The Boarding House was a snowboard/skateboard shop owned by world-champion Team Burton snowboarder Andy Coghlan, whose name I recognized from *International Snowboard Magazine*—the first and only snowboard magazine I'd ever seen, which wasn't surprising since it was pretty much impossible to find.

Joel Muzzey and the boys were pretty much my link to staying up to date with skateboarding while I was in college. Vert and pool skating were really popular at the time, so the vert contests always attracted the best skaters. Joel asked me about my best contest results, and he thought I was full of it when I admitted I'd never entered

I used to borrow Muzzey's clothes to fit in with the rough blue-collar kids. Here he is in full skate-and-destroy mode.

a vert contest. I'd done well in my two street contests, so I figured, "Why not?" Finding one to enter became my next goal. Joel and the boys were a super-supportive crew, and I think they wanted to see me take skateboarding to the next level. They called me "marathon man" because I could drop in on a ramp and go forever without falling. But their confidence might have wavered a bit when they saw me faced with my first real vert competition at CT Bike Exchange in Connecticut. I was so nervous, I felt like I would barf my brains out before my run. I also sweated a lot. Muzzey took some photos of me while I warmed up in hopes of sending the shots to magazines, but there was a big sweat ring around my butt hole that ruined every good shot. The more nervous I got, the more I sweated.

When I stood up on the deck in front of the substantial crowd and prepared to drop in, my legs began shaking uncontrollably. I could feel the ass sweat dripping down my legs, and it was like someone turned a faucet on under my arms. My feet and my legs went tingly and numb, like they weren't even mine—I couldn't even feel them. I dropped in and sketched out in the flat bottom, and that was that. Game over. No second chance. My reaction surprised me because I'd always been pretty calm and collected during street contests, but something about being on a big ramp in front of everybody turned my stomach. I was also intimidated because there were lots of really good skaters.

Muzzey and the crew didn't say anything, but I knew that they knew I'd choked—and bad. After the contest, I replayed the bail a zillion times in my head and tried to dissect why I'd messed up. That's when I realized why I'd always practiced so damn much. I had a serious complex: No matter how well I did, I thought I sucked, so I'd run myself into the ground practicing. Up there on the ramp, I started thinking about sucking, panicked, and fell. It was something I had to work on. I wanted to redeem myself so I would feel better.

Skate Rats Unite

By Thanksgiving of my freshman year, things were looking bright. I had skate friends to motivate me and ten minutes away, in Gilford, New Hampshire, was Gunstock Ski Area. Gunstock had a 1,400-foot vertical drop and 215 acres, so it was massive as far as I was concerned, and all of a sudden I wasn't so bummed winter was upon me. I was starting to get amped about snowboarding, which was great and all, except that my parents weren't paying for me to get fired up about my old high school hobbies. My study and attendance patterns started to mimic those of my high school years. I did just enough in school to pass my classes so that my parents would keep the money flowing.

Skateboarding magazines always won out over schoolbooks, and I'd also taken a new interest in snowboarding literature. *International Snowboard Magazine* was the hard-to-find original, but TransWorld Publications had just come out with a new snowboarding magazine named, appropriately, *TransWorld SNOWboarding,* followed by Surfer Publications' *Snowboarder.* Inside one of those magazines was a Sims advertisement showing Terry Kidwell tweaking out a method above a quarterpipe with a round-tailed "freestyle" snowboard. A method air is a classic skateboarding trick performed on the backside wall of a halfpipe or off launch ramps, where the skater pulls the board up behind his back with bent legs, and his hand is on the heelside edge of

Me without pads at some ramp in Laconia—
confident or stupid?

the board. The more stylish skaters would push their back leg out straight while at the apex of the jump, giving the trick a smooth, "tweaked-out" appearance in the air. As far as I was concerned, a person's style could be gauged by his or her methods.

Kidwell translated this skate trick to his snowboard like nobody else at the time. Sims was a California skateboard brand, and Kidwell sealed the deal for me: I had to get a Sims freestyle board. Burton was the East Coast favorite, but all the Burton advertisements I'd seen had racing photos—which didn't interest me at all—or a few air shots of guys in red Burton team suits with bad riding style (i.e., bent "stinky" legs and no tweak). Don't get me wrong—I looked up to anyone who had a name or photo in a magazine. It just seemed that the Sims riders had more style, and speed didn't matter. I was fascinated by images of the skateboarding-inspired tricks that people were pulling off on snowboards. Out West—which to me included Wisconsin to the Pacific Coast—was supposedly the promise land of halfpipes made of snow. Ever since my freshman year in high school, I'd wanted to get out to California to go skateboarding, and now I had the same bug with snowboarding.

I was skating with the boys one day in early November and noticed a COMING SOON, SKATEBOARD/SNOWBOARD SHOP sign in a crappy little strip mall in downtown Laconia. The shop was called New Wave Sports, and the owner, Perry, was either a business genius with years of foresight, a money-laundering opportunist, or a self-destructive entrepreneur. As far as we could tell, the four of us *were* the entire skateboarding population of Laconia. Simply put, there was not a huge customer base.

Perry's judgment in employees wasn't so great, either, because he hired me to run the register and sell shit—and I could barely count. At first, the shop only had a metal cash box and a calculator, which was manageable with the three or four customers we'd get per day. Then we got a cash register in time for Christmas and, surprisingly, the shop became packed with people. I was running the cash register by myself when it went down. Just blew up. People were buying complete skate set-ups, with wheels and bearings and decks and griptape, with all these different prices and tax, and the calculator had disappeared.

My mind seized up. I couldn't figure out anything in my head or on paper fast enough to appease the mutinous crowd of pissed-off East Coast holiday shoppers. In the interest of self-preservation, I rounded everything down to whole numbers and didn't charge any tax. If something didn't have a price tag, I either guessed or threw it into the bag for free. Word of this filtered back through the line, "Hey, the stupid skateboard kid is giving shit away so mellow out."

I don't know how much money the shop made that day, but it was a lot—enough that Perry didn't notice how much I screwed up. God only knows how much I gave away. One thing was for certain: It was a Merry Christmas in Laconia.

First trip to Breckenridge, where a damn fine pipe awaited me. I turned this shot into a Christmas card.

My First Switchblade

I went home for the Christmas vacation during my first semester in college, and Mom and Dad came through with a combo Christmas/eighteenth birthday present: a new Sims "freestyle" snowboard. Compared to the swallowtail 1500 FE board I'd been riding, the Switchblade was amazing. It actually flexed (my other boards were as stiff as ironing boards) and had a slightly kicked-up tail that looked more like a skateboard. It was white, with a blue and hot pink Sims logo—the epitome of cool.

I immediately hit up anything with snow and an incline—the sledding hill behind my house or my old haunt, Mount Wachusett. The board's design was super-forgiving, and I could land more airs off moguls. I started to try handplants like I did on a skateboard. After a few tries I could get inverted on little bumps or banks, but I couldn't quite hold them for more than a couple seconds. In skateboarding, I had them so wired I could stall out inverts for days on flat ground or any transition.

At night, I began to dream about snowboarding. Skateboarding had done the same thing to me for years, but with snowboarding it seemed there was more room to explore. I'd always looked up to the veteran skateboarders, and now, here was this new thing to do that was really fun, but it seemed hardly anybody was clued into it. That, I think, is what made it extra appealing. I felt like I was breaking new ground every day I went out. I wasn't just trying to copy the tricks I'd seen other skaters try at a vert ramp, I was out in the snow creating my own and that gave my mind something to chew on. At first, snowboarding had been something to do to pass the winter. I'd hunt out small jumps and land on my butt while trying tricks. It wasn't pretty, but I'd laugh it off. But that winter, I was 100 percent focused on snowboarding—totally devoted—and not willing to accept poor performances. When I fell trying something, I'd get pissed and have to go back up and redeem myself or it would eat at me.

As a result of my newfound passion, I decided I needed a season's pass to Gunstock. Bad. I knew my parents would never kick down for a midweek pass since I was supposed to be in class, so I looked into getting another part-time job (New Wave Sports had become a super-sporadic part-time gig after the holiday rush). I applied at Gunstock and told them I knew how to snowboard, so I was instantly qualified as a snowboard instructor. Back then if you could stand up and make it down an entire run without falling, you were ripping.

So I became the backup instructor in the snowboard division of the ski school, which was quite an honor considering there were only two of us who taught. My first paycheck was twenty dollars—the first time I ever got paid to snowboard. Being an instructor was the next best thing to being sponsored. You got a free season's pass, wore what I considered to be a cool uniform (a red CB jacket), and got to say, "I'm an instructor at Gunstock," which didn't have the goon factor some people associate with it nowadays.

At Gunstock, when I wasn't instructing, I concentrated on my riding the same way I'd always done with skateboarding. I'd find a snow bank on the side of a run where a rock was protruding, and I'd practice handplants over and over and over again. Or I'd find a knoll and work on my method airs. Called a number of things by snowboarders who didn't come from a skateboarding background—suitcase air, Burton Curl, backscratcher air—it was, in reality, a bastardized version of a skateboarding method. Even though I was completely captivated by snowboarding, I knew that skateboarding was more difficult because on a skateboard, your feet aren't locked onto the board. You can't skateboard down the street and just jump up in the air (if you did, you'd just jump off the board and it would keep rolling away). Air on a skateboard required a high level of technique that, simply stated, kept the skateboarder attached to the skateboard. This freedom of movement with your feet allowed you to contort, or "tweak" your legs because the soles of your shoes could pivot on the deck of the skateboard. With my feet locked into bindings on a snowboard, it was easy to jump off anything because the board stayed with me, but I couldn't pivot like I could while skating. This meant I could not extend (bone out) my back leg no matter how hard I tried. I had to rethink the mechanics of my body and learn to tweak by bending at the ankle—a mental and physical block that tormented me.

Part of the reason was the horrible equipment of the day. Snowboards, boots, bindings—everything was ghetto.

The Worst New Sport

Before 1988, most of the world didn't even know snowboarding existed, and those who did didn't consider it a legitimate sport. This changed when *Time* magazine labeled snowboarding the "Worst New Sport" in its January 1988 issue. Finally, credibility! By this time there had been a few different contest series going on for a few years, which consisted mostly of races. The rippers in the early to mid-eighties were the guys and girls who could actually control their boards while sliding at semi-high speeds through racecourses made for skiers. Professional snowboarders were ranked based upon their giant slalom and slalom racing results, especially on the East Coast. By the late eighties, these snowboarders were actually carving turns thanks to better board shapes and a newly adopted science, the "sidecut," which is the curve put on the edge that allows the board to travel in an arc. Speeds approached sixty miles per hour on the bigger racecourses. Things were getting serious—and seriously sketchy on that hoopty equipment.

The West Coast was way more freestyle oriented. A guy named Mike Anolik reportedly discovered the first snowboard halfpipe in 1979 near the Tahoe City, California, dump. That "halfpipe" was really a natural gully with a couple vertical wall hits for tricks; it received its first real publicity in the March 1985 premiere issue of the world's first snowboarding magazine, which was called *Absolutely Radical*. (Publisher Tom Hsieh changed the name to *International Snowboard Magazine* after one issue because his advertisers thought *Absolutely Radical* was too hardcore of a name for a magazine depicting a sport trying desperately to attract mainstream consumers.)

The cover of that all-newsprint issue featured a bearded Keith Kimmel pulling an early snowboarding version of a lien air by grabbing the heelside of the board on a frontside wall and leaning over the tip to spot the landing—a trick taken from skate-boarding and invented by skate legend Neil Blender ("lien" is "Neil" spelled backward). Inside the issue, there were shots of Bob Klein, Allen Arnbrister, and Terry Kidwell blasting backside airs and sketchy-looking handplants—riders and tricks that were

Trevor's portrait photography has improved a lot over the years—as has my fashion sense.

Brushie ripping at the Tenney Mountain Board Bash, 1988.

"The Kid with the Helmet" (i.e., me), Tenney Board Bash.

ahead of their time. In Washington that same year, Mount Baker held a "banked slalom" event with a racecourse snaking down a natural gully—probably the first event customized for snowboarding. Following the Mount Baker banked slalom, bona fide halfpipe contests sprung up on the West Coast, mainly in Tahoe, but as the sport gained momentum, I'd still never heard of a single snow halfpipe on the East Coast.

Finally in early 1988, I got word that the first-ever East Coast halfpipe was going to be built at Tenney Mountain, New Hampshire, for the Funky/Bolle/Tenney Mountain Snowboard Bash. Two things happened the day after I arrived: I entered my first snowboard contest and turned pro at the same time. I was eighteen, and since there was only a men's pro division—no "sponsored" or amateur category—I was pro. That was February 20, 1988.

I was blown away by the sight of the halfpipe. In hindsight that pipe was horrible, but I didn't know any better at the time and thought it was the raddest thing on snow. There was a huge crowd of snowboarders, more than I'd ever seen in one place, probably around thirty or forty riders. And they were mostly good riders, sponsored kids from Burton, Kemper, Flite, all the brands—not the usual beginners struggling down the mountain.

I recognized Jeff Brushie and Kris Swierz from our summer skate session in Burlington. A lot of the riders just carved down the pipe, using the transitions as banked turns with an air thrown in at the bottom, but Brushie was working the walls like he was skating them, catching air on one wall, and then pumping into another air across the wall—combination tricks that you'd do on a skateboard vert ramp. He was all decked out in hand-me-down Team Burton gear he'd scored from world-champion Andy Coghlan.

Brushie was known as the "little kid who rips," and I was soon dubbed the "kid with the helmet." Helmets definitely weren't a fashion statement back then, and I was the only person there wearing one. A helmet was standard safety equipment on concrete and wood vert ramps, and I was used to having one on my head. I was too oblivious, snowboarding in my little world, to notice the snickering about the headgear. But I think other riders eventually forgave this fashion faux pas because I'd become really good at handplants (which also helped get the blood flowing to my head). I found a few places in the halfpipe where they worked and stalled the shit out of them, which resulted in some cheers and hoots.

After a few runs, I was hiking back up the pipe when a guy who looked almost as dorky as me approached. He was skinny and pimple-faced, and he had a camera around his neck. "Hi, I'm Trevor Graves with *International Snowboard Magazine*. You're ripping," he said, holding up his camera to convey the point. At that moment, I thought I was part of something huge. After all, here was this guy from "*International*" *Snowboard Magazine* taking photos of me.

As he walked away, I noted that his blue skin-tight North Face outfit had an *ISM* logo screened on its back. Super official. I had no idea that Trevor was living in his car at the time and using his credentials to get free lift tickets. *ISM* barely paid enough to cover his film and processing. His secret goal at these events was to take pictures of riders that he'd try and sell to them at the next contest.

That little bit of Kodak motivation got me riding harder than I ever had. In the contest, I took fifth place in the men's division. There were probably only a couple dozen competitors, but I was stoked. I'd pulled a few good airs and was fired up that Brushie won, especially because he was technically a junior at seventeen years old. But he had whooped everyone in the men's division—guys with names I recognized from the magazines like Chris Karol, Bud Keene, and Dave Lemieux, who placed second, third, and fourth.

When the contest had ended, Andy Coghlan came up to me in his neon green

The reigning world champion Andy Coghlan at Tenney Mountain, 1988.

and black Life's a Beach batwing jacket and said, "You were shredding." I was floored. The world champion thought I was shredding? Then my old friend from Paxton, Rob LaVigne (who took fourth in the slalom event), patted me on the back and said, "Wow, you could have a future in this." Unbeknownst to me, there was a talent scout watching me. Well, sort of. He was the seedy local rep for Funky Snowboards, which, along with Bolle, had sponsored the event. Perry Silverstein, my boss from New Wave Sports, had told the rep to check me out.

As I was getting ready to leave Tenney, the rep, a slightly overweight guy with spiky-bleached punk-rock Rod-Stewart hair and a Team Funky jacket walked up to me. This was my first encounter with a sales rep in the snowboard industry. He was the classic stereotype from that era: a guy who wasn't all that in touch with the sport, loved the party scene, and could talk the shit out of anything he knew nothing about. Once he cut through the bullshit, he told me he was stoked on my riding and held out a brand new Funky snowboard. "I'd like you to ride this," he said.

I accepted the board with multiple thanks, then drove straight back to my apartment because I had a Monday morning test to pretend-study for. I alternated between staring at my schoolbooks and the shiny Funky snowboard leaned up in the corner of my room. I was sponsored! Un-fricking-believable. I picked up the phone and called my parents—and then everybody else I knew—to tell them the great news.

When I finally realized I wasn't going to get any studying done, I went to a local ski shop where they drilled the board and mounted bindings on it (Funky boards, along with a lot of other boards during this era, were sold like skis, without pre-drilled holes for bindings). The next day at 2:30, after I bombed my test, I picked up Joel Muzzey at his school and we drove to Tenney. It was pouring rain and nearly dark when we arrived, but I was determined to ride that pipe until I couldn't see a thing. I was soaked, cold, and loving it. I wasn't, however, loving the Funky, which was stiff, ugly, and as heavy as a small Volkswagen. Even though the board my parents had bought me—the Sims Switchblade—was way better, I was prepared to deal with the Funky. After all, I was sponsored by the company.

I went back to Tenney every day for the next three days and then, on Friday, the half-pipe was gone. The groomers had leveled it. I was furious. Why would they get rid of that beautiful pipe? It never occurred to me that the pipe was ruining a perfectly good ski run, and that me and a couple other guys were the only people who had ridden it since the contest ended. Another kid, who was hanging out with his snowboard looking equally dismayed that the pipe was gone, confirmed the rumor that the next event of the New England Cup, which was the East Coast's main contest circuit, would have a pipe, too. The location: Nashoba Valley outside of Boston. And it was only two weeks away.

The day before the Nashoba contest, I called Funky Snowboards and asked for

Mr. Party Rep Guy, figuring he'd kick down for the next contest entry fee or maybe give me a T-shirt or something. I got transferred to Mr. Bitter Guy, who informed me, "Uhhh, yeah. Mr. Party Rep Guy no longer works for Funky and we didn't authorize him to sponsor you." I was like, "Oh." Then he said, "And that board. Can I get that back?"

_Cross Rocket, East Coast style,
Waterville Valley, 1989.

ONE-TRACK MIND/
MY BOARDERLINE OBSESSION

We rolled up to Nashoba on February 28, 1988, and there was another amazing—i.e., ghetto—halfpipe staring me in the face. It looked like someone had plowed their driveway. I pulled a bunch of handplants on my Funky (I used it for this contest because I didn't want anybody to know my sponsorship had only lasted two weeks), and Jeff Brushie along with this guy Jason Ford, who was riding a Sims, pulled huge Burton Curls. The skaters in the crowd found the name "Burton Curl" offensive because they were "method airs" in our terminology. My handplants were good enough to get me fourth place, and Brushie won again. After that contest, Brushie became "super pro." That was the last time I saw him for a while because he started traveling with the Burton team. The rest of us kept on slumming it at our little New England Cup events.

Me on my Funky at Nashoba, 1989.

I began to notice a division between the snowboarders: There were the experienced alpine snowboarders who kept the board on the ground, and there were the scrub skater guys like myself who wanted to get in the air as much as possible, mimicking skateboarding heroes of the day like Gator, Chris Miller, Kevin Staab, and others.

I ended up selling the Funky board to a friend of mine for a couple hundred bucks. He told me later that the board sucked and I'd ripped him off. To be honest, I agreed with him, but he knew the rules. It was a dog eat dog world. Kids bartered and sold stuff all the time. Ripping off your friends was totally acceptable if they were stupid enough to pay the price.

In March, I returned to work at Gunstock on my trusted Sims. My friends were telling me, "With your skills, you gotta get hooked up," but I wasn't sure I was good enough for a legit sponsor. Then I saw Team Kemper Guy. TKG was the other instructor who worked with me at Gunstock. Somehow he'd gotten hooked up since I'd last seen him. You could see him from a mile away, all decked out in Team Kemper gear: jumpsuit, hat, boots, and snowboard with Team Kemper stickers stuck on every square inch of deck. TKG was an okay snowboarder, but he wasn't what I considered pro caliber. In fact, I hope he doesn't read this, but he was really horrible. Like so horrible, I figured his family owned the company or something and gave him the gear because they felt sorry for him. Right then and there, I realized, "Yeah, maybe I am good enough."

Hook Me Up

Dave Lemieux, who had beaten me at the Tenney Board Bash, rode for Gnu Snowboards. I'd originally met him a few years earlier at a skateboard ramp in Paxton where we'd bonded over eggplants and lien to tails. Although he didn't have enough clout to help me out, he insisted that I deserved to get hooked up with a company. Amy Howat, one of Gnu's top pros, was touring on the East Coast at the time, and Dave thought we'd have fun riding together and maybe I'd get to network a little. Amy had photos in magazines, so she'd already earned my respect. She was from the West Coast—Mount Baker, Washington, where her father was the mountain manager—and was known to ride with the Mount Baker Hard Cores, a group of snowboarders that included Jeff Fulton, Dan Donnely, Mike Ranquet, and Craig Kelly.

Craig, especially, was one of the sport's most successful competitors, having chalked up some twenty first-place finishes during the last couple of years, mostly as a racer for Sims, but he was also a ripping freestyler. He was having some unusual sponsorship issues: He had two companies fighting over him. He signed on with Burton

Snowboards when his contract with Sims was still valid, and a federal judge had ordered him to ride on a black snowboard with no visible company logos until the smoke cleared. I figured that Craig must have signed on with Burton for a lot of money if the two companies were duking it out in court over him. It made me realize that there *were* career opportunities in snowboarding, or at the very least, lots of free product to be had.

With this in mind, I met up with Dave Lemieux and Amy Howat at Snows Mountain, a tiny ski area across the street from New Hampshire's Waterville Valley. I rode with her that day, trying really hard to impress her since she was the only big pro snowboarder I'd ever had this kind of one-on-one contact with. Going in, my expectations of her skills was pretty low. Magazines or not, she was a girl, and all the girls I'd seen ride were pretty bad. There were girls who could race and girls who could carve the pipe, but as far as freestyle tricks went, I hadn't seen much.

Amy, on the other hand, hit big jumps and grabbed airs: rocket airs, mutes, methods. She used skate terminology, which I thought was rad. She knew what she was doing and what she was talking about, which made me really nervous around her. Near the end of the day, I finally worked up the courage to talk business, babbling at her on the chairlift. "I'm. Like. Well. I'm sorta trying to hook up with Gnu. You think? Could I? Maybe? Do you think I could use you as a reference?" She said, "Yeah, sure no problem." And that was it. She didn't say I ripped or anything, but she said "no problem," and that was good enough for me.

I Want to Be Terry Kidwell

On March 6, 1988, Loon Mountain in New Hampshire (one of a handful of resorts in New England that were allowing us on their slopes) held a giant slalom race that I had no interest in entering. But I heard that Terry Kidwell was going to be there, so I had to weigh out the whole "drive to Loon and see my hero ride or stay home and study" predicament. The answer was obvious.

Loon Mountain was the first mountain I'd flailed my way down on a snowboard, and it felt good to ride around the place without feeling like a complete idiot. I don't remember much about the contest there, except for one thing: Terry Kidwell. After the unremarkable race, mountain management opened up the freestyle ski jumps, where hot dog skiers would practice gainers and spread eagles and stuff. These jumps looked like skateboarding quarterpipes, and some were eight or nine feet tall and pointed straight up like rocket launch pads. The ski patrol insisted anyone hitting them wear a helmet.

I was in the crowd of gawkers on the sidelines when I saw him strapping into his red Terry Kidwell Signature Pro Model—the first pro model snowboard *ever*. The world stopped, and in my mind the theme song from *Chariots of Fire* came on as he slid in slow motion toward the giant kicker and floated the most stylish, gigantic method air. He was airborne like twenty feet up with his back leg kicked out straight. He held the grab forever and then absorbed the landing on the steep downhill as effortlessly as though he was pumping the wall of a skateboard halfpipe. He repeated the performance over and over again with tweaked-out mute airs and tuck-knee Indies, proving himself worthy of the title he would lay claim to: "father of freestyle snowboarding."

Kidwell was the first person I saw ride who looked like he should be doing it. He was made to be in the air on a snowboard—smooth, effortless, and godlike. I wanted that session to last forever so I could soak up every bit of his style. From that moment forward, I wanted to be Terry Kidwell.

Shortly after the Loon Mountain event, Muzzey and I were driving home from riding. I was spaced out in my Kidwell/pro snowboarder fantasy world while Muzzey sat shotgun and checked out my newest skateboard, a Chris Miller, Schmitt Stix. He started pulling Miller's signature crossbone leins with the skateboard out in front of him, having a good old time until he jammed the skateboard against the shifter and rammed it into reverse while we were at fifty miles per hour. A sickening metal-on-metal grinding sound caused the entire car to shudder, and I instinctively smacked the shifter back into drive and kept going.

To retaliate, I ejected his new Zodiac Mindwarp tape out of the stereo and air-mailed it out the window. Didn't even slow down. I knew he was seriously pissed off at what I'd just done, but it was all part of the "airmail game" we'd been "playing" since we met. You had to act like you didn't care when your shit got jettisoned. A few miles down the road, my Cult, Love tape met the same fate. We never pulled over for any of it: wallets, watches, skate wheels. Nothing was sacred. The laughs were worth way more than the crap we tossed out.

The Historic 1988 U.S. Open
(And Why I Missed It)

The biggest event in snowboarding was—and still is—the U.S. Open, held yearly at Stratton Mountain, Vermont. It was the first contest that Burton snowboards really got behind and helped to organize, and it was the talk of snowboarding circles the world over. Joel Muzzey describes it as the Olympics, Mardi Gras, and a mosh pit rolled up in one insane week of competitive snowboarding. Since it's an open event, anyone can qualify. Every year since 1986, snowboarders from around the world have converged at Stratton to try their luck against the international field or just to watch the best snowboarding on the planet. Back then, it was probably the closest thing snowboarding had to a world championship, even though it was the "U.S." Open.

Of course, to the mainstream, snowboarding was still a fringe sport. The International Olympic Committee (IOC) considered it a fad that was about as athletic as sledding on a silver saucer. The majority of ski areas didn't allow us on their slopes because they considered us an insurance liability and didn't want to upset their longtime skiing clientele. Money would eventually change the minds of ski resorts and the IOC, but in the winter of 1988, we were outcasts, viewed negatively—or at least warily—by public opinion. This only fueled the fire of the snowboarding youth movement.

I was determined to get to the 1988 U.S. Open, but my car had been acting up ever since the ram-it-in-reverse-at-50-mph incident. I wasn't ready for the level of competition, but I wanted to watch Kidwell and other top pros kill it in what was predicted to be the best halfpipe in the world.

Instead, I ended up teaching a kid how not to break his wrists while he fell repeatedly during a half-day lesson at Gunstock. I found out later that week that the halfpipe *had* been insane. A pro-skater-turned-snowboarder named Bert LaMar took second in the men's pro division by pulling handplants and Miller Flips (a skateboarding trick), and Kidwell won by pulling huge slob airs, methods, mutes, and a 540 helicopter (they weren't calling them "spins" back then). I wasn't really into racing but Andy Coghlan, a full-fledged veteran by that time, won the downhill event one-hundredth of a second ahead of West Germany's Peter Bauer. The Euros were known for kicking ass in racing and bad fashion. When an American local, who had personally complimented my riding, took first, I felt some serious American pride. Turns out that Andy had taken his gloves off before his run to reduce wind friction—way before Jamie Lynn became widely known as the pro who would ride without gloves, no matter the conditions.

Not too many people were shooting video of snowboarding events, and even the biggest one in the world—sponsored by Suzuki Samurai that year—didn't get play on television. So that was it. I missed the opportunity to watch Kidwell take the U.S. Open. Damn. I'm still pissed about that one.

Shortly after the Open, Gunstock jumped on the bandwagon and held a contest, but I couldn't talk the mountain management into building a halfpipe. Snowboarding was not a big draw for customers. Groomed runs and moguls for skiers brought in the big bucks. So, in true skier-crossover mentality, the mountain held a snowboarding slalom race. I didn't bother to enter, but I did use the opportunity to stalk the Gnu rep who showed up to demo boards in the parking lot.

It never occurred to me that there were certain channels to go through to get sponsored. As far as I was concerned, here was this guy with a Gnu sticker on his van and a bunch of Gnu snowboards in the back, and I had a reference from professional snowboarder Amy Howat, so why wouldn't he give me a board? After practicing various approaches, I decided on the casual, confident touch. I walked up to him and said, "Hi, I'm Todd Richards. Amy Howat said you could give me a board."

He tried his best to brush me off by looking as though he was busy working. Only problem was that nobody was standing in line to try out Gnu Snowboards, so eventually he had to talk to me. He agreed to let me "demo" a board for the day. I don't think he trusted me because he also made me give him my driver's license. But it was a start, and I figured I could work on the rep later.

Gnu was being touted as the future in snowboard designs, and the company was claiming that their boards carved like no other when you set them on edge. After one run, I absolutely hated it. It was stiff as hell, and the Elfgin bindings were like bear traps on my feet. I fell just trying to ride down the mountain, and catching air on that thing was a joke compared to my soft and flexible Switchblade. I returned the board after three runs, got my license back, and figured I'd give Gnu a few years to catch up with Sims.

My last snowboarding trip of the season was to Attitash Mountain with some friends, and I was determined to nail a method or a mute—any trick where I had to straighten out my back leg in the air. The snowboarding magazines had photo after photo of riders simultaneously grabbing their boards and straightening their back legs just like in skating. I could do it on my bed, but I couldn't figure out how they were doing it in the air. It was like my body wouldn't work that way.

At Attitash, I said, "I'm gonna do it or I'm gonna die trying." On my last run, I launched off a slushy knoll with a bunch of speed and, bam!, kicked my back leg as hard as I could. It locked out straight and the nose of the board came right up into my hand. I was so shocked, I didn't let go and ate crap. But I was pumped that I finally got my body in that position. That day was the last time I'd ride until the following November, but it was a huge breakthrough.

Snake or Be Snaked

There is a certain etiquette to skateboarding on vert ramps. In simplest terms: You want to give other people their turn.

I, on the other hand, was ruthless when I dropped in. Once I got rolling on the ramp, I would totally zone out, oblivious that people were waiting for me. Indoor skate ramps had become fashionable on the East Coast by summer 1988, and Muzzey and I acted like we owned the big one at Zero Gravity in Nashua, New Hampshire. We'd take almost every

Andrecht handplant, 1989.

other run until the Vert Police told us we were hogging the ramp. We'd say we were sorry or pretended to be sorry, then walk back to the ramp and do it again.

All the edginess came from skating with ruthless kids when I was growing up. I learned how to snake really early because there were no such things as respectful pauses in which I could drop in, and that was the only way I'd get runs. The standard motto was "snake or be snaked." So I was always quick on the draw, getting my tail out, not looking when I dropped in. I was lucky that I never really slammed into anybody, although that same summer I did hit a dog. I was at Z.T. Maximus, an indoor spot in Boston, and it was a heated snake session loaded with local hotshots. I timed going after a guy bailed, dropping in without looking, just as somebody's dog wandered onto the ramp.

When a dog gets hit by a car—or a skateboard—all its sweat glands open up. I smacked into the dog and was instantly covered with dog stink. To make matters worse, I heard, "Oh shit, my dog!" and there was one of my heroes—East Coast pro Fred Smith—running toward me and the equally dazed canine. Fred ignored me. He checked out his mutt (which was fine), and I limped off the opposite side of the ramp thinking, "Damn, I just T-boned Fred Smith's dog."

Second Year of College, Barely

New Hampshire Vocational Technical College almost didn't let me back for the 1988/1989 school year because my grades were so terrible. I was still super-pumped on skateboarding, but this was the first summer that I couldn't wait for snow.

Somehow, I convinced my parents to keep paying for school—and to get me an early Christmas present: a Sims Terry Kidwell signature model snowboard with folding Sims highback bindings and a pair of Quimbola Man snowboarding pants. Kidwell wore Quimbola Man, as did Tim Windell and a lot of the other skater-influenced riders. They were the shit, but the Sims board is the reason I am where I am today.

When it turned cold enough in November, Gunstock started blowing snow and I was there the minute a run was rideable. The run had little jumps on its edges, and in one day it all came together for me. I don't know if it was the magic of that Kidwell board or the countless hours I'd spent strapped into the board on my bed doing repetitions. (I'd seriously worked out, like ten mute air grabs in a row, then I'd catch my breath, lie on my stomach, and practice methods, ten in a row, until the board felt like it was a thousand pounds.) Whatever the reason, that opening day at Gunstock in 1988 was the first time I learned how to get my tweak on: rocket airs, double-handed rockets, mutes, methods, anything you could do by grabbing the tip of your board and sticking your back leg out.

Around the time I turned nineteen, the January 1989 issue of *ISM* showed up,

International SNOWBoard Magazine ™

January 1989 Vol. 4 No. 5
U.S. $2.50 CAN. $3.00

The First Mag, The Last Word.

WARNING:

This mag contains explicit and graphic photos of snowboarding. Excessively excitable readers should be lashed down before whipping out the

BIG DICTIONAIRY

or else someone could get seriously hurt. And what about those never-before-released, nude photos of Marilyn Monroe

SURFING THE SUMMIT

out on top of a long mogul run, about to

YO BLAZE AND SLICE

her way down to the base lodge? Those sure would be nice, but no one has those photos and even if we did they wouldn't tell you anything thing about

HOW TO LAND AIRS

HOW TO INSPECT A COURSE

HOW TO RENT EQUIPMENT

But this snowboard magazine will. So get your mind out of the gutter and buy it. Read it. Read it again. Wear it out. Buy another one.

Kidwell doing what he was meant to do on the cover of *ISM,* January, 1989.

and it had Terry Kidwell on the cover doing a mute air from the kicker session at Loon the year before. Trevor Graves had shot the photo, and I had been there. I stared at the magazine cover for about an hour, feeling like I was on the inside of something really big.

During Christmas break, me and Team Kemper Guy took a road trip to Sugarloaf ski resort in Maine because we'd heard they had a halfpipe. When we got there, I attacked the pipe armed with my new grab tricks. I found that the tricks I'd been learning were easier in the halfpipe, and "boning out" my back leg actually helped with balance and landing the tricks. TKG and I took turns snapping photos of each other with my Kodak Disk Camera, and then, when we weren't riding, I'd study the snowboarding magazines I'd brought along and try to figure out variations of the tricks I felt comfortable with. On the hill, I began to think I could actually ride a half-pipe, and told myself, *I'm going to win some contests this winter.*

The first contest of the 1989 New England Cup was at Gunstock, but it was only a slalom, so I didn't even enter. The next event was in February at Sunday River, Maine. I fell on my first run in the halfpipe and ended up back in the pipe practicing while the awards ceremony was going on. Jason Ford, who was following in Craig Kelly's footsteps as the all-around guy who ripped at racing and freestyle, won that event. That was the first time people really took notice of his freestyle abilities.

Waterville Valley was next, and a guy my age named Noah Brandon was there. On my wall at school I had a photo of Noah wearing a *Thrasher* magazine T-shirt, with dread-locks flowing behind him, pulling a big method air. *Guaranteed, he's going to obliterate me in the pipe,* I thought to myself as I watched Noah practice. I saw his skate style. He was so damn good, so damn cool, and so damn nice at the same time. He was the first person I met who came across as a gentleman snowboarder. No attitude—he let his snowboarding do the talking. And that, I thought, was something to aspire to.

Jeff Brushie showed up at Waterville, too. He'd been off riding with Craig Kelly, whose all-black board was called the "Mystery Air." It wasn't really a mystery, since everybody knew the story behind the Burton versus Sims sponsorship ordeal. Once it was settled, the Mystery Air would become the Craig Kelly pro model.

Brushie's halfpipe style and skills had really progressed since the previous winter. He was wearing tongues on his boots (a Craig Kelly trademark that helped increase edge control with your board) and, shit . . . he was riding backward, doing half-Cabs, and looking even more like a skateboarder. I went into that halfpipe contest thinking I was hot shit, but when I saw Brushie, I realized I wasn't. There were maybe thirty guys in the men's division and about twelve in the women's—steep competition. I got third place, Jason Ford took second (and won the race), and Brushie won.

Kris Swierz (one of the kids I'd met while trying to skate the vert ramp at the University of Vermont the year before) and I rode together a lot the winter of my second year in college. I'd drive out to Vermont instead of going to my classes, and we'd try to push each other to learn new tricks. If we could find a halfpipe, or just something resembling a bank of snow, forget about it. We camped out for hours. This was an era when, if you could put your hand on your board in midair, you were a standout on the mountain, and we got used to confused New England skiers stopping to watch us hit jumps. They didn't get it. One day a skier came up and asked me, "Why do you grab your ski-board like that?" and I told him, "So it won't get away." Somehow this sarcasm escaped him (a board can't get away, it's attached to your feet). He nodded and went back to his friends, who had elected him to come and talk to the weird skiboarder. They all nodded in agreement, and some of them waved at us. It was fun to toy with unsuspecting wanker-two-plankers; I'm certain they considered us equally pathetic. Snowboarders were a novelty to skiers, and skiers were old news to snowboarders. There was an utter lack of understanding, which made the early days so much fun.

_The East Coast crew invades the West. Left to right: Jeff Brushie, Lisa Vincinguerra, Kris Swierz, Andy Coughlan, and me at the 1990 Vision Pro at Squaw.

SHRED AND DESTROY/
SNOWSKATERS ON ICE

Kris Swierz and I were at the same level, and we felt confident enough to go to the U.S. Open in March. We pulled up to the Stratton Mountain lot and immediately started picking out pros we'd seen in the magazines: Shaun Palmer, Tim Windell, Kevin Delaney, Keith "Duckboy" Wallace, Rob Morrow, and Andy Coghlan. As we were gearing up to catch the gondola, Coghlan introduced us to Brad Steward, the team manager for Sims. "These are the guys I was telling you about," Coghlan said. Brad was like, "Right on, good to meet you," and that was that.

Swierz and I were silent as we got on the gondola. We were both thinking, *Holy shit, Andy Coghlan has been talking about us?* Later, we found out that photographer Trevor Graves, as well as Andy and some other established pros were heralding us as up-and-comers.

I looked out the window of the gondola and saw a line of three snowboarders wearing black and ripping down the mountain. They were airing off rollers, pulling super slow-motion half-Cabs, and grabbing tight next to their bindings, which is total skate style (unlike me with my nose grabs). We saw them later at the halfpipe. The leader was Chris Roach, who had bleached white hair flowing out from a black beanie. He was with Mike Ranquet and Tucker Fransen—NorCal guys from the West Coast. Over the next few days, I kept an eye out for these three, especially Roach.

The Open had a slalom, giant slalom, and halfpipe event. Swierz and I only entered the halfpipe, and we had a lot of fun practicing in the best pipe we'd ever ridden. I stalled out at least one handplant every practice run, timing a few directly in front of the Sims team manager, Brad Steward, who was camped out near one of the better hits. In the competition itself, we both did shitty. I don't think I even qualified for the final heats, we were so far out of our league.

Craig Kelly took first, Bert LaMar second, Terry Kidwell third, then Delaney,

Palmer, and, way down in eighth place, Chris Roach. Kidwell was still my hero, but Roach's NorCal style, though not as smooth as Kidwell's or Kelly's, was raw and tight. It looked so skatey, and the second he was in the air, he rotated so slow and grabbed his board for so long it was like you were watching a movie in slow motion. From that contest forward, I wanted to ride like Chris Roach.

After the contest, Brad Steward came up to me and explained that even though I hadn't placed well, he saw a lot of potential in my riding and thought I fit the Sims image. He said they'd been looking to add some East Coast talent to their predominantly West Coast team. My jaw dropped as he handed over a used Sims Halfpipe snowboard with a white topsheet and the coveted Sims Team logo on the nose—a hand-me-down from Kevin Delaney, who had just received next-year's model. Then Steward gave me a couple of Sims sweatshirts, a stack of stickers, and a pair of gloves. Swierz got hooked up, too.

So here we were, East Coast regional riders for Sims, on the same team as Kidwell, Roach, and Palmer. It was the best day of my life. I geared up, adjusted the bindings on my new board, and went to the halfpipe, where Trevor Graves was running around like a chicken with its head cut off, trying to get the best photos of the best snowboarders in the world. I pointed out the Sims Team logo on the board, and he gave me a thumb's up. He already knew. In between shooting the real pros, Trevor took a few photos of me grabbing the nose of my board. Life couldn't have been better.

National Collegiate Snowboarding Championships, 1989

While at the Open, I heard about the first-ever National Collegiate Snowboarding Championships, scheduled to take place at Stratton a couple weeks later.

After a painful explanation to my college's sports program advisor about the legitimacy of snowboarding, she agreed to pony up the hundred-dollar entry fee. So I found myself back at Stratton Mountain in April for the inaugural NCSC. I signed up, got my bib, and headed to the halfpipe, where I overheard a couple of kids saying, "There's this Sims Team guy here who's going to take it." I looked around for a while trying to find the other Sims Team rider, before I finally figured out they were talking about me.

I didn't enter the NCSC slalom race. I skipped it because that's what Chris Roach did at the Open. In general, he either boycotted races or rode the courses backward (fakie) on his board, showboating by airing out of the ruts. He was more interested in riding style than speed. Winning a race meant nothing to him. It was a good thing I skipped the race, too, since I would have suffered a beating from the girls' division.

"Holy shit, I just got sponsored by Sims?!"
1989 U.S. Open.

Although it was mainly an East Coast event, people came from as far away as the University of Utah. Lisa Vinciguerra, representing George Washington University in Vermont, won both the slalom and the pipe and was named the overall women's champion. I came through and won the halfpipe by hitting one big method air and a handplant, and I even pulled around a frontside 540. Winning my first halfpipe event was really cool but it wasn't like winning a pro event. I think everybody else fell on their runs, so I didn't get too cocky. That would come later in my career.

I called Sims to tell them, "Check it out, I won this contest." The reaction was, "What contest? Collegiate what? Never heard of it." I got the impression that they didn't care. My self-defeatism took over, and I thought that maybe they didn't remember giving me the free board. Likewise, my parents' reaction was nonchalant. At that point, they didn't understand the magnitude of winning a contest, kind of like the skateboarding events I'd won in the past. I'd tell them, "Hey, Mom and Dad, I won the contest. I took first place." The response was basically, "That's nice, sweetie. Can you pass the milk?"

But I still had a free Sims team board, team sweatshirt, and team gloves, and it didn't bum me out that much that my parents didn't get it. They were on the same page as the rest of the world. Snowboarding was a fad. It would fade away into the next one. I couldn't blame them. It wasn't like snowboarding was in the Olympics or anything.

Sponsored Pro—Rookie Year

I should probably mention that I graduated from college (it was a two-year program) in May 1989 with an associate's degree in graphic stupidity. My entire education was rendered obsolete by a keystroke—that same year computers started to replace drawing boards, and layouts were being done on-screen. The highlight of graduation was throwing my shit into my Chevette and getting out of Laconia as fast as possible.

So I was done with school, living with my parents, and thinking, "What am I going to do now?" My parents read my mind and answered, "You've got to get a job." Landing a job would be extremely difficult, what with my busy summer skateboarding schedule and all. Then I received a letter in the mail from Sims that began with, "I would like to take this opportunity to confirm that SIMS Snowboards, Inc., is interested in retaining your services for the Sims Snowboard Team for the 1989-1990 season." Sims *did* know who I was. And not only that, they wanted to retain my services! I read that letter about a hundred times. It basically asked me to confirm that I wasn't riding for anybody else, didn't have any medical problems, and that I'd get a bunch of free stuff in exchange for my "services." A contract was supposed to show up a few weeks later, but never did.

≡SIMS≡

SNOWBOARDS
714.972.9777
1395 S. LYON ST.
SANTA ANA, CA.
9 2 7 0 5

June 16, 1989

Mr. Todd Richards
135 Pleasant Street
Paxton, Mass. 01612

Dear Todd:

   I would like to take this opportunity to confirm that SIMS Snowboards, Inc., is interested in retaining your services for the SIMS Snowboard team for the 1989 - 1990 season.

   The following summarizes and outlines the basic terms and conditions which were agreed upon by yourself and SIMS.

   SIMS shall provide you with assorted free goods in an amount to be determined in SIMS sole discretion, consisting of snowboards, bindings, and related accessories. You will be designated as a SIMS Snowboard team rider for the 1989 - 1990 season.

   You shall use your best efforts when riding or competing on behalf of the SIMS Snowboard team.

   You represent that you are healthy and suffer from no illness or disability which would inhibit your ability to ride or otherwise compete for the SIMS Snowboard team. You further represent that you are not bound by any other contract for the endorsement of the same or similiar products or accessories as those which you will represent/endorse for SIMS.

   A formal team rider agreement shall be forwarded to you within the next few weeks. Should you decide not to enter the subsequent team rider agreement, then you agree to return all free goods given to you pursuant to this letter of intent. You agree to pay, at retail cost, for any goods not returned, or returned in a damaged or destroyed condition.

I read this letter 2000 times and taped it to my wall.

In September Trevor Graves called me to say, "I think you might be in the next issue of *ISM*. What's your address?" I got a package the following week. Inside was the October 1989 issue of *International Snowboard Magazine* with a note that read, "You're in the magazines now, kid." On the cover was Noah Salasnek with the blurb SHRED & DESTROY: THE SKATER INFLUENCE ON SNOWBOARDING.

Flipping through the magazine, I paused on the page Trevor had marked. I stared at a photo of this guy dorking around inside the lodge at Tenney, pulling a streetplant on his skateboard with snowboard gloves on his feet—and I realized it was me. My first photo in a magazine: a three-quarter-page black-and-white. I was a little bummed that I wasn't snowboarding in the shot, but I really couldn't complain. Next to my photo was Mike Ranquet, flipping off the camera with a caption that read ATTI-TUDE IN ACTION. On the opposite page was a shot of pro skater Kevin Staab. Shaun Palmer, Dave Lemieux, Jeff Brushie, Andy "Pretzel" Hetzel, skating legend Gator, and Matt Cummins were shown on the following pages. I was surrounded by greatness in both the skating and snowboarding worlds.

From that day forward, whenever I flipped through magazines, I kept a shame-less eye out for shots of myself. Still, I never thought I was good enough to be in the mags. I felt like I'd tricked everybody.

Fall rolled around, and my dad explained to me that "two free T-shirts" and "that photo in the snowboarding magazine" were great and all, but, "Really, you *need* to get a job." Dragging my feet on the job issue wasn't going to carry me through the winter. I passed on the opportunity to pour concrete for a construction company, and winter pizza delivery on the East Coast was way too hazardous. I ended up going to work at the Ski Market, a ski shop at the base of Mount Wachusett. Shortly after I got the job, Brown Santa brought me a bunch of boxes—big boxes from Sims that con-tained two new black-graphic snowboards, sweatshirts, T-shirts, gloves, and a purple-and-green team outfit with a Sims Team logo and my name embroidered on the chest pocket. I called Kris Swierz to see if Santa had visited his place, too (he had), then put my stuff on, strapped into one of the snowboards, and jumped around on my bed until I was soaked with sweat.

The Ski Market required me to attend a bunch of mandatory sales clinics so I could learn about the different skis, boots, and bindings I'd be selling. I didn't pay attention. I was only there for the free Mount Wachusett season pass and to appease my parents so they'd continue to let me live at home rent-free. Somehow, I actually sold skis to people, like a used car salesman. The best thing about the job was the hours. I'd ride every morning, then work the afternoon to closing shift.

There weren't very many snowboarders on the hill, and an even smaller crew of sponsored riders. Back then if you had a team jacket, you were special. In my case, I

INTERNATIONAL

SNOW
Board

October 1989 Vol.5 No.2 U.S. $2.95 CAN. $3.95

THE FIRST MAG. THE LAST WORD. ™

SHRED & DESTROY ?

The Skater Influence on Snowboarding

47940

Noah Salasnek on the cover of the October 1989 *ISM*. Inside was my first published photo . . .

Attitude in action: Mike Ranquet.

Photo: Trevor Graves

M ost skaters don't go around beating up drunks and stealing people's mail...

"Hey, you with the gloves on your feet! No skating in the lodge!" Todd Richards at the "Habitrail."

. . . Of course, this shot has nothing to do with snowboarding, except for the gloves on my feet.

felt like the big fish in a little pond, but I was really just a minnow in a puddle. I wore that team jacket everywhere to show it off, even if it was sixty degrees out. It was the best thing since sliced bread.

Mid-December, Trevor Graves called with a cool Christmas present. He said I had a photo in the January *ISM,* a nice surprise because I'd begun to think the "Shred and Destroy" article might have been my five seconds of fame. I was barely off the phone before I was in the car, trying to hunt the issue down. Only two places in a hundred-mile radius carried *ISM,* and they rarely had more than two copies. I don't know who the other two snowboarders in Massachusetts who read *ISM* were, but both shops were sold out and I was pissed.

I drove around for another two hours and finally stopped at a little bookstore in Fitchburg, forty-five minutes from Paxton. There it was in the magazine rack, the January 1990 *ISM* with Craig Kelly on the cover. Inside was the article my old friend Rob LaVigne had written about the inaugural Collegiate Championships, and a three-by-five inch color shot of me doing a method air with a caption that read, TODD RICHARDS

Finally, a magazine shot of me on a snowboard. From my first win at the 1989 Collegiate Championships.

DOING HIS BEST SHAUN PALMER LOOK-ALIKE AIR. As Palmer was widely regarded as the most stylish method-man, I was flattered. Then I read the article twice, just to make sure Rob had really forgotten to mention that I won the halfpipe event! He mentioned the overall winners, Steve Hayes and Lisa Vinciguerra, who had both raced and competed in the pipe, but I got barred. So much for knowing the writer.

Despite my superhero team jacket and superhero team board, I was still a mild-mannered wanna-be. I wasn't very good at drinking and didn't do drugs—so courage was something I couldn't find in a bottle. (The last time I'd drunk anything was senior prom when I barfed all over my car and myself, rolled around in it, and went to sleep.) Those magazine photos, however, did great things for confidence, and I took first place and second place at the first two 1990 New England Cup contests at Sugarloaf, Maine, and Waterville Valley, New Hampshire. Kris Swierz took second and first respectively, so we were doing a good job of representing Sims on the East Coast. We won big glass goblets and a couple hundred bucks each—huge as far as I was concerned. My dad told me not to quit my day job.

Late in January 1990, the new Sims team manager, Miki Keller, called me. "The Vision/Sims Pro in the Snow contest is coming up at Squaw Valley," she said. "I'll give you and Swierz a place to stay, but you gotta get your butts out to California."

I asked my manager at the Ski Market for the week off, and he wasn't happy about it. He'd nicknamed me—the only snowboarder who worked at the shop—"Agro" as in, I was "like, the totally way rad, and like agro surfer/skater on snow dude." "The schedule's not looking good, Agro," the manager told me, shaking his head. I laid down the law."Look," I said, "I gotta go. I'm out of here. I quit if you can't give me the time off." Or maybe I groveled a bunch and he finally caved. Either way, I got the time off.

All Expenses Not Paid

I'd flown in an airplane only once before, to Florida when I was seven, so the trip to Tahoe, all the way across the country, was huge. I double-checked my gear, stuffed money in different pockets, and carried double IDs. My parents were very adept at planning for everything that could go wrong. Kiss, kiss, "Call us when you get there," said my mom.

Kris Swierz and I landed in Reno (the closest airport to the California/Tahoe mountain resorts) and met Miki Keller, our team manager, and most of the Sims A Team in the baggage area. I was twenty, but felt like a three-year-old in front of Mickey Mouse at Disneyland. Tucker Fransen, Terry Kidwell, Kevin Delaney, Kris

Jamieson—they were all there, just hanging out, waiting for their bags, just like us! Swierz and I hung back and whispered to each other, "Dude, look at all these pros." Then Swierz's older brother, who worked at Heavenly (another resort in Tahoe), showed up, and we waved good-bye to the guys we really wanted to hang out with. We'd come four days before the event with the understanding that we'd couch surf at Swierz's brother's place for a couple of days until our hotel room with the team was available. But it appeared as though he was our chaperone when he picked us up, and I felt stupid. That didn't last long, though, because I was in *California*. Actually, I was in Nevada, but in my mind I was already in California. All the way to Heavenly, I couldn't stop saying, "I can't believe we're in California."

The next morning we headed into a whole new world. It snowed two feet the night before, the biggest dump I'd ever seen. The Sierra Mountains could have been the Himalayas as far as I was concerned. I couldn't believe that people snowboarded this type of terrain. The expert runs were so steep that if you fell you'd roll all the way to the bottom of the mountain, and they didn't have cheesy East Coast names like "White Heat," "Nubian Nightmare," or "The Corn Cobber." There were huge cliffs that people were jumping off of, and the runs were so long, I couldn't ride one top to bottom without stopping to rest my legs, and lungs. It was the complete opposite of the gentle, rolling hills I was accustomed to back home.

Heavenly was Shaun Palmer's zone. That day, Swierz and I were wearing our magic purple jumpsuits, hoping he'd recognize us as fellow Sims Team riders. Sure enough, Palmer came up to us at a lift line, wearing some older Sims gear that was torn up and held together with duct tape. I took a deep breath and tried to be cool, casually sticking my chest out to display the embroidered Sims Team logo.

"Hey, what's up?" he said, looking at Swierz. "Didn't I hook up with your sister at the Open?" He talked to us for a minute, then said, "See ya later," and got on the chairlift. Swierz knew about the hook-up with his sister, and he could have cared less. What he cared about, like me, was that Shaun Palmer had talked to us. In public! It was the coolest thing in the world. Palmer was a jerk, but he was cool at the same time. I respected the shit out of him. And I respected him even more after riding Heavenly. It took us a while to get used to riding in deep powder, but after that, we started following other locals around the mountain. They rode in the trees at speeds I thought were fast on open runs, and there were times that I was intimidated by the bigness of it all. It was humbling, but at the same time inspiring.

Two days later, we jumped a bus to Squaw Valley. The resort hadn't always been receptive to snowboarding. According to legend, in 1988 the president of Squaw Valley wrote a letter to *ISM* that said, "We do not believe that snowboarding is truly compatible with regular alpine skiing for several reasons, not the least of which is safety: lack of releasable bindings, loading and unloading lifts, and acrobatics, just to name a few." The following summer, pro snowboarder Tom Burt ran into Squaw's president on a beach in Mexico and introduced himself. Burt taught him how to surf, and Squaw Valley changed its policy the following winter.

Swierz and I met Miki at the Squaw Valley Inn then went up to the counter to register, figuring we'd have to pay despite the original deal. To our surprise, and relief, Miki had reserved a room for us, which we thought was great because we weren't on the A Team (which got paid and had expenses covered) or the B Team (which got free gear and expenses covered). We were on the supersecret East Coast C Team. I think Swierz and I were Sims' East Coast experiment, to see if freestyle was really alive east of the Mississippi. Anything we got above and beyond free gear was gravy.

After Miki handed us our room keys, she held up the just-released February 1990 *ISM* and said, "Have you seen this?" The cover featured Tom Burt busting through a wall of trees straight toward the camera, wearing a flaming pastel orange and yellow tie-dye jacket, blue gloves, and neon pink Bolle goggles. That was totally acceptable fashion; in fact, most brands encouraged mixing pastels, primaries, and neons. "Check page thirty-seven, full-page, full-color," Miki said. I flipped to a Trevor Graves shot of me doing an East Coast double-handed rocket air in Stratton's pipe, taken right after the U.S. Open. I was stoked until I closed the mag and saw that on the back cover was a Sims ad featuring Chris Roach pulling a full West Coast, Chris Miller skate style, frontside nosebone grab, his hand tight next to his foot. I flipped back and forth from my shot to his, and it was like night and day. I was in the dark ages with my

My unstylish nose grab inside the February 1990 *ISM* paled in comparison to Chris Roach's back cover.

The back cover of the February 1990 issue of *ISM*. This shot of Roach with pure skate style told me it was time to get my shit together.

My money move in 1990 was the handplant. This one became a double-page spread in *TransWorld*.

grab near the nose of my board. He was on point with his skate-style grab so close to his bindings. I had to get my shit together.

That night, to our surprise, Swierz and I were actually invited to the A Team meeting, which took place in Miki's hotel room. We had no idea what went on at a snowboard meeting, but it sounded pretty important. It ended up being a casual discussion about how the boards were riding, who would be featured in the next ads, and a bunch of mutual heckling and chest pounding. Swierz and I kept our mouths shut and stayed in the shadows until Miki made a phone call to Brad Steward, who had been promoted to marketing director. The phone was passed from pro to pro to me.

"Hey Todd, how's it going, glad you're there, blah, blah, blah . . ."

This guy knows I'm here? I thought.

"What do you need?" he asked.

"A new Halfpipe freestyle board and a Kidwell?" I said tentatively.

"Okay," he said. "And do you need any shirts or anything?"

I was tempted, but the C Team had a policy that if you got new gear, you had to turn in your old stuff to the factory. I liked how my Kidwell was worked in—nice and soft like a banana—and didn't want to give it up. The red Vision (the distributor for Sims) sweatshirt I'd been wearing in all my published snowboarding photos thus far was lucky, and I didn't want to part with it for superstitious reasons. So I told him I was all set.

On the way back to our room, I asked Swierz what he'd ordered. He'd spent a lot of time with Jeff Brushie, who had been coached by Andy Coghlan and a long line of in-the-know scam artists. "I ordered four boards, boots, sweatshirts, new gloves, and a half-dozen T-shirts," he told me. Damn, I blew it.

My First, and Last, Police Lineup

We went to Mi Casa, a Mexican restaurant, with the Sims team that night: Shaun Palmer, Scott "Upside" Downey, Kevin Delaney, Tim Windell, Kris Jamieson, Lisa Vinciguerra, Paul Parsons, Bill Harris, Terry Kidwell, Tucker Fransen, and Gator (the only pro skateboarder of the group who was also a sponsored pro snowboarder). Plus, pro snowboarder Matt Cummins was there representing Lib Tech, a new company born on the West Coast. It was a who's who of all the heroes in the videos and magazines. To be part of the Sims team was incredible. This meal was such a milestone in my life, it's still like a photograph in my mind.

I sat between Gator and a guy named John Bradshaw, who was a friend of Brad Steward and Kevin Staab (a Sims pro skateboarder). I'd never heard of him, but I'll never forget him. He was the king of doing weird things, like folding a napkin into a dick, or a dragon, or this strange crying baby thing, all of which made me shoot food out of my nose. People were drinking, but I was too young, and not into partying anyway.

So these guys were going nuts on sponsored beer and margaritas, and all I wanted to do was talk to Gator about skateboarding. Finally, he brought up skateboarding, and I blurted out, "Dude, I skate. I'm a skater." That opened up the conversation. We talked about photos in recent skate mags, and I rambled on about Fred Smith, the Canton ramp, Maximus, Todd Squad, and tricks that could be crossed over into snowboarding. I probably talked his ear off, but I got the impression he was stoked that I was the youngest-looking guy at the table but could hold my own regarding skateboarding trivia. At the end of the night, I shook his hand, and it felt like we were bros. Swierz and I both felt accepted, despite the fact that during dinner, Jamieson had ripped on both of us relentlessly, ordering us milk because we were underage and shit like that. We ate it up.

After dinner, most of the pros headed to the hotel bar or the hot tub or wherever post-twenty-one superheroes go, but Swierz and I went to sleep so we'd be well rested to ride.

We were woken at six-thirty the next morning by Miki pounding on our room door. She was going down the hallway to each of the riders' rooms, yelling, "Everybody outside in the parking lot. We have a problem." Outside, two cop cars were parked alongside an impromptu police lineup of the Sims team, minus Gator and Cummins. *What the hell is going on?* I thought to myself as a cop ushered me and Swierz to the end of the line. Some guy with a bandage on his head got out of a police car and walked up and down the line, glaring suspiciously at each of us. The guy huddled with the cops for a few tense minutes, then we were released to go about our "business."

Inside the lobby, Tucker filled us in: "Something gnarly went down in the hot tub last night, and they thought it was one of us." Then he whispered, "We think it was Gator. Got in an argument with that dude and whacked him on the head with a bottle." The guy woke up on the edge of the spa, and all he could remember was a couple of derelict snowboarders who'd been talking shit.

Swierz and I were wide-eyed. I'd had a pretty sheltered existence to that point, and this was serious. It kind of bummed me out. It hit me much harder the following winter when Gator raped and murdered a twenty-one-year-old girl—the best friend of his estranged girlfriend—stuffed her body into a surfboard bag, and buried her in the California desert. He is now serving a life sentence. When I heard this news, I flashed back to that night at Mi Casa and how stoked Gator had been while talking about skateboarding. How could that same guy commit such a horrible crime? The whole thing really creeped me out. It kind of gave me some insight into a life that I could have lived without. This whole snowboarding/skateboarding fantasy world wasn't supposed to include the evils of the real world. Unfortunately, I learned that there's no escaping reality.

Riding with Legends

After the lineup, we packed into a van to Donner Summit for slalom practice because back then, most sponsored riders did every event. Sims wanted well-rounded riders and overall results. Considering that 95 percent of the Sims team were freestyle snowboarders, it was pretty pointless. But, at the time, there were no halfpipe specialists, which was exactly how I thought of myself. Even Palmer, one of the top freestyle pipe riders in the world, ripped at racing, and Kidwell had been known to take a top five in the gates. I flailed my way through practice, taking some gates to the dome (getting whacked in the head by the poles), and when we were finally excused, I felt like a kid at recess.

Chris Roach and his brother Monty, Tucker Fransen, and this other Tahoe local named Devon Ryerson took off toward Donner's little excuse for a halfpipe with Swierz and me hot on their tails. This session was just for fun, but I still felt pressure to perform and hopefully salvage some dignity after my horrible slalom racing performance. It had been a year since we'd seen these guys snowboard in person, but we'd been studying their riding in a snowboarding movie called *The Western Front,* the first snowboard video I bought. It was produced by Fall Line Films, which specialized in freestyle snowboarding shot in Tahoe. I watched it a million times. Seriously, I wore that tape out.

The guys had longer bleach blond hair, updated Sims clothes, and cool sticker jobs on their boards. They had "Tahoe style"—not only their riding, but their look. They were everything that we wanted to be, but just didn't know enough about.

It was hard to ride and watch them at the same time. They were pulling unbelievable shit like fakie to fakie 360s (taking off backward and landing backward) and switch (i.e., fakie, both of which mean "done while riding backward") Indys, though they called them "rewinds." I was thinking, *What the hell is that?* I only rode backward when I accidentally slid out, and then I got back around as quick as possible before I wiped out or ran someone over.

The pipe was essentially a crappy ditch with chopped-up snow and big frozen snow boulders pushed up on the sides. If you hit a snow boulder the right way, it could pop you into the middle of the halfpipe. It sounds funny now, but halfpipes were dangerous then. Most of the hits would send you into the adjacent trees if you weren't careful. Terry Kidwell showed up and started hitting the same spot everybody else was. Tucker was doing frontside inverts off it, and I was like *What? Someone can do frontside inverts on a snowboard?* The only time I'd seen someone do one that clean was Bert LaMar—in a photo.

The entrance of the halfpipe was just this meager snow bank, but I could snap up into an invert on nothing: a mogul, even flat ground if there was a tiny bump. I waited for a gap in the action, dropped in, snapped up into an Andrecht on that little wall, stalled the living shit out of it, and then casually laid it down. I looked around and noticed Tucker and Kidwell were staring at me. Kidwell said, "Dude, that's messed up!" and Tucker followed with, "How did you do that? There's nothing there."

Nothing compares to that moment in the shitty Donner pipe when Terry Kidwell and the Tahoe crew paid me a compliment for my riding. Nothing.

Holy Fricking Halfpipe!

The next day, January 23, 1990, was halfpipe practice at Squaw. When I took a look at that pipe, all I could think was, *Damn. It's big.* The Squaw pipe was an actual pipe with transitions. It had eight-foot walls that were difficult to get used to after all the crappy pipes I'd ridden in the East, not to mention the little ditch at Donner. Here, you had to make your own line because there weren't highway ruts guiding you from hit to hit. Plus, it was steep so Swierz and I were legitimately intimidated.

What freaked me out the most was riding with Damian Sanders. Damian was a hard-boot, bleach-blond, neon-spandex-wearing psycho who rode for Avalanche Snowboards. He went bigger than anybody else. He would tuck the entire halfpipe, build speed, and then do a single huge air, like a contorted, ultra–tweaked out cross-rocket that made him look double-jointed, or a progressive 360 (grabbing his board's tip on the first 180 and its tail on the second 180) while ten feet above the lip, easy.

It was like Twistah's ramp all over again—a pipe crawling with talent, and I was out of my league. Burton had sent a team salvo from the East Coast known as the Burton Army: Jeff Davis, Mike Jacoby, Jimi Scott (a vertical roller skater turned snowboarder), Jason Ford, and Noah Brandon. They were up against our West Coast–dominated Sims squad and other big names like Don Szabo and Victor Coyne from Nectar, Dan Donnelly from K2 (the first ski company to charge into the snowboard market), Andy Hetzel representing Kemper, Brian Harper for Look, Mike Estes and Jon

Boyer for Barfoot, and Rob Morrow, an ex-Sims rider who was riding the first board of his new company Morrow Snowboards. Not many companies made snowboards in the late 1980s and early 1990s, but as I learned, this was changing fast. This was just the beginning of an onslaught of new copycat companies, all vying for a piece of the snowboarding industry pie.

Once we got used to the sheer size of the pipe, Swierz and I started doing pretty well. After one run, I met Tom Sims, who not only founded Sims, but was a photographer as well. I introduced myself and, despite his stoked demeanor, I was positive he had no idea who I was. He set up on one of the pipe's big frontside hits, where I pulled a big stiffy—shoved my board right in his face and looked straight into the camera. I heard the camera go click, and Tom let out this loud and clear "Yeah!"—a verbal high-five from the founder of Sims.

The Vision/Sims Pro in the Snow contest got rolling on my fourth day in Tahoe.

Kris Swierz, Tom Sims, and me at the Vision/Sims Pro in the Snow, Squaw Valley, 1990.

Lee Crane, the managing editor of *TransWorld SNOWboarding* magazine was co-announcing the event with Wiley Asher, the senior editor of *TransWorld*'s competitor, *International Snowboard Magazine*. The two were calling out tricks, and their heckling of each other and each other's magazines between runs grew more competitive as the contest went on. Wiley finally asked Lee something derogatory about his mother over the loudspeaker, and Lee responded with, "My mother? Why don't you ask her, she's right there," and pointed out his mom, who had come to watch her son as he announced the event. Luckily, she was laughing.

Shortly thereafter, my run came up. It was a head-to-head format. I can't remember who I was up against—but it was somebody I was convinced was better than me, and I got the jitters. Halfway through, I fell when re-entering the pipe after a pretty big method. I wanted to ride straight down the middle of the pipe and go hide, but something made me finish my run. I grunted out a handplant at the bottom and stalled it as long as I could. As I held it, I heard the crowd cheering, which gave me some redemption. And it wasn't like I had expected to beat any of these people anyway. At least not this time.

As I was leaving, a guy wearing a *TransWorld SNOWboarding* sweatshirt walked up to me and introduced himself. Formerly a sponsored East Coast skateboarder who I remembered seeing in a 1985 Kryptonics Skateboard ad, Fran Richards was now selling ads for *TransWorld*. "Hey Todd, I'd like you to have this," he said and threw me a *TransWorld* sweatshirt. Then he handed me the February 1990 issue with Jon Boyer on the cover. Inside was an article called "The Eastern Front," which had a photo from the Open of me doing a double-handed handplant at Stratton. The caption read TODD RICHARDS HAS BEEN TURNING HEADS ON THE NEW ENGLAND CUP FOR THE LAST FEW YEARS. The photo was taken by Jon Foster, whom I vaguely remembered meeting at the event, a guy with a big bushy beard and a bunch of cameras hanging around his neck. He looked like Chong, from Cheech and Chong. Needless to say, I was happier than a pig in shit.

The next two days the slalom and super G were held, and I figured if I didn't compete in them, Sims would drop me. Suffice it to say I was terrible (got disqualified for missing gates), and Kris Jamieson won both racing events.

Back Down to Earth

The mandatory post-contest party was held at someone's house in nearby Donner. I thought I was pretty cool in my new *TransWorld* sweatshirt. Plus I'd just competed in an invitational pro snowboarding contest. And Tom Hsieh, the publisher of *ISM*, came

Me and my method, during a photo shoot just after the Vision Pro at Squaw.

up to me with photographer John Sposeto, who said he'd gotten some great shots of me. Hell yeah, I was badass.

Swierz and I were getting pushed around in this sea of people, when some girl asked us, "So who are you guys?"

Swierz said, "I'm Kris," and I said, "I'm Todd Richards."

She flattened me with one fell swoop.

"Do you always introduce yourself with your full name?" she said. I was a stuttering idiot at that point, but she went on. "Why do you have to introduce yourself as Todd Richards? Do you think I'll recognize your name or something? I don't care if you are some pro, so get over yourself."

Swierz slinked off, and the girl waited a second for me to respond. When I didn't, she said, "Whatever," and melted into the crowd. I stood there swearing that I would never ever again introduce myself by my full name. This wouldn't have been so horrible if she hadn't been so right on it. Truth be told, I knew there was a little bit of a buzz going on about me, and I wanted to impress her. Being pro had been my biggest goal. It wasn't working out in skating, but it was looking good for snowboarding, and I flaunted it a bit. Boy, that girl chopped my ego in half. She also made me realize something important, and that is, "Who cares?" It's only snowboarding, and when you're not on the hill, you're just like everybody else. In fact, even when you *are* on the hill, you're just like everybody else. Case in point: I found out later that the girl was a pro snowboarder herself.

As the night wore on, the crowd grew even bigger and started pitching and rolling. Then there was a blood-curdling scream. Kris Jamieson, the champ of the event, had been pushed into a wood-burning stove and caught himself with both hands. He was rushed off in an ambulance, and I jumped at the opportunity to leave early with Miki Keller and Lisa Vinciguerra. As we were driving down a snowy road, the headlights caught a slumped-over figure sitting in the snow. It was Chris Roach, wasted, with a bloody nose. We got him into the car and brought him back to the hotel. Chris had been dating a pro named Heather Mills and during an argument, she had apparently walloped him and shoved him out of her car and took off. Chris would forever claim that he didn't remember anything from that night, but I never missed a chance to remind him that he got his ass kicked by a girl.

On the way to the airport a couple days later, I remembered that I never called my parents to let them know that I'd gotten to Tahoe okay. I'd been away from home for nine days by the time I got home only to find out they'd been checking in with Swierz's parents. They were more bummed than angry that I hadn't called. I never forgot to call and check in ever again.

I'd only been home for a couple days when Miki called and said she wanted me to go to the OP Pro at Copper Mountain, Colorado, in February. Apparently I'd done something right in Tahoe.

It was the same deal. I had to get there, and Sims would cover everything else. I knew leaving again so soon was the kiss of death for my job at the Ski Market, so I psyched myself up to ask my parents for help. Perhaps Miki had gotten to them first because they said they'd been saving some money for a rainy day (quite possibly a four-year college education for me) and were excited that my snowboarding seemed to be taking me somewhere.

Swierz didn't get invited to this one, so I flew to Denver alone, then took a three-hour shuttle up to Copper, where I recognized Jon Boyer, the Barfoot rider I'd seen at Squaw. His nickname was Jon Boy Air. He was a red-haired Canadian Danny Bonaduce—your typical class clown with stand-up potential. We ended up going over to Brecken-ridge together to practice on the halfpipe.

At Brek, I met Noah Salasnek, one of the few pro snowboarders who was also a sponsored skateboarder. Andy Hetzel and Mike Ranquet were there, along with a couple locals named Matty Goodman and Ken Block. I was pretty quiet riding with these guys. Even though I wanted to be hard core punk like Ranquet, my personality wreaked of conservative East Coast guy.

Driving with the Enemy

At the end of the day, the Brek locals started talking about going to Fort Skate in Fort Collins, Colorado, a couple hours away. I immediately thought, *Oh shit, here's my chance,* and jumped in the back of Ken Block's black Volkswagen GTI with Matty Goodman. Ranquet sat up front, and seconds later the car was filled with smoke, beers were cracked, and Ken was driving like an idiot—at least ninety miles per hour on a winter road. The nervous, sheltered kid in me came out. I was shitting my pants, at the mercy of a maniac behind the wheel.

Ken skimmed past a row of orange traffic cones on the right-hand side of the road at light speed. All of a sudden Ranquet yelled, "Door prize!" opened his door, and whacked a cone. The entire way through the Eisenhower Tunnel, Ranquet blasted cones. All I heard was Ken laughing and "Door prize!" Boom! "Door prize!" Boom! "Door prize!" Boom! To top it off, I looked over at Matty, and he was picking huge boogers out of his nose and wiping them on the back of Ken's seat. Matty gave me a look that was like, "Go ahead, kid, it's fun." So I dug deep and started smearing boogers too. Anything to look like I wasn't scared shitless.

Somehow we made it to Fort Skate, and some guy let us in to skate the session for free. Noah Salasnek showed up with Andy Hetzel, and he was doing crazy tricks like Caballerial Indy nose bones to superhigh chicken wings. He was pro and you could tell. Matty Goodman was also a good skater. He was friends with Kevin Staab and was even wearing one of Kevin's "90" sweatshirts. Kevin's company was pretty underground, which gave Matty instant credibility. I had a great session and stalled a sad plant to fakie for what seemed like a half-hour, first one ever for me. I proved myself to these guys, which was important because there weren't too many pro snowboarders who were also good skaters.

The OP Pro halfpipe contest was the next day, February 11, and it was head-to-head. I went up against Mike Jacoby, who was all over the magazines. Just seeing his name next to mine on the board was enough to punch myself out. The halfpipe was perfect for my handplants, but everybody was doing airs. I figured, *I better do airs, too. Or maybe I should do a handplant. No! Yes? No?* I was completely confused as I dropped in. Zero focus.

This was back when one trick could win your run, and everything else was just filler. My airs were mediocre, and Jacoby won and advanced with his J-Tear cartwheel shit. After my run Shaun Palmer came up to me. He was so pissed I thought he was going to slug me, but he only said, "Shit, man. Why the hell didn't you do your handplant? You would have beat him for sure." All I could say in response was, "Fuck!"

I thought, *From here on out, I'm going to do what I'm good at, not what everybody else is doing.*

Apparently I'd become known as the "handplant guy" because at the photo shoot after the contest a bunch of photographers kept asking me to pull them. Ken Achenbach, a Canadian rider and photographer from Whistler, BC, got a shot of one that became a double-page spread in a *TransWorld* article the following January. (Yes, an entire year later.) That day, I was coerced into doing handplants so Tim Windell could air over me. Going doubles was sketchy in skateboarding and hadn't been tried very much in snowboarding—too many sharp edges being hucked around. With cameras aimed at us, I'd stall each handplant out until I saw Windell riding across the bottom of the pipe, which a lot of people thought was pretty rad. That whole time, I was praying that I wouldn't get flattened by my doubles partner.

I returned to Massachusetts in time to finish off the New England Cup at Magic Mountain on February 18, 1990. I was surprised to see a crowd that probably topped one hundred spectators, not including the competitors. The riders were getting better and better, too. I started incorporating more fakie riding into my routine, with some half-Cabs, and I considered spinning a 540 but didn't risk it. My handplants were still a crowd pleaser, and my tricks were enough to edge out Swierz who was my closest competition. I won the event and was named the New England Cup Halfpipe Champion for the winter of 1989/1990. I got three hundred dollars for the overall title and another goblet.

My dad's eyes were starting to open. He began attending some East Coast events where he saw the contest banners, sponsors, and teams. He liked the camaraderie and high-fives among competitors and realized why snowboarding and skateboarding meant so much to me. It made him proud to watch me in my element, vastly different from the Little League practices he'd taken me to when I was a kid. Then, nobody had wanted me on their team; now I was getting attention and respect from announcers and competitors alike. When some of the parents and riders noticed me hanging with him, they'd come up and say things like, "You're Todd's dad? You've got a hell of a son there." I could tell he was proud of me, and likewise, I was stoked that he was taking an active interest in my riding, and me.

International Man of Mystery

OP sponsored an international pro invitational series in Canada, and I got invited to compete, thanks to Sims and Miki Keller who picked me for one of the team rider slots. I had never left the United States, so before I committed I made sure that there would be some riders I knew attending. Dave Lemieux, Kris Swierz, and I made the arduous drive to Quebec, a few hours away from Paxton. The border crossing freaked me out. I thought the guards might give me a cavity search just for the hell of it. Though innocent, I felt paranoid, and as we drove through the checkpoint, I actually turned around and took what I thought could be a last look at America.

The Mont Avila contest was a joke: It was pouring rain, and the pipe was unimaginably small and lame, even worse than the pipes in the New England Cup. But all the big names were there, and I placed fourth behind Rob Morrow, Andy Hetzel, and Noah Salasnek, who got first, second, and third, respectively. Jason Ford, in his purple pastels and Oakley factory pilot sunglasses, won the races, proving that he was no longer just following in Craig Kelly's footsteps as a diverse rider, but a thunderous force to be reckoned with.

The 1990 U.S. Open

The following weekend, March 29, 1990, was the U.S. Open. My dad suggested that both he and my mom come to watch, which made me feel like I had my whole family behind me. It also increased the pressure—I really wanted to do well in front of them. For some reason, I felt that was more important than anything.

That's Jason Ford trying to grab the tail of
my board in 1989 at Waterville Valley.

I showed up a couple days early to practice. The pipe had just been built by a legendary pipe cutter who worked at Stratton. Lyle used what we called the "scooper machine" to create an amazing pipe. It was basically a standard bucket-loader tractor attachment, but he was the first to use it for this purpose. It was way different than the eventual Pipe Dragons (pipe shaping and grooming machines) of the future, but with Lyle's touch, cutting pipes was an art form. At this particular U.S. Open, the pipe was like a brand-new skate ramp with perfect transitions and the perfect amount of vert—the type of pipe you can take one look at and know how it will perform. I'll never forget the smell of that pipe: crisp morning air mixed with the grease from the chairlifts overhead. I love that smell. I was allowed to session the pipe early by Burton police, along with proven competitors like Mike Jacoby, Craig Kelly, Kelly Jo Legaz, Joe Jackson, Bret Johnson, Dave Seoane, and Jason Ford. Normally, the newer kids had to wait and practice with the other open-class riders, but I was invited inside the fence when they saw me watching. I had graduated from the minors, even though I still felt like a bat boy.

Sims had rented a big house next to Stratton, and the first person I encountered when I got there after practice was Mario Paolo Dabbeni, an Italian powerhouse who raced and rode pipe equally well. I'd never met anybody from another country (except for English-speaking Canadians), let alone somebody who walked around the house wearing skin-tight Speedos. Mario was also one of the first guys to wear a helmet consistently in the halfpipe. Since that first contest at Tenney in 1988, when I'd gotten so much shit for it, I hadn't put mine on once.

Stratton is known for its raging parties during the Open, a collision of east and west coasts, with Europeans and the occasional Japanese thrown in. This was the era when pro riders were starting to realize they needed to be good on the mountain, but they also had to rage equally hard at bars and parties in order to establish the "right reputation." After the races were over (the first three days of the Open), the parties got into full swing. I did not want to increase my odds of puking the following morning, which was the day of the halfpipe competition, so I took it easy. The butterflies in my stomach were already circling like vultures, so I called it a night early.

At three in the morning I woke to the sight of blurry humanoids all around me. One was rapping me on the forehead with his knuckles. It was Andy Coghlan, who was grumbling angrily, "Where's Palmer?" I looked around at his equally pissed-off lynch mob that included Mark Sullivan and Russell Winfield, thought it was a bad dream, and closed my eyes. Coghlan whacked me on the forehead again, looking ready to rip my head right off. "Where the fuck is Palmer?" he repeated, and I sputtered, "I don't know, man. I don't know."

I found out quickly enough that Shaun Palmer had gone to the Sunset Bay Snowboard Shop party and "lost" his wallet. After he couldn't find it, he decided someone had stolen it. When nobody came clean, he threw a log through a window and bailed. Andy Coghlan, who was a sort of East Coast riders' representative, didn't tolerate that kind of punk-ass bullshit in his hometown and was determined to hunt Palmer down.

The mob of Burton riders left my room, banging on the walls as they tore the Sims house apart from top to bottom. They finally found Palmer passed out in a basement room with Chris Roach. Swierz and I ran down to witness what we were sure was going to be a brawl. We saw Coghlan in the doorway to Palmer's room, and he was on fire.

"You come to my house [the East Coast], and you disrespect me like that with this bullshit?" he yelled at Palmer. "You can't do that shit around here!"

Just then, Paolo, who was in the room next door, stumbled out in his banana-hammock bikini bottom, rubbing his eyes and saying in his heavy drawl, "You'a can't-a be-a doing this-a in this house-a. I need sleep-a. I've got to ride in the morning." Seeing this stopped Coghlan in his tracks. He looked Mario up and down, shook his head, and left.

I went back to sleep with a heavy heart, because I figured Coghlan was pissed at me for being associated with the whole scandal. Coghlan had watched over me and all the East Coast kids. He was responsible for hooking up a lot of young riders, myself included, by helping them get noticed by teams looking for talent. The first thing I did when I hit the hill the next day was track him down to apologize. I hung my head low and said, "Dude, I am so sorry about last night." Coghlan's response was, "Don't worry about it. It had nothing to do with you. We were pissed at Palmer." With that weight lifted, I was ready to compete.

I saw my parents on the side of the pipe when I practiced and felt that overwhelming nervousness that had ruined me in my first vert skating contest back in college. My legs started to shake, probably from hiking the pipe, but I equated it to the "jitters." At the top of the pipe, I walked away from everybody and tried to pull myself together. I envisioned myself falling all over the place, making a fool of myself in front of my parents and letting down the team. I looked at my older, more seasoned teammates, and they seemed so confident and carefree as they prepared to drop in, so I tried to adopt that attitude. I strutted over to the pipe, took a deep breath, and did my thing. Fortunately, I had a great practice run, and then another—just stringing together tricks. When the pipe closed for practice, I replayed my practice runs over and over again in my head, and tried not to talk to anybody for fear that it would trip up my facade of total confidence.

When the competition began I was one of the first riders to go, and damned if I didn't fall. Seriously. I *didn't* fall! I felt pretty good and sat back to watch the other riders do their runs, figuring I'd learn something. There was a little fifteen year old from Norway named Terje Haakonsen who dropped in and blew the crowd away with big airs that seemed even bigger because of his size. Everybody who watched him ride that day suspected they might be watching the next Craig Kelly. Youth combined with skill was a scary combo, and his attitude was cool as ice. Here I was freaking out, terrified of my next run, and he was enjoying himself. When all the scores were tallied, I found my name—for the first time—as a qualifier in the finals of the U.S. Open!

Making the finals lifted a huge weight off my shoulders, and I actually enjoyed the recognition for about a half hour. Then the main event began. Before my run, I told myself, once again, to ride like I was practicing. At the top of the pipe, it was tunnel vision. I didn't look over at my parents or the crowd. As I entered the pipe, I shut out the world and everything I'd been practicing came together—Indy air, air to fakies, half-Cabs—not too high, but I tried to keep everything smooth like Chris Roach. Most important, I made sure I didn't forget to do my handplant. At the bottom, it was like somebody turned the volume back up because I could suddenly hear the crowd. Miki ran up to me and said, "Look! Look at the scores! You're in second! You're in second!"

"Second to what?" I said.

She slapped me on the head and said, "Second place!"

Jeff Brushie was in the top spot, but then Palmer came down and bumped him to second. Miki was still jumping around screaming, "You're in third! You're still top three!" Then it was Craig Kelly's turn. Mr. Consistent took first, and I came in fourth, which was winning as far as I was concerned. I'd beaten back the evil dark side of my mind. The other guys beat me with bigger airs, but the tricks weren't super-technical compared to mine. *I'll have to grow a set and go bigger next time,* I thought.

Miki was patting me on the back, my mom and dad gave me hugs, and I was on top of the world. Plus, I won five hundred bucks. I didn't know it then, but the guys I stood alongside on that winner's podium would go down in history as some of the most influential freestyle riders in the history of the sport. That would come to mean almost as much to me as my parents being there to see it.

After the awards ceremony, Kevin Kinnear, founding editor of *TransWorld SNOWboarding,* told my mom and dad, "Todd's a big up-and-comer. Congratulations on whatever you've done to get him here." Even though my parents had never really taken my snowboarding or skating seriously, they had pulled through that winter with travel expenses and emotional support. I was sponsored by Sims, but I was also sponsored by my mom and dad. Despite their reluctance over the years, they'd always come through with equipment and money, and they instilled in me a work ethic that I transferred into fun things, like learning new tricks. I also couldn't overlook the fact that they first introduced me to the art of sliding on snow.

I was determined to master that art and someday actually win the U.S. Open with them in the crowd. Big plans coming from a kid who, a few hours earlier, was a nervous wreck. Competition stress, I sensed, would be my greatest nemesis.

At the 1990 U.S. Open (left to right), Jimmy Scott, me, Jeff Brushie, Shaun Palmer, and Craig Kelly. I'll always be thankful that my dad got to see me ride well and take fourth place that day.

THE YOUNG AND THE FEARLESS

Full Name: Brandt Todd Richards

Birth Date: December 28, 1969

Born In: Holden, Massachusetts

Mother's Maiden Name: Farley

Stick it in Your Ear:
1. Bad Brains- Sailin' On
2. The Cult-Nirvana
3. Public Enemy- Miuzi Ways a Ton

Snowboarder Hall of Fame:
1. Tim Windell
2. Jason Ford
3. Tucker Fransen

Dork Patrol:
1. Day-glo
2. Copers on skate trucks
3. People who don't use turn signals

Dream Day:
Waking up to two feet of fresh snow at Squaw Valley, then going riding with Chris Swires, Tucker Fransen and Chris Roach, going nuts and flying off everything.

Videorgy:
1. Tales from the Dark Side
2. Fast Times at Ridgemont High
3. Bill and Ted's Excellent Adventure

King for a Day:
I'd like to change a lot of attitudes. I'd like to see people wake up one day and have more acceptance of new ideas.

Halfpipe Yo:
1. Perfect trannies with one foot of vert
2. Spines
3. All pipes built to the same specs

Halfpipe No:
1. Cartwheel flips
2. Teeny amounts of flat
3. Rock-hard pipes

_My first "interview" in *Snowboarder Magazine*, 1991.

TEAM MOM, DAD, AND SIMS/
EMOTIONAL ROLLERCOASTER

After I placed fourth in the Open, Sims agreed to pay my travel expenses in full. The very next day, they flew me out to Breckenridge for the TDK Snowboarding World Championship. There was no time to be nervous; it was all just exciting and unbelievable. I felt like I was in a dream.

Sims rented a big house in a neighborhood at the edge of Brek called Warrior's Mark where a lot of locals lived. After an entire winter of traveling together, we were starting to feel like an extended family. But there was always some sort of scandal brewing, and it usually involved Shaun Palmer, Chris Roach, or Mike Ranquet.

Our first night there, Roach met a girl while he was walking back from the Breckenridge Brewery. He must have made quite an impact on this pedestrian because she immediately returned to the house with him. When he realized I was already asleep in the room we were sharing, Roach, ever the gentleman, humped the girl in the hallway, and then they both came into the room and passed out in his bed.

The next morning, I was at the kitchen table with the rest of the team eating breakfast when this strange girl walked in with messed-up hair and her "out" clothes on. She looked around, squeaked out a timid, "What's up?" then did the walk of shame right out the front door. We all looked at one another like, "Who the hell was that?" The second the door slammed, Roach sauntered into the kitchen, looking refreshed, and fixed himself a bowl of cereal. He tried to maintain a straight face, but a grin betrayed him, and we eventually got the story out of him. For me, life with the team and on the road was like the college experience I didn't have—a constant party and just as insane as everything that went down on snow.

At Brek that year, the extracurricular activities were fun (even though I didn't hook up), but the event was a flop. I couldn't get my game-face on, and I fell during the finals of the second biggest contest of the year. I took unlucky thirteenth place in the pipe and was certain that Sims was going to drop me. Miki, however, gave me the cup-is-half-full response saying, "You almost made top ten."

At the awards ceremony, a local pro named Shawn Farmer stole the show. He was one of the sport's strongest freeriders, attacking terrain, any terrain, with fearless style. The lines he rode were death defying and scary. Even the best riders were wary and often said, "Don't follow Farm." Off the mountain, he was known to jump through windows and run through sliding glass doors for the entertainment value. But on this occasion, he performed a snowboarding rap song. I can't remember the lyrics, but he had everybody rolling.

I loved the halfpipe and didn't understand people's attraction to riding powder. On these contest trips, the pros would go and ride pow when it snowed, and I'd hike the pipe. I always had it to myself on those days. During these solo sessions I'd get into my training mind-set, picking one trick to do over and over again until I could practically do it with my eyes closed. Then I'd pick another. I lived for the riding days before and after events. The resorts didn't really maintain the pipes very well for the general public, but they were usually best just before and just after contests—and if it wasn't snowing, the pipe would be packed with pros and photographers. These prac- tice and photo sessions were electric. The energy was all positive—no contest jitters and no judges to impress—so nobody held back. That was where I really progressed. Riding with people who were better than me was the best motivation, and I kept mental notes on the tricks I saw and heard about, which was a crossover habit from skateboarding. During the post-contest session at Brek, for example, in the search for my next money trick, I practiced Cab methods, tweaked out like I'd seen Palmer do his airs, and even tried a few frontside 540s. I failed miserably, but I kept on pushing.

Later that day, I watched Tucker Fransen do the first-ever fakie 720 in a halfpipe. At the time, not many riders could pull off a backside 540; even fewer did frontside 540s and only a handful grabbed them, so his 720 was groundbreaking. I don't think anyone else saw him and I kept quiet about it because I thought it was his new secret weapon. Years later, I confessed to Tucker about that day. He remembered the same moment and said that he knew he'd done something new, but hadn't wanted to claim it, which says a lot about Tucker.

To Canada, Again

Sims surprised me once again by keeping me on the team and sending me, along with Lisa Vinciguerra and seasoned pro/smooth talker Kevin Delaney, to an invitational Op Pro event at Lake Louise, near Banff, Canada. Delaney had been around the block and had

Handplant on a snow boulder at A-Basin, Colorado, in 1990.

accumulated lots of sponsors, and he was making a consistent living through snow-boarding. He had all sorts of insight into the business aspect of the sport and was willing to share his knowledge. The overall moral of his story was, "You gotta start getting paid." At the time, I had a couple thousand dollars in contest winnings in the bank. I thought I was rich, but Kevin Delaney, along with Andy Coghlan, taught me that prize money was only the beginning. They knew there was more money to be had in endorse-ments and didn't want to see me and other riders taken advantage of. I appreciated their guidance and vowed to do the same for up-and-comers later on in my career.

I was beginning to see that I had a lot to learn both on and off the snow if I was going to take this career route. I realized how lucky I was to be able to make money off of something that was so fun, but it would require some bona fide work along the way. I kept my ears open while on the road and learned as much in cars, buses, planes, and hotel rooms as I did on the mountains.

When we got to Banff in mid-April 1990, there were no affordable rooms avail-able in the entire town. Since the trip had been put together at the last minute, Sims hadn't been able to make us a reservation. Somehow Delaney charmed a hotel recep-tionist into giving us a suite at a reduced rate. I don't know how he did it, considering our reputation in ski towns. Snowboard teams had become known as hotel vandals and room thrashers, so a lot of places were on alert and suddenly "all booked up" when they saw our motley day-glo crews approaching the counter. Many team man-agers had to be creative when making reservations saying things such as, "Could I please have a block of ten rooms, ground level, smoking, with a mini bar? Hold that for the Washington Avenue Baptist Church. Thank you. God bless you."

At Lake Louise I started trusting myself with more speed and higher airs. Once I real-ized more hang time was actually safer—it gave me more time to do the trick and land—I began to smooth out my style, which had been a little jerky before. With this newfound

In Gotcha gear at Mount Hood, 1990—my first experience "modeling" clothes.

revelation, I grabbed fourth place and left with another six hundred fifty bucks. The OP contests were known among riders as "The OP Pro Free Money Giveaway Series" because they awarded cash prizes up to sixteenth place. Finally, snowboarding was becoming lucrative. I hadn't been home in weeks and hadn't had a chance to spend any of the money I'd earned. My savings topped three thousand dollars—more than I'd ever dreamed of saving in my life.

Life Isn't Always Fair

I returned to Paxton on April 10 thinking I was pretty damn cool.

When I got home that night, I filled my parents in on my travels. The next afternoon, my on-again-off-again girlfriend Carrie (whom I'd been dating since college in Laconia) agreed to help shuttle me back to Vermont where I'd left my car after the U.S. Open. My dad came home early from work just as we were leaving. He told me he felt pretty sick. I told my dad I had to go get my car, and he asked me to call my mom and tell her to come home from her telecommunications job (Hair Unlimited had turned into a part-time gig). He said he had this crazy pain in his knee that he'd never experienced before, but thought it was just an old hockey injury. Then his nausea got worse and he started to throw up pretty violently. I asked him if there was anything I could do, but he said no since my mom was on her way home to take care of him, so I left thinking he had the flu.

By the time Carrie dropped me off at my car it was dark, so I hopped in and headed straight back to Paxton. In Gardner, Massachusetts, an hour from my house, I saw out of the corner of my eye a strange, bright blue flash on the side of the road. I glanced around and realized I was driving past a cemetery. By this time, I was used to driving on creepy New England roads, but this really turned on a switch in me.

Three miles from my house I saw more flashes, but these came from behind me and were accompanied by a shrieking siren. I pulled over and the ambulance roared by. A weird sense of dread overcame me, and I stepped on the gas. I knew something was wrong at home.

I came over a hill and saw the ambulance pulling into my driveway. I parked, ran inside, and found the paramedics in the kitchen, trying to resuscitate my dad. I started to walk in, but my mom pulled me away. Then, after a few minutes, we heard somebody say that they didn't have a pulse. My mom lost it and became hysterical.

My mind couldn't process it all. I watched my mom getting into the ambulance while my dad was being lifted onto a gurney. As the ambulance took off, my dad's brother, Uncle Ron, arrived and told me to get into the car. He put his hand on my shoulder as we drove to the hospital and said, "Todd, this just doesn't look good."

That night, April 11, 1990, my father died from a heart attack, which the doctors said was probably the result of a blood clot in his leg. He was only forty-six.

I don't think I reacted the way a kid should when he loses his dad—especially a dad he truly loves and cares for. I was sad but just kind of pushed the grief aside. I wasn't like, "Oh god, my dad died, it's the end of my world." I think I was in shock. During the weeks after the funeral, my mom grieved enough for both of us. Seeing her in so much pain made me wonder, *What am I supposed to feel? Am I broken because I don't feel the way my mom does?* At the time, all I wanted to do was go snowboarding to escape the pain and sadness that I refused to let surface. I never cried.

I knew that my mom needed me, so I made it a point to stay at home and help out as much as possible. It was a tough time, and I've mostly blocked it out of my memory. For a couple weeks, my life consisted of hanging out with my mom and having meals together on a regular basis, which was something we'd never really done when my dad was around. Occasionally I'd go skate someplace close to home, alone. I didn't want to run into any friends because I didn't want to deal with them saying, "So how's everything going?" and me having to say, "Oh, my dad died." I also didn't want to put the people who knew about my dad through awkward condolences. I guess I just needed to be alone for a while.

Miki called a week after my dad died and was very sympathetic. She told me how sorry she was, and then, as gently as possible, she told me the reason for calling.

"I don't know what your deal is right now," she said, "and don't take this the wrong way. There's no pressure at all, but I wanted you to know there is this late-season contest coming up at Arapahoe Basin. If you're interested, let me know." I wanted to say, "Yes!" right then and there, but I needed to feel out the situation with my mom.

One night at dinner I told her about the contest. It was scheduled for May 12, so I only had about a week before it was time to go. I was half-scared to bring it up because I thought she might say something like, "How can you even think about snowboarding right now?" But I didn't give her enough credit. She knew me better than I thought and without hesitation said, "You should go. I want you to go. Your dad would want you to go." And so on May 7, I left for A-Basin in Colorado for the Body Glove Pro.

Back in Action

With a summit elevation of 13,500 feet, Arapahoe Basin in the Colorado Rockies is the highest resort in North America. In the east, I never needed to worry about elevation issues like dehydration and sun intensity. In fact, I don't think I'd ever used sunscreen in my life. Back home, my dad used to put baby oil on us when we went skiing in the spring so we'd get nice and bronzed. But in Colorado, altitude sickness and sunburns are pretty common among out-of-state visitors.

The contest took place during three or four of the sunniest days in Colorado history, and I got the sunburn to prove it. It all started when Scott "Upside" Downey took Kris Swierz and me freeriding at A-Basin, pointing out mogul fields, cornices, and rocks to jump off—all above treeline.

Sims hired Trevor Graves to come along and shoot photos of us riding the newest Sims board—Shaun Palmer's first pro model. We were getting ready to jump off this rock near the East Wall when Matty Goodman rode up and told me to put on some sunscreen because I was looking pretty red. I ignored him.

I continued to get fried and when I started feeling dizzy, I went into the lodge to get a drink of water. I was standing inside the entrance when I saw Craig Kelly walking up the steps. Craig was the world champion, and I was still a star-struck fan at heart. As he went by (even though I figured he wouldn't recognize me), I said, "Hi, Craig," as casually as possible. He turned, looked at me, and with just the right amount of cool composure said, "Hey, T.R." In doing so, he gave me the nickname that would stick throughout my entire career.

Late that afternoon, altitude sickness and sun poisoning hit Kris Swierz, Trevor Graves, and me like a Mack truck. We could barely climb the five stairs to the condo, and when we did, we just plopped on the floor and moaned. As the night wore on, Trevor began puking his guts to the point of dry heaves, while blisters formed on my face, ears, and neck. The next morning, my nose was a ball of puss, but all three of us had to drag ourselves out of bed for the contest. I drank a gallon of water to try and rehydrate and then practiced in the pipe.

By Colorado standards, the pipe conditions sucked.

"Be careful," warned Brad Steward. "This thing's super icy."

"Are you kidding?" I said. "I'm from the East Coast. This thing's perfect."

Halfway down the right side of the pipe there was a big tombstone of snow that Andy Hetzel was doing huge air to fakies on while wearing a cool 7-Eleven store uniform, paying tribute to the snowboarder's main nutrition source. Below the hit was this huge unrideable snow boulder that was smashed into the wall of the pipe. So I went smaller on the tombstone hit, hit the snow boulder everybody else avoided, and stalled out an Andrecht handplant on top of it. I saw a couple people try and hit the boulder after I did, but nobody could pop up there. It was like they'd run into a brick wall. I knew I'd found my ace in the hole for the contest. It was nice to have a little bit of confidence, because my stomach was grumbling and I felt like lying down in the snow and going to sleep.

The boulder and my handplants served me well, but by the time I made the finals, I had a lot of gas from the altitude sickness and was polluting the air around the starting area. To top it off, the event was televised, which was a big deal. The World Championships in Brek had been on television earlier that winter, but camera crews were still a pretty rare sight back then. At this event, most riders, myself included, were acutely aware of the big cameras that were constantly trained on us. Here's what I later watched: Me poised in the starting gate for the finals. The camera zooms in on my severely charred face, and the voice-over says, "Here, we have Todd Richards from Paxton, Massachusetts, riding for Sims." I look around briefly. Then I stop, stare upward into space for a second with this look of confusion, then my face wrinkles up into a grimace.

That was the exact second I shit my pants. Just blew out, spackling the inside of my magic purple Sims jumpsuit. The announcer said, "Go!" and I didn't have a choice. I dropped in and dealt with the load in my pants. It's a good thing I semi-blacked out during my runs or I might have realized that my pants were filled with poop soup and all the tweaks and handplants were spreading the love, so to speak. Despite the gross factor, I pulled all my tricks and straight-lined it to the bathroom.

I was a mess. I had to take my boots and pants off and wipe my ass with the leg sections of my long underwear (the ass part was pure mud). After my clean-up, I just threw them in the trash. I got back to the pipe to find out that Kevin Delaney had won, Craig Kelly took second, Shaun Palmer third, Andy Hetzel fourth. I had become the first snowboarder to take fifth and mud his drawers on national television.

The story was too funny not to share with a few close friends, which eventually became a few hundred friends. Eventually I was inducted into Jeff Brushie's prestigious Team Dookie. Brushie coined the phrase after sharing a story of how he had been pushed through a wall of Sheetrock when he was younger: "Dude, this guy pushed me so hard, I went through the wall, and this little piece of dookie came out." That's what gave him the idea for the team. Team Dookie required the obvious for membership, and all the Burlington kids, as well as Craig Kelly, had, at one time, shit his pants and become a member. We all put Team Dookie stickers on our boards. That same year, Burton came out with a video called *Chill*, in which there's an interview where you can hear Jason Ford in the background chanting, "Team Dookie, Team Dookie, Team Dookie!"

I returned home on May 15 and felt semi-normal again. I could still feel the void left by my dad's passing, but snowboarding had pushed it off to the side. I wasn't ready for the season to end, but on the East Coast, summer was in full swing. The snow had melted at our low-altitude resorts, and I turned to skateboarding.

The Endless Winter

Early in June 1990, I got a letter from Miki explaining that Sims was having some issues with its distributor, Vision. Apparently, Tom Sims wanted control of his company because he wasn't happy with Vision's business and manufacturing practices. Vision, however, didn't want to give up rights to the Sims trademark.

For me and a bunch of other Sims riders, this meant not knowing if we were still sponsored. The team was kind of left in the dark while Tom and Vision figured things out. I was just settling in for a summer of skateboarding around Paxton when I found out that other pro snowboarders were still riding despite the snow-melting heat of summer!

For years Mount Hood, Oregon, and Blackcomb, British Columbia, had been summer training grounds for U.S. Ski Team racers who set gates on the mountain's glacier. As snowboarding picked up momentum, so did snowboarding summer camps. Tim Windell, Craig Kelly, and Ken Achenbach were three of the first pros to organize summer camps for snowboarders. They set up slalom courses and halfpipes, and kids flocked to the summer snowfields.

My summer took a turn for the better when Jason Ford invited me to join him on a cross-country road trip to Mount Hood and Blackcomb during July. He rolled up to my house in a brand-new purple Toyota van, and my mom dragged out one of my dad's money socks and presented it to me. I almost declined, but I knew my mom saw it as a symbol of my father being part of this cross-country adventure. We cashed it in for about three hundred bucks on the way out of town, and we got the most out of every penny.

The last time I was in Colorado, all of the cool West Coasters had been talking about this awesome Mexican fast-food restaurant, and this road trip was the first time I ever had the pleasure of experiencing Taco Bell. I can't remember the exact location, but it was definitely west of Wisconsin. I was amazed at the sheer volume of food you could buy for a couple bucks.

Our plan for the trip was to stop off and see my fellow Sims team member Tim Windell in Boulder and meet up with Jason's Burton team pal Noah Brandon, whom I'd met during the New England Cup. Colorado in the summer was amazing. We saw Midnight Oil at the famous Redrocks Amphitheatre, and I spent a lot of time at the infamous Fort Skate park getting my game back on the vert ramp. Before we left, I pulled off a bastardized version of a McTwist, an inverted aerial named after skateboarder Mike McGill. You approach the wall riding forward, rotate 540 degrees in a backside direction while performing a front flip, and land riding forward. It was an insanely hard vert trick to learn. My version was a backside 540 mute, and I basically

Jason Ford, pre-Burton, on a Sims at Nashoba in 1988.

squatted the living shit out of it. It wasn't pretty, I just gutted it around—probably slid the last 180—but I didn't slam. I was stoked.

In 1990, I wouldn't have considered trying a McTwist on the snow. It didn't even enter my mind. Going upside down was not cool in snowboarding. Mike Ranquet, Chris Roach, and Shaun Palmer all told me that flipping was gay. The previous winter, Mike Jacoby had done this thing called a J-Tear-Air that was basically a backflip cart-wheel in the halfpipe where he put his hand down like a handplant as he was reenter-ing the pipe. Inverted aerials were prohibited in competition for safety (and insurance) reasons, so putting his hand down made it a legit competition trick. In retrospect it was a pivotal move for snowboarding, but at the time a lot of people bagged on it, calling it the Gay-Tear-Air. Jacoby took the shit in stride though, and his trick paved the way for the inverted tricks to come.

After a couple weeks on the road, Jason and I rolled up to Government Camp, the small Oregon town at the base of Mount Hood. For a couple weeks, all I did was snowboard, skateboard, eat, and occasionally shower. We were sleeping in Jason's van to save money, so we'd have to sneak into High Cascade Snowboard Camp to shower, which is where I met a girl named Gretta (Re-Gretta). She was learning how to snowboard, and I was into her. I started showering more often after we met, which was important because my sweating problem kicked in during female encounters. It was the summer of love. Carrie and I had broken up again, so I was free to enjoy it.

Hood was (and still is) a magnet for snowboarders. They come from all over, and among this crowd was a significant number of skateboarders. Andy Hetzel and I skated a lot with veteran snowboarders Don Szabo, Noah Salasnek, and John Cardiel. These guys traveled around the world to snowboard in the winter, and in the summer they hung out at a glacier to ride and skateboard their asses off. Could life get any better?

Jon Foster, the photographer from *TransWorld,* came up to me one day at Hood carrying a pile of purple clothing from a surf company called Gotcha. He dropped them in front of me and asked if I'd mind wearing them for some of his photos. I was like, "Sure, why not?" Even though I was still wearing the Sims Team gear, I had no idea what the deal was. For all I knew, the company had gone under. I was so confused, I even drew a big black question mark over the Sims logo on the bottom of my board.

Jason, Windell, and a bunch of other riders encouraged me to put together a snowboarding résumé and get hooked up with more sponsors, especially those that would pay me cash money, not just product. I called my mom to check in and told her about the résumé idea. She said we could work on it when I got back home. I found out later that as soon as we hung up, she'd begun getting my contest results in order. My dad's passing had done something to her. She started reading the snowboarding magazines I had around my room and decided that if I was going to be a pro snowboarder, she was going to support me as much as possible. Helping me with a résumé was the perfect opportunity for her to get involved. She clipped the photos of me from magazines and began the process of making me appear to be some sort of organized professional athlete. She became my first manager that summer.

That same week, Jon Foster got the photos processed and told me he was really excited about the results. He told me I could expect a call from Gotcha because they were putting together a snowboard team. He handed me a business card and said, "If they don't call you, make sure you call them. If you have any problems, give me a call."

Foster also introduced me to Mike and Tina Basich, brother and sister pro riders, who carpooled with me and Jason up to Blackcomb resort in Whistler, BC, for the final OP Pro event of the year. I still couldn't believe a snowboarding contest was taking place in the middle of the summer. At Blackcomb, I hung out with Mike Ranquet as much as possible, because he's the shit both on and off the hill. He messed with me constantly, pushed me into girls in the lift lines and ran me into poles on the T-Bar. He

This 1990 handplant photo led to my first major money sponsor
(Gotcha forked over 1,000 bucks a month).

called me "Preppy Boy" because I was from the East Coast. Despite (or maybe because of) all the shit he gave me, he became one of my good friends whom I'll always look up to.

At the OP competition at Blackcomb, I took fourth place again, good enough to restock my wallet. Jason won the races and the overall OP series, so he got a serious wad of cash. He decided to use it to drive down to California to visit the magazines (*ISM* was in San Francisco and *TransWorld* and *Snowboarder* were in Southern California). Going to California's skateboarding hotbeds was tempting, but I was getting pretty homesick, so my mom bought me a plane ticket, and I flew back to Massachusetts.

_Showing off the Morrow colors.

SNOW JOB/ OBJECTIVE: TO BE THE WORLD'S BEST SNOWBOARDER

When I got home in late August 1990, my mom was gung-ho to get my résumé out. She had already gone through the magazines and put together a list of potential sponsors we could hit up. Sunglasses, watches, outerwear—every company that had an ad in a snowboarding magazine was a target. She even had addresses for some big corporations: Some pro snowboarders had done television commercials with McDonald's and Wrigley's chewing gum, but the corporate jury was still out in the land of big business. Snowboarders just weren't considered marketable.

My mom typed up a résumé, which began with my goals, the first of which was to become "the world's most recognized freestyle rider." Then we mass-mailed fifty résumés and waited. Within days, I got a call from Gotcha, not because of my résumé, but because of the shots Jon Foster had taken of me at Mount Hood. They were stoked on the photos and wanted to sign me as part of their first snowboard outerwear team, which was a bit of a departure from their roots as a surfing-oriented company.

I didn't commit immediately. Other pros had schooled me a little on the importance of image. I didn't want to be associated with a lame company, and I knew I had to negotiate, not just settle for a "free stuff" contract. I also knew that Gotcha based everything on their pro surfer pay scale. Unlike snowboarding, surfing was established, and its athletes were considered marketable. So I was ready to get offered something like a hundred dollars a month during the winter. I figured I'd counter with two hundred but would happily settle for a hundred and fifty. Their first offer was a thousand dollars a month for an entire year. I told my manager (Mom), and she responded with sound business advice: "Here's the pen. Sign." I was stoked about the money, but still uncertain about the brand. All I knew about the company was that pro skater Steve Caballero rode for them, and its logo was a shark holding a flag.

```
                        BRANDT TODD RICHARDS
                        135 PLEASANT STREET
                        PAXTON, MA  01612
                HOME TELEPHONE :  (508) 791-2735

   GOALS:
            To become the world's most recognized free style rider.
            To professionally enhance snowboarding and skateboarding
                 in the public's eye.
            To market specific product lines through sponsorship both
                 in the northeast as well as on the west coast.
            To keep the spirit of snowboarding alive.
            To one day own my own company.

   OBJECTIVES:
            To train and teach continually through snowboard camps,
                 skateboarding, excercise programs, and diet.
            To work at sponsorship opportunities related to both
                 snowboarding and skateboarding.
            To concentrate on training in slalom events, an area in
                 which I need to improve.
            To continually educate myself in business skills.
            To set a positive image in whatever I do and wherever I go.
            To actively and aggressively promote all sponsors' products
                 and accessories and to enhance the image and reputation
                 of sponsors.

   QUALIFICATIONS:
            1990-91    Demonstrated contest achievements as a Pro snow-
                       boarder, Morrow, Gotcha Sportswear, X-Isle sun-
                       glasses, Airwalk boots, Sessions Snowboards Shops.
            1990       Sales and marketing of specific product lines as a
                       full time professional snowboarder representing
                       Morrow Snowboards, Gotcha Sportswear, X-Isle
                       glasses and goggles and Sorel boots.
            1989-90    Demonstrated contest schievement as a Pro
                       snowboarder, Sims Snowboard Company, Santa Ana, CA.
            1986-90    Demonstrated contest achievement as an Amateur
                       skateboarder.

   EXPIERENCE:
            1991-92    Part-time sales position, B.C. Surf & Sport (snow-
                       board & skateboard paraphernalia), Boulder, CO
            1990-91    Planned and executed demonstrations, exhinitions,
                       and contest tours 1990-91 season World Cup and
                       North American Series in U.S., Canada, Japan, and
                       Europe.  Involved in design and production of
                       products at company headquarters, Morrow Snowboards
                       and Gotcha Sportswear.
            1989-90    Head of snowboard department, Ski Market at Mt.
                       Wachusett, Princeton, MA
            1987-89    Snowboard instructor, Gunstock Mt., Gilford, NH
```

Page one from my first résumé (Thanks, Mom).

Brad Steward called a few days later and told me that he'd jumped ship from Sims. He asked me about my situation and I told him I was on the fence (i.e., I had no fucking idea if I was riding for Sims). "Good," he said. He went on to explain that he was hooked up with Scott Clum, who had done art direction for Sims and other brands I respected. They were teaming up with Rob Morrow to take Morrow Snowboards to the next level. They wanted to compete with established names like Sims, Burton, Kemper, Avalanche, and Barfoot. Morrow, as far as I knew, was a logo on the bottom of a snowboard that Rob Morrow rode. But I trusted Brad, I liked Rob, and Miki Keller also quit Sims and signed up as the team manager, so I took a leap of faith and signed with Morrow for two hundred dollars a month, plus traveling expenses.

I had some mixed feelings about leaving my first sponsor. I really respected Sims, and their riders were important inspirations for me. I liked being associated with them, but I had begun to notice snowboarders regularly jumping around from sponsor to sponsor. The whole "team unity" thing was fading, and riders were becoming their own private entities. I was lucky enough to be part of the Sims team during an influential era when your team was your family. The company and its riders had supported me when I was nothing more than a kid with potential, and I'll never forget that. But it was time to move on, and that's what I did.

I really wanted to get hooked up with Xisle sunglasses. Roach, Ranquet, and Palmer rode for them, so the image of the company was just what I was after. Per my mom's suggestion, I asked Ranquet to call the Xisle marketing department and ask them to check out the résumé I'd sent. A few weeks later, I got a box of sunglasses and a surprise contract for a hundred dollars a month.

My hard work and my mom's management really paid off. For the 1990/1991 season, I was hooked up with Morrow Snowboards, Gotcha clothing, Xisle optics, and Sessions Snowboard Shop. I was slated to receive thirteen hundred dollars a month from Morrow, Gotcha, and Xisle combined. Sessions wasn't coughing up any cash, but I didn't care. I probably would have paid *them,* because if you legitimately had a Sessions sticker on your board, you were part of an elite crew.

Go West, Young Man

It was a tough time for my mom because she knew I had one foot out the door. She'd lost her life partner, and her only child was gearing up to leave the house forever. But she held up really well and only encouraged me. I think part of her strength came from knowing that my dad had just started to see my career take off, and she was going to see it through.

When Carrie decided she wanted to go to a photography school in Denver, we started talking seriously about moving. We were back together and getting along great, and Colorado seemed like the logical place for my career as well. We decided to relocate to Boulder, because I would be fairly close to the mountain resorts and Carrie would have a reasonable commute to school in the city.

My parents had always taught me to be patient and really think things through: *Always have plenty of money in your pocket if you're going to be in a strange city.*

Have your hotel reservation in advance. Leave for the airport early in case there's traffic. As a result, I didn't live by the seat of my pants. When I brought up the Boulder idea to my mom, she was all carpe diem and urged me to go for it. I figured she had gone nuts. Within hours, she'd cashed in the savings from my inheritance, bought me a new Volkswagen GTI, and handed me the remainder of the cash as a cushion. She cautioned me to make it last and gave me some tips on budgeting and bank accounts.

Two weeks later, on September 1, Carrie and I were in a crappy one-bedroom apartment in one of the cheaper parts of Boulder, and we were stoked. I was living in Colorado! I had barely settled in when Morrow told me to get to the Action Sports Retailer (ASR) trade show in San Diego so I could see the new line of Morrow boards. Lucky for me, Gotcha and Xisle would be there, too.

Carrie and I drove from Colorado to Orange County, where we met Gotcha's team manager, Mike Cruckshank. He invited me to come by the Gotcha headquarters to "get some clothes." I figured he'd hand me a stack of shark/flag T-shirts, shake my hand, and say, "Welcome to the team."

When I got to Mike's office, he threw me for a loop saying, "Let's head over to the warehouse." The warehouse was straight out of *Raiders of the Lost Ark,* a massive building with rows upon rows upon rows of clothes. Mike grabbed an industrial-sized shopping cart and said, "Fill it up." *Are you kidding me?* I went up and down the aisles, picking up pants, shorts, button-downs, T-shirts, sweatshirts, board shorts, jackets . . . and if I looked at something for too long, Mike would just grab it and throw it into the basket. He said, "You can get some new outerwear, too, but we'll have next year's stuff to you by the time the snow flies." We hit the duffel bag and backpack section last and grabbed some bags to stuff all the gear into. Then, it was off to the trade show the next day, farther south in San Diego.

My mom, being my manager and all, met Carrie and me at the San Diego convention center. She wanted to have a little face time with my sponsors to show that I had someone watching over me. Fortunately, she met Bea Morrow, Rob's mom, who assured her that when I was on the road with the Morrow team, I'd be looked after. Inside the convention center itself were booths for all the skateboard brands, pro skaters mingling everywhere, and bikini models walking around in high heels. There was a big buzz at the show about Morrow because it was the first company started by a pro rider who had left a major sponsor. A lot of people came by the booth to check out the new company in town. I think other pro riders saw what Rob was doing and it got their wheels turning.

The highlight of the trip to San Diego came soon after I met Grant Brittain, the photo editor for *TransWorld SKATEboarding.* They needed some shots of "crossover"

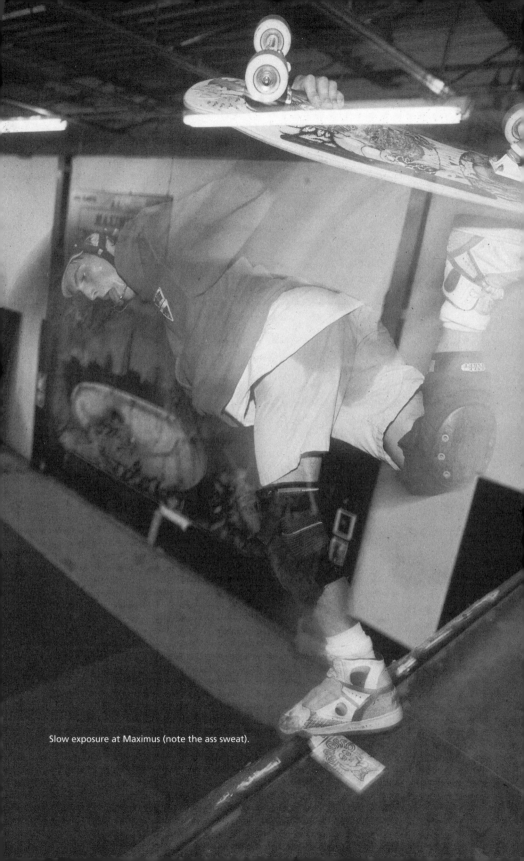

Slow exposure at Maximus (note the ass sweat).

athletes who could skate and snowboard. Grant had been told that I could skate and asked me if I'd be into hitting up a vert ramp. I jumped at the chance and found myself at Tony Hawk's house in Fallbrook, California!

Tony's ramp was the most insane private ramp I'd ever seen. I stood up on top of the giant decks, looked down at the perfectly surfaced ramp, and compared it to what I'd grown up with. I remember wishing that I could transport the ramp back to when I was a sophomore in high school, and plop it into the middle of downtown Paxton. Even though I didn't get to skate with Tony (he was out of town, but Grant had the keys), just being on his ramp was amazing.

Snowboarders had been pegged by pro skaters as the guys who couldn't make it as skateboarding professionals, which was pretty damn true in most cases. So when Grant asked me if I wanted to do a disaster and I countered with, "Frontside or backside?" he was stoked. He was like, "You can do both?"

I've often told reporters for mainstream magazines, "Snowboarding is just an excuse to suck at skating." That quote was certainly true for me, but I could still hold my own. The magic of skating on Tony's ramp helped me a lot, and being photographed by the legendary Grant Brittain was an honor beyond words.

Inside the Industry

In October, I visited the Morrow factory in Salem, Oregon, and hung out for three days. It was cool because I got to pick out the boards I'd be riding the coming winter. At first I felt like a kid with a free pass in a candy store, but as soon as I tried flexing the boards, I got concerned. They were all stiff, and I liked mine soft like a cooked noodle. I tried one out on the glacier at nearby Mount Hood, and it rode horribly. Rob assured me that once I got used to it, I'd never go back to a soft board. As it turned out, he was right, but at the time I was more than a little skeptical. The Morrow board designer grilled me for information on how much sidecut I liked, what kind of nose shape, camber, edge contact, and a bunch of technical terms that made me go, "Huh?" All I said was, "Make it soft."

While in Salem, I met the rest of the riders who had been recruited to be the first Morrow team: Noah Brandon, Tucker Fransen, a girl named Shannon Dunn, and of course Rob Morrow. Bea Morrow cooked us big dinners at the Morrow house, and we had a family vibe going right from the start.

When I got back to Boulder, Morrow put me to work. Justin Hostynek, a photographer, made plans to introduce me to a different kind of run at Breckenridge. The Whales are huge piles of man-made snow that the resort stockpiles on the upper runs

Rob Morrow busting skis with kung-fu power for a Morrow ad.

"Maybe stiff boards aren't so bad . . ." Getting the Morrow wired with a frontside air tow in.

of Peak 9 on cold nights. If Mother Nature doesn't puke her guts by the scheduled Thanksgiving opening day, the piles are groomed into a long single run. Snowboarders and skiers took advantage of these fall snow patches to build kickers and "warm up" for the coming season. When Justin and I showed up for a photo shoot in early November, it was like watching a circus in the snow. After watching the people slam over and over again, I thought a more appropriate preseason warm-up would consist of running full-speed into a wall a few times to toughen up their bodies.

That day at the Whales was the second time I rode a Morrow board. It still felt stiff as hell, and the stance was centered on the board. I was used to my Sims, which had a lot more nose and a lot less tail, for a sense of security when landing. On the Morrow, I felt like I was going to go over the handlebars on every landing. Another problem was the bindings. I missed my Sims bindings, which were widely known as the best on the market. Morrow's bindings sucked, and, as I'd find out later, would simply rip off when you least expected it. The brains at Morrow said that pre-drilled inserts limited foot placement on the board, so they left their boards clean, requiring riders to choose and drill holes in the board for binding placement. This was a bad idea for three reasons. First, snowboarders didn't want to deal with this type of decision; second, without inserts, the screws you put in didn't hold; and third, after a board had been re-drilled a dozen times, it looked like it had been blasted at close range by a shotgun.

I'd put twenty screws on a binding and the thing would still rip off the board, which is terrifying when you're going forty miles per hour toward a wall of trees. I would eventually learn to keep a battery-operated drill in my car so that if I needed to, I could ride down the mountain on one foot and drill new holes to re-attach a binding that was still locked to my boot. There were days this happened so often, I considered carrying the drill around in a holster like a six-shooter. All the team riders complained, and Morrow eventually started using inserts.

I would soon learn about the negative aspects of my Gotcha outerwear, too. Gotcha was a surf company that was just getting the hang of its new customers' climate. At the time (fifteen years ago), its snowboarding clothing was apparently made to be worn at the beach. It didn't work in cold, wet, snowy weather. The stuff might as well have been made out of a sponge. In fact, it seemed like the sole purpose of the outerwear was to get you as soaked as possible.

Snowboarding itself was coming on strong, but the gear was at an all-time low. And it wasn't just me. A lot of riders were bummed about the functionality of their equipment. Yet we had to deal with it because that's what we were getting paid to do. We'd grit our teeth, smile, and say, "I'm so stoked. My gear is the best in the world!"

Despite my budding equipment problems, I knew Justin Hostynek needed shots of me that could be submitted to the magazines before the season began. This was to be Morrow's first year with sponsored riders, and they needed new photos in order to catch up with other companies.

Hiking the Whales for Justin that day made me realize snowboarding *was* a job. Granted, a really fun job, but I didn't have the option to call it a day and head to the lodge if I felt like it. I had a responsibility to not only do well in contests, but to get my photos in magazines. There was pressure to perform, and that's really hard to do when you're riding a new board you don't like. I know Justin blew a lot of film on horrible shots of me with bad style, but gradually I began to understand the benefits of a centered stance and stiffer board, and we ended up getting one usable shot out of a few hundred.

Street Style on Snow

There were suddenly lots of pros in Colorado, including a number of East Coast and Midwest riders, who'd probably decided to move after seeing all the magazine and television

An early jib experiment at the Mont Avila Pro, Quebec, 1990.

coverage of the big contests at A-Basin and Breckenridge. I got a Ski-the-Summit season pass—which included Breckenridge, Copper Mountain, Arapaho Basin, and Keystone (a resort that didn't allow snowboarding at the time)—just before Thanksgiving. When the snow finally arrived in late November, I was jonzing for a halfpipe, but it would take months before there was enough snow on the ground in Summit County for a halfpipe to be built. So, I did like everyone else and made the best of what I had.

Jibbing was a new phenomenon in snowboarding then. There are different theories of where it started, who did it, and what inspired it. My understanding is that Brek locals, including Andy Hetzel, Bret Johnson, Nick Perata, Zach Bingham, and Shawn Farmer, started jibbing in the 1988/1989 season on a run called the Burn on Breckenridge's Peak 8. The Burn had a bunch of protruding tree stumps and logs left over from a forest fire and the punk thing to do was ride over the obstacles, instead of around them. I'm sure it derived from street skateboarding, which at the time was really popular because many skate parks—and therefore vert ramps—had been forced to close down in the late eighties.

When I saw it for the first time, jibbing was in its infant stage. If you could ollie up onto a log and slide across it for more than five feet without catching an edge and knocking your teeth out, you were ripping. Landings were purely incidental. What happened in the air was most important. Soon riders were jumping off of anything and everything, and resorts began to think twice about where they put their picnic tables.

I wasn't very good at jumping or jibbing, probably because I was so used to landing on transitions in halfpipes. But slowly, I built myself up to bigger and bigger airs with flatter and flatter landings—and I beat up my body with the rest of the riders.

We're at War—Let's Go Snowboarding.

Just after my twenty-first birthday, I flew to Reno to hit the OP Pro at June Mountain, California. The day before the contest, January 16, 1991, Operation Desert Storm began. That night in the hotel we watched CNN's coverage of the anti-aircraft fire, while Wolf Blitzer reported on the airstrikes in Baghdad. We heard about the atrocities committed by Saddam Hussein's Iraqi forces in Kuwait, and here we were, in our safe little bubble in America, preparing to go snowboarding. No one would have considered canceling the contest because of the war, but it made a lot of us think about how lucky we were. I know it opened my eyes to the world outside. Up until then, my entire life revolved around skateboarding and snowboarding—nothing else mattered. International politics? Whatever. Now I was worried that I'd get drafted. One of my rocket scientist friends told me that since I was the last Richards male in my family, I was ineligible for the draft. It was bullshit, but it put my mind at ease. Eventually I caught on to the fact that there was never a draft in the first place.

The afternoon before the halfpipe event, I went to Steve Klassen's house to give his trampoline a shot. Tramp-training had become a semi-standard practice for snowboarders, and Steve, a pro rider who owned the Wave Rave snowboard shop in Mammoth, had only one rule of engagement for his trampoline: If you're going to jump with your board on, you gotta duct tape your edges.

After a few good jumps, I felt a twinge of pain, almost like an electric shock in my spine. I rolled off the tramp, walked a few steps, and it hit me again. I mellowed out for the rest of the day and felt normal until the next morning. Hiking up the pipe, my whole body seized up in pain, and I had to lie down right there on the side of the run. Something was seriously wrong.

I skipped the contest and saw a doctor back in Colorado who told me that I'd partially herniated a disk on my lower spine—the result, he presumed, of bouncing on the trampoline. I realized then that it would have been nice to have medical insurance. Between the pain and the substantial medical bills, I was basically screwed. *My career's just started, and now it's over,* I thought. The fact that injuries go with the territory didn't even enter my mind. My mom bailed me out by paying my doctor bills and then helped me secure medical insurance for any future injuries. Eventually I learned that getting worked goes hand in hand with pro snowboarding. It's only a matter of time. Sooner or later, you're going to get hurt. It's not a question of "if." It's a question of "how bad."

If there is one thing I recommend to future pro snowboarders, it's medical insurance. The companies that sponsor us are more than happy to see us beat ourselves senseless while learning new tricks, but they won't put us on their insurance policies. We're too much of a liability. Personally, I think it's bullshit, but at the end of the day, I guess we're just independent contractors, responsible for our own bodies. I know one pro who injured himself really badly when he hit some rocks—blew out his spleen, broke ribs, limbs, a huge mess. He didn't have insurance, and he ended up sneaking out of the hospital that treated him. He's still on the run from a five-figure doctor's bill.

At the time of my first real injury medical insurance was the least of my concerns, and if my mom hadn't insisted, I might have blown it off. All I could think was that every contest I missed meant people were getting better than me—and it drove me crazy. I was in the gutter. Carrie, who was glad at first to have me home, kept her distance when I started spitting venom. Mostly, I played Nintendo to calm my nerves and used physical therapy as an outlet for the adrenaline that boiled in my veins. The injury had ignited a whole new competitive spirit—it wasn't just me versus myself, but me versus all the other guys who were out there improving while I sat on my ass. In hindsight, I was overreacting, big time. I should have stayed off it for a few weeks, but I pushed it and planned to get back on the snow in a week.

One Tuesday afternoon, about five days after my injury, I got home from a doctor's appointment to find a bunch of weird messages waiting on my answering machine. They were all collect calls from Brek local Matty Goodman, who'd been trying to reach me from the Boulder jail all morning.

As I tried to make sense of the messages, the phone rang again. I picked up to an electronic operator saying, "Do you accept a collect call from . . . " and then Matty saying, "Can I have my freedom please?" I accepted the call, and Matty, who had been in jail since Friday night, explained his predicament.

He had gone bar hopping in Boulder with Andy Hetzel, Shawn Farmer, Shaun Palmer, and a few others known to party pretty hard. They showed up at a bar with their Long Beach 1986 look—beanies, flannels, chain wallets—and started performing the bullfrog mating dance, a move Matty had invented using Bullfrog sunscreen. He'd lean back on his heels, reach between his legs from behind, and spray Bullfrog sunscreen forward onto perspective mates. In the bar that Friday, they'd used bottles of beer and targeted a group of girls.

The girls kind of liked it, but some meathead frat boys weren't impressed. They shoved Matty and crew toward the door, shouting things like, "Go back to Denver, you bunch of motherfucking dirtbags." One of the snowboarders, whom I won't identify, said, "You want dirtbag? I'll show you dirtbag!" and pulled down his pants, squatted right there on the street, and shit into his hand. The fratboys scattered like someone had pulled the pin out of a grenade. The shit handler chased them, yelling like a wild man. He launched the fecal-bomb, which tumbled end over end, broke up in mid-flight, and peppered the sidewalk with shrapnel.

Later that night Matty ended up with a different crew of snowboarders at a different bar, but more trouble was brewing—this time with a bouncer. Matty watched the bouncer pushing a guy he knew into a wall and grinding his face toward the floor. He didn't think this kind of force was necessary, so he put the bouncer in a headlock. When the guy ran out of the bar, Matty let go and made a quick exit himself.

Outside, the roughed-up snowboarder put his jacket on and a handgun fell on the sidewalk. All the riders were shocked, especially Matty, who had just liberated the idiot. Matty yelled, "You've got a fucking gun?" and *that* was what got the cops involved.

Every snowboarder (or anybody else wearing a flannel and beanie) within a two-block radius was hauled into the station. They were all cleared by midnight, even the guy who had the gun (apparently, he had a license for it). How the hell that happened is beyond me. In Boulder, you can't even skate down Pearl Street without getting a ticket. I guess it's okay to carry firearms though. Matty, who had a string of unpaid parking tickets, wasn't so lucky. On top of it all, Monday was a municipal holiday of some sort, and the judge couldn't hear his case until Tuesday, which was when I got the call and bailed him out.

This story mutated into a huge scandal in the snowboarding world and beyond. Within weeks, urban legends involving gun-wielding snowboarders were circulating like wildfire. Major newspapers talked about gangs of Colorado snowboarders invading ski areas and prompting turf wars on the slopes.

What the general population didn't realize was that snowboarders really were pretty harmless. They might have been wearing gangster fashion, but it was just that—fashion. We went from Miami Beach to Venice Beach, making a mockery of real gangs. It was the next logical step after pastels and neon.

Changing of the Guard

I was laid up for a grand total of six days—a fast recovery. Probably too fast, but I was going certifiably crazy. Luckily, a huge storm hit the Rockies, and a kid who lived nearby called me up to see if I wanted to go to Berthoud Pass to ride pow.

Jim took me to a bunch of crazy chutes and treelines where the powder was up to my waist. I'd never before ridden anything so light and deep; it was like riding on helium crystals. It felt so smooth and natural, like how I imagined surfing would be. I thought, *Oh my god, I've been missing this?* And I finally understood why I had been all alone hiking the pipe on powder days.

The TDK World Championship was scheduled for February 1, 1991, in Breckenridge. At that time in snowboarding, "world championship" was a confusing term because a number of governing bodies were sanctioning different events around the world. But the TDK was a prestigious event by anyone's standards, and most of the top pros showed up.

The crowd was massive, with people crammed shoulder-to-shoulder on all sides of the pipe. Jeff Brushie won the halfpipe with huge, ultra-smooth airs; Bertrand Denervaud from Switzerland took second with smaller, precise tricks; Andy Hetzel took third with a combination of technical spins and big airs; and I pulled together a fourth, though I have no idea what I did. The performance calmed my paranoia about my back injury and my sponsors dropping me. A couple weeks later, I entered a Rocky Mountain Snowboard Series event at Eldora, Colorado. Events in this series were localized contests with both pro and amateur divisions so they didn't attract as many big names. I nailed a second-place finish, which should have fired me up, but I didn't think it was a big deal because all the top pros weren't there.

In March 1991, I traveled back east to Stowe, Vermont, for the Professional Snowboard Tour of America (PSTA), an event my mom attended. Once again, I was unable to crack the top three, and I was starting to think I was cursed.

The U.S. Open at Stratton was approaching, but my back had been acting up since the Stowe contest. During practice the morning of the event, it seized up again. I was in pain but figured that since this was one of the last big events of the season, I might as well push through it and worry about healing over the summer. I qualified for the finals and while waiting for my last run, I alternated between holding snowballs against my lower back and eating Advil like jelly beans.

I was wary of twisting my spine, so most of my tricks were seriously compromised by the injury. I took eleventh—an accomplishment I would never have imagined two years before. Now all of a sudden it wasn't good enough for me. I told myself I sucked and would continue to suck until I broke the fourth place hex at a major event.

That was the last year Craig Kelly competed actively. By the end of the season, he was a four-time world champion, a three-time U.S. Open champion, and the most successful competitor in snowboarding, pulling in six figures from sponsors alone, not including contest winnings. He walked away from all of it to embark on a new phase in his career: professional freeriding. I found out years later that one of the reasons

Craig stepped down from the pro circuit was that he didn't like the person he became when he competed. It consumed his entire life, so he took the route that three Avalanche team riders pioneered a few years before.

In 1988, Tom Burt, Bonnie Learey, and Jim Zellers had walked away from a contest on a perfect powder day and never returned—to organized competition at least. The trio started climbing mountains and riding powder with photographers in tow. During that first year, they kept close tabs on the magazines to see how their experiment was panning out. The next year, their coverage quadrupled, and their love for and skills in big-mountain conditions expanded exponentially. Burt, Zellers, and Learey had invented a new way to make a living from snowboarding. In 1989, *ISM* honored them for the risks they'd taken by leaving the contest circuit by naming them the "Snowboarders of the Year."

I enjoyed keeping up with the trio's adventures and thought riding powder was fun, but I was still just a skateboarder on snow. The halfpipe was what motivated me, and competition seemed to be the seed of progression for freestyle tricks.

When Craig retired after the 1990/1991 season, people started wondering who would dominate the overall titles in the coming year. I wasn't concerned about the overall and, fortunately, Morrow didn't care if I ever entered a race. The halfpipe was up for grabs, and lots of gung-ho pipe jocks were up to the challenge. Veteran riders like Jeff Brushie, Jimi Scott, Noah Brandon, Jason Ford, Andy Hetzel, Keith "Duckboy" Wallace, Shaun Palmer, and Euros like Terje Haakonsen, Camille Brichet, and Bertrand Denervaud were all gunning for halfpipe supremacy. The halfpipe is physically and mentally trying, and competitors got burnt out as fast as the sport was evolving. Riders I considered mentors just two years before had dropped off the map in halfpipe competition.

I worked really hard on rehabbing my back with a physical therapist for the first half of the summer, and when I felt great again, I went skating. Then it was off to Morrow headquarters in Salem and then Mount Hood two hours away for summer training. I scammed my way into different camps, including Windell's and High Cascade, under the guise of "guest coach," but all I really did was ride. Every now and then, I'd give kids pointers, but I was never much of a teacher. I was too busy focusing on the next trick, and that was fine by my sponsor.

Morrow was searching for an identity that would make it stand out from other companies. Thanks to a well-chosen team and top-notch graphic designer Scott Clum, Morrow began to carve out its own niche. Scott's abstract computer-graphic designs and low-impact fonts and logos gave Morrow a more artsy feel. The vibe was more mellow than in your face, and that, along with a talented team, was what made Morrow stand out.

Make It or Naked

That fall, I had trouble finding snowboarders who were into skateboarding so I skated solo a lot. Then I met the guys from Las Vegas, and my life was never the same.

One night in October, I was in Denver skating at Jamaican Jim's. There were no parents lurking during the 10 P.M. to 1 A.M. session, so all the skaters were serious business. At around 11:30 P.M. a group of semi-normal looking college-aged kids showed up and took over the park. They were doing hard tricks and obviously knew what they were doing.

I was getting ready to drop in on the vert ramp when I glanced at this guy standing a foot away from me and saw that he was wearing nothing but shoes, a helmet, kneepads, and a thong. This was years before anything like *Jackass* was on television, so I didn't know what to think.

Before long I figured out that this guy was losing bad in a game they called

Skate or die!

"Make It or Naked," a bizarre combination of strip poker and skateboard "horse" where every time you blew the trick, you had to take an article of clothing off. A few minutes later, he was trying to pull kickflip Indys totally naked.

I struck up a conversation with one guy who still had most of his clothing on. His name was Palmer Brown, but everybody called him "Balls." He gave me the rundown on the crew, Team Cheese: Brian "Booker" Bessold, Travis "Crabs" Price, and Brett Davies. They were all about twenty and had grown up together in Las Vegas. They were all straight-edge, but to make up for the lack of alcohol or any other mind-altering substances, they'd do the craziest shit, like walk butt-naked two city blocks in the middle of the day to a 7-Eleven convenience store, go inside, buy a Big Gulp, and walk back (this was actually their original rite of passage).

Team Cheese was attending the University of Colorado at Boulder, so it turned out that we were neighbors. One night, Balls invited Carrie and me to a party they were having in the dorms. It was a raging party, and it took us a while to wade within sight of Balls's band, Finger, which was made up of the Vegas guys rocking out in G-strings. A few minutes later Balls was completely naked at the mic, singing a really bad rendition of a Dag Nasty song. I'd never met such insane people in my life.

Getting to know the Vegas crew helped me break out of my shell and, at the same time, instigated the beginning of the end of my relationship with Carrie. Their nickname for me was Shred, and they were always saying, "Shred, when are you gonna drop the baggage?" or "Lose the e-brake." I was in the middle because I liked them both.

I'd go to rager frat and sorority parties with Team Cheese, and they'd drink huge bottles of IBC root beer while everybody else got wasted. The girls liked them because they were so funny and different, and most of the frat boys thought they were too weird to be a threat to their women. But, every once in a while, a frat boy would pull attitude: "Who *are* you? Why are *you* here?" The Vegas crew would agree to leave saying, "Let me just find my friends first." Before leaving, they'd mark territory by peeing in random places all over the house and uppertanking the toilets, which I personally witnessed. The tank lid on the toilet is removed, shat in, then replaced. The bathroom is then polluted with constant post-bowel-movement stench, and every flush thereafter is spackled with brown water. It requires a rubber glove cleanup—a dry heaver, for sure.

The Winter of Balls

It started snowing in November, and I was more fired up than ever about snowboarding. In December, I went home to the East Coast for Christmas, and then, back in Boulder, Team Cheese bought me a G-string for my twenty-second birthday. Even though I didn't get naked, they had accepted me into their circle of freaks and changed my nickname from Shred to Ronnie for reasons unknown.

My two closest friends in the group, Brett and Balls, had moved into a house together, and I crashed there one night so we could go snowboarding early the next morning. I woke up, jumped in the shower, and the next thing I know, Balls is in there with me, then Crabs is lathering up, and I'm in the corner, thinking, *I don't get it.* They slapped my butt, called me Renaldo—their gay version of Ronnie—and finally let me go. They loved pulling stunts like this, pretending they were homosexual. They were all rated PG, "part gay."

Before I met the Vegas guys, snowboarding was serious business. Riding with Team Cheese at Copper Mountain that winter was a reality check. They didn't give a shit about snowboarding and reminded me not to take myself so seriously. They'd drop their snowboarding outfits—one-piece gas station attendant suits—around their ankles in the lift lines and dance in their G-strings. The lift operators got to know them and they'd request dances. Balls and Crabs helped me remember that snowboarding is fun.

One day in January, Balls whacked into a tree while riding with the Vegas crew. I wasn't there, but the guys told me that when the ski patrol got to him he was unconscious, so they took him down on a backboard. Down in the first aid hut, while they were waiting for the ambulance, the ski patrol checked him out. They unzipped Balls's one-piece suit and found he was wearing a thong with a bird head, orange bird legs dangling between his legs, and a yellow beak pointing out with a message that read, "Squeeze me." The patrol squeezed it, and it started playing "Whistle While You Work." The two patrollers looked at each other like, *We've got a situation here.* That bird really disturbed them. Here they were in a life and death situation—unconscious snowboarder with a head injury—and the victim was wearing a novelty thong.

The story is funny, but Balls's condition wasn't. He was in a coma for about a week. Then he woke up, none the worse for wear, and was back to normal soon enough.

After he came out of his coma, Balls became a sort of big brother figure to me (even though he's younger). He came from a family with money and I was living on Ramen, so he covered me all the time and really took me under his wing. Plus, he gave me a lot of good advice, like, "Figure out what's really important in life. Fuck the rest of it."

_My first trip to Europe. Just another blond boy in Spain.

SNOWBOARDING/
THE INTERNATIONAL
LANGUAGE

The winter of 1991/1992 was my first real year "on the road" because I had to get a passport. I had signed the dotted line with Morrow for another year, so they owned me. They could send me to compete anywhere in the world they wanted, and I had to be ready to perform my services.

There was a lot of political drama in snowboarding regarding rival sanctioning bodies and multiple pro tours. In America, the PSTA (Professional Snowboard Tour of America) and USASA (United States Amateur Snowboard Association) events were the main contest circuits that most riders gravitated to. There was a mostly American tour sponsored by Nissan and the more internationally oriented World Cup series—not to mention all sorts of localized pro/am events. Had I given it any thought, I would have been extremely confused about which contest to enter. Luckily, Morrow became my baby-sitter and made it simple for me with one-syllable instructions: "You. Todd. Go there. Now."

About half of the companies and riders were looking toward the Olympics as the ultimate competitive forum that would legitimize the sport. The other half didn't give a damn about the Olympics because it reeked of skiing—a stuffy, by-the-books sport with an attitude that was the kiss of death for snowboarding's irreverent spirit. At this time, you had to be an amateur in order to be eligible for Olympic competition. Once you collected money in contest winnings or via sponsorships, you basically became a pro athlete, thus not Olympic material. There were all sorts of loopholes, though, and the 1994 Olympics were still a long way off. A number of forward-thinking individuals wanted to be ready. I personally wanted to make a living doing something that I loved without worrying about the politics. I just wanted to ride.

Morrow based all their decisions about everything I did on what would get the most coverage. Snowboarding was a business, and I was essentially selling snowboards. Magazine editors, for the most part, looked at contest results to help them figure out who deserved to be on their covers. Kids looked at magazines and bought snowboards based on who was riding them. The marketability, and thus the success, of all companies was directly related to the exposure their team riders were able to secure.

Morrow knew what they were doing. To motivate its team to do well in contests (which led to more photos in the mags, which led to bigger sales) they invented an ingenious incentive plan called "The Five Top Fives." If you got five top-five finishes at five different contests, you'd receive a bonus of at least a couple thousand dollars at the end of the season.

Beating the Boy Wonder, but Not Really

Terje Haakonsen had raised a few eyebrows as a ripping fifteen-year-old Norwegian who took fifth place back at the 1990 TDK World Championships in Breckenridge. Two years later he was the odds-on favorite for every event he entered. Americans had always been known as the best freestyle (halfpipe) riders; now, Terje was giving notice that the Europeans had been practicing.

Terje's nickname was "The Cat" because he always landed on his feet. The kid stuck everything, and everything he did was on a huge scale. He made all the pipe riders nervous. Jeff Galbraith, a snowboard writer for *TransWorld,* interviewed us for an article about Terje. I compared the Boy Wonder and his style to the transporter on *Star Trek: The Next Generation.* I said that Terje's riding style had a bio filter on it that wouldn't transport diseases or imperfections. He'd see someone do a trick, then run it through his filters, and when he did it, the trick would come out flawless.

To take on the über-Viking at the World Cup at Snowmass, Colorado, on February 6, 1992, I had to pull out my own bio-filtered trick. People were just starting to spin *and* grab their tricks in the halfpipe, so freestyle was still in the dark ages. (Remember, back then spins were "cool," but flips were "gay." Flips were upside down, and spins weren't inverted—yet.) Most contest runs consisted of big straight airs, with maybe an alley-oop, air to fakie, Cab trick, basic spins (360 or 540), or the occasional grabbing 360 spin as a money move. In practice before the event, I began with grabbing 360s, then started gutting around 540 grabs. When I finally hit it with enough speed and grabbed, the 540 spin felt like no trick I'd ever done before. It was totally natural, and I knew I had a heavy new contest trick. I pulled it clean halfway through my World Cup qualifying run and ended with a handplant—still a crowd pleaser—but I mixed it up by doing the handplant to fakie (landing backward).

I got the highest qualifying score—and even beat Terje. Of course, winning the qualifying run means nothing overall; you still have to compete in the finals. As far as

I was concerned, I could have packed it up and gone home with a grin on my face. That's how rad it felt to beat the Cat.

I was really sick of getting fourth place and really wanted a top-three finish. It was frustrating because I had the tricks in me, I just hadn't been able to pull them clean during contest finals. People would beat me with easier tricks and a higher degree of consistency. With my high-scoring qualifying run behind me I wanted to keep the momentum flowing, but the 540 grab didn't work for me in the finals. I hesitated and fell. Terje won (in fact, he won every halfpipe event he entered that winter), and I got tenth, which was a pisser. But I told myself that my qualifying run score proved that I had it in me, not only to take top three, but to win.

Have Snowboard, Will Travel

Mid-February, *TransWorld*'s photo editor, Jon Foster, called me to say, "Guess what? We're going to Spain. Morrow already okayed it. Brad Steward is coming, and so is Jason Ford." I asked if there was a contest or something, and he said, "Nope. We're just going to drink sangria and go snowboarding. It'll be a feature story in *TransWorld*. You know, exotic world travel. You've got a passport, right?"

I was fired up to go to Europe, but I was also a homebody. I liked my nearby resorts, shooting photos off familiar jumps, and playing Nintendo in my shitty little apartment in Boulder with my girlfriend. I was a little scared and needed some advice to feel out the situation.

I talked to Jason Ford and he told me about the beautiful Spanish girls we were going to meet, which was great and all, but I had a girlfriend. I consulted with Balls and he reinforced his ongoing philosophy: "A trip to Spain or stay here for a shitty contest? Go to Spain."

Locked and Loaded

We landed at the Bilbao airport in northern Spain and met our guide, Javier, who was also the co-owner of *Tres 60 Surf* magazine. Javier was thinking of starting up a snowboarding magazine and had invited Jon Foster out to see the Spanish scene. Javier gave us the keys to our micro car with Basque license plates and said, "Follow me." Thus began our road trip through the Pyrenees mountains, complete with an ever-present contingent of Spanish *amigos*-aka-*amibros*.

The schedule was tough. We didn't eat dinner until midnight, and then it was time to "make party," which lasted until five in the morning. Then we'd sleep a couple hours, go snowboarding until the late afternoon siesta, sleep until around 10 P.M., and start it all over again. And again. And again.

I loved Spain, though. There were skateboard parks everywhere, the girls *were* beautiful, and I found I could handle the alcohol, at least the kind that was sweet and had an umbrella in it. I quickly discovered a local drink that combined wine and Coca-Cola. This dis-intimidator helped me interact with the forward Spanish women who scared the shit out of me by stroking the long, severely fried blond hair protruding from under my ever-present baseball cap, which I turned around backward. None of the other guys in Spain wore caps, and the ladies apparently dug mine and my bleached-white locks. When they made eyes at me I tried to be a man and stare back, but I always got embarrassed and looked away. This made them even more determined, probably because they knew they had a young inexperienced American to play with. Unfortunately, I never let it go any further.

One morning, while en route from the heart of Basque country to a resort called Candanchu, we noticed a lot of military and police vehicles on the road. The resort was located in an area that had been recently bombed by a Basque "terrorist" group. For years, the Basque people had been trying to secede from Spain—a conflict I didn't understand at the time. Later I learned that we had been in the northernmost section of Basque country, i.e., the "hot zone," of this loosely termed "civil war." And we looked pretty shady.

The recent bombing was probably the reason for the vast amount of firepower being displayed at an impromptu checkpoint that appeared in the road ahead of us while we were driving into the mountains. I immediately started sweating while Foster casually reminded us that he spoke Spanish and not to worry. The truth was, Foster spoke enough Spanish to confidently order Jack Daniels at the bar, but to the guards we were babbling foreigners with suspect-looking snowboard bags strapped to the roof of our car. A uniformed army guy next to the *alto* (stop) sign eyed them, then asked for our papers in Spanish.

Papers? Foster and Brad Steward, the writer, handed over their passports, and I whispered to Jason, who was digging around in a pocket, "You're supposed to keep your passport with you?" He nodded, and I got really nervous. The guy checked out Foster's and Brad's passports, then tapped his machine gun on our back window, the international Morse code for, "Roll down the window, or get shot." I realized then that I was really in a different country. We didn't have military checkpoints back home. Occasionally, we'd get stopped by cops, but they were pretty subdued and carried around mellow little revolvers. The rest of the world was strapped with hand-cannons or machine guns. Our cops carry Mace; theirs, grenades.

A big powder roller, one of my favorite jumps in Spain.

Brad, apparently bucking for a job with *National Geographic,* saw an opportunity for a Pulitzer Prize and discreetly pointed his camera at the soldier from between the seats. I saw him setting up and as calmly as possible, looked him in the eyes, smiled, and said, "Are you retarded? You want to get us shot? Put. That. Away." I was totally about to lose it. I had never even dreamed of situations this bad. These soldiers seemed really shifty, like they were just looking for a reason to pop off a few rounds, and if we got in the way, so be it. I kept it together long enough to explain to the guy that I left my passport in the hotel room. He must have understood English, because he said, "American," sounding as if he meant "stupid American," and let us go.

At the Candanchu resort, there were some amazing freeriding terrain—big avalanche chutes with giant roller jumps we called *Sexos Con Gordos* after an adult video we saw for sale at a gas station. We checked out a halfpipe contest at a neighboring resort the following day. Our guide, Javier, introduced us as "American superstar snowboarders" over a little amplifier speaker and microphone and the locals freaked out, thinking Jason and I were there to sandbag the event and take away their prize money. We didn't compete, but it was cool to see where snowboarding was at in Spain. This was one of the country's early halfpipe events, and the setup reminded me of the crappy New England Cup pipes of the late eighties. Here, we were at the "cell" stage of snowboarding evolution, maybe a tadpole . . .

One night, we traded in our comfy hotel for a coed youth hostel because it would "add to the story," and because most of the mag's readers wouldn't be able to afford anything more. When we walked in the door, it was like we were instantly enveloped by a big fart. A bunch of people were walking around naked from the shower or changing in front of everybody. Modesty wasn't an issue. That night I heard people snoring and doing the eight-legged love dance. The next morning, I was on a lower bunk putting on my snowboarding pants when a naked Spanish guy in his twenties swung down from the upper bed and sat next to me to talk. *This guy should go bowling with the Vegas Crew,* I thought.

I loved Spain, but after ten days, I was homesick and ready to go back to the States. While traveling abroad, I had to deal with things like the phones, almost getting hit crossing the street because pedestrians have no right of way, and having guns pointed at me. A seasoned traveler would probably consider that stuff part of the fun, but I was a far cry from being a seasoned traveler.

That trip was my first glimpse into a very interesting perk of pro snowboarding. Everybody has an angle that allows them to see the world on somebody else's dime—writers, photographers, snowboarders, filmmakers, team managers, designers. The

The three amibros—Brad, Jason, and me—doing the museum thing in Spain.

Spain story was *TransWorld SNOWboarding*'s version of a *Travel and Leisure* feature. "Here's a hot tip for you travelers. Go to Spain!" But in reality, it was just a reason for Jon and Brad to take a snowboarding vacation. Jason and I had been invited along for legitimacy, to hit a few jumps while we toured the countryside. This was a formula I'd learn to appreciate—and exploit—for years to come.

Godzilla Country

My next major assignment for Morrow was to travel to Japan. Japan!? I was incredibly nervous on the trans Pacific flight—Asia was a whole other world, after all—but then I remembered it was the home of Godzilla, which turned my trepidation into excitement. The Big Greenie was everywhere—amazing memorabilia, models, and toy shops—and I became captivated by the Japanese culture. My goal was to seek out as many Godzilla stores as possible, and, oh, try to get my fourth top five of the season.

We were headed to the island of Hokkaido to hit the 1992 World Cup at Rusutsu Resort, which was like a gigantic amusement park with rides and a carnival next to the ski area. In addition, vending machines that sell beer were located every twenty feet.

The resort had gained notoriety in the snowboarding world the year before because Shaun Palmer and Chris Roach had become obsessed with the carnival game in which you put a plastic frog on a launcher, smack it with a hammer, and try to land the flying frog on a lily pad. They were trying to win stuffed animals for their girl-friends back home, but all their frogs were landing in the water, and Palmer and Roach were getting really bitter about it. Their multiple trips to the beer vending machines didn't help their launching skills or their punk attitudes. Several losses later, Palmer and Roach replaced the frogs with half-full beer cans and began launching them at confused Japanese employees. They were escorted out of the resort by the police and told not to return.

This year, all the visiting pros received stern warnings from the contest organizers that were immediately forgotten. The international snowboarding community descended on the place, and mayhem ensued. Even Palmer was allowed back. When we arrived at Rusutsu Resort, the mountain had just gotten four feet of snow. The resort had all sorts of slides and playground equipment for kids at the bottom of runs, so it was transformed from an actual playground into jib heaven—we called it Super Mario Land for Snowboarding.

On the runs themselves, Japanese skiers and snowboarders made their way down in an orderly fashion, staying inside the ropes like cattle. Any "off trail" riding or skiing was, for some reason, prohibited. The visiting snowboarders, on the other hand, ducked under (or aired over) the ropes and rode the amazing powder between the runs. It was paradise.

The ski patrol tried to stand between us and the closed powder fields. They'd blow whistles, wave their arms, and point at the rope saying, "No!" We'd just dodge them, yelling, "I'm American!"

We were blatant American assholes, and I feel bad about it now, but that's how we were. It was mob mentality. One person did it, and everybody followed. These days, I have a greater respect for the Japanese people and their culture. If I have to break the rules, I do it very discreetly.

Experimental freeriding at A-Basin and one of the few times I left the pipe in 1990.

Our fun continued off the slopes as well. The Rusutsu Resort hotel we stayed at during the World Cup had an indoor waterpark/wave pool with a spiral slide at one end (the Japanese are full on about packing as much stuff as possible into a small area). Add to that forty out-of-control snowboarders drunk on vending machine beer, and things get ugly. We watched the vacationing Japanese couples hit the spiral slide going down two at a time in a little train, controlling their speed so they went really slow, and at the bottom yelling, "Weeeeeeeh!" as they plopped into the pool. They were laughing and having a great time.

It took us about five minutes to discover that if we lubed up our butts and backs with liquid soap from the bathroom, we became bullets. We'd let a Japanese couple go and wait until they were halfway down before jumping into the tube one after the other like paratroopers exiting a plane. The couples would splash into the pool, and before they could wipe the water from their eyes, fifteen soaped-up snowboarders would shoot out of the tube like rapid-fire cannonballs and land on top of them. The pool was a foamy mess. There was only one lifeguard in this Olympic-sized pool/slide complex and it was beyond his control. He didn't even try to stop us. Wherever we went on that trip, we terrorized the Japanese. We were Godzilla.

The World Cup contest got going after three days of round-the-clock madness. Shaun Palmer (who had been on his best behavior due to the frog incident the year before) pulled something much bigger. At the time, halfpipe judging was at an all-time low. Scores seemed to be based more on a person's reputation than actual halfpipe runs. Brushie had been winning most of the halfpipe events (unless Terje was there), and Palmer, who *had* been the reigning American in past years, hadn't been able to beat him in quite a while.

So the two switched identities: clothes, goggles, snowboards, everything. Palmer did a run as Brushie, and Brushie did a run as Palmer to see if judging was biased. When the real Palmer, disguised as Brushie, got better scores than the real Brushie, disguised as Palmer, they proved their point. Later, when Ted Martin, the technical delegate of the World Cup, saw Brushie and Palmer blatantly changing out of their disguises, he freaked and threatened to ban both of them from the International Snowboard Federation.

Terje Haakonsen won the event, pulling the first 720 I'd seen in competition. Palmer as Brushie took second, Brushie as Palmer took third, and I got another fourth with my money-move 540 and a handplant.

After two and a half weeks in Japan, I was ready to go home. It was the longest I'd ever been away. I despised fish, and my rice, candy, sports drink, Coke, and beer diet was starting to get to me, but my fascination with Japan had just begun. I didn't have enough money to take advantage of the gadgets in Electric Town, Tokyo, but I filled my luggage with Godzilla toys and flew home with a whole new appreciation for world travel.

Another day. Another trick. Another dollar.

PIPE DRAGON/
TRICKS OF FURY

After the World Cup, I hit the halfpipe and trained like crazy. I began to grab my board in different places for the 540, trying to figure out what worked well and looked stylish. I found that the more I tweaked it, the easier the spins were to get around and land. A tweaked-out lein 540 felt the best, so for days I hiked the pipe, doing the same trick over and over until it was easy. All the riders I'd ever admired made tricks look effortless, and I figured this was the best way to get to their level. By the time the 1992 U.S. Open rolled around in March, I was so sick of tweaked-out lein 540s that I wanted to puke.

I made the finals, and before dropping in for the main event, I talked to my dad in my head, which was something I started doing the winter after he passed away. I found it calmed me down and gave me someone to lean on, if only in my mind. Relying solely on myself was too much pressure.

I nailed my entire run, including one of the bigger lein 540s I'd ever done. The judges liked it, and I took third place behind Jimi Scott and, of course, Terje. This secured my "Five Top Fives" bonus from Morrow, which was great. More important, though, I'd capped off the season with a top three finish at the U.S. Open.

The European Tour

That June, I went back to Mount Hood. The freestyle aspect of snowboarding was really taking off, and I was excited to see all the new tricks people were pulling. Creativity was in the air.

I'd only been there a couple weeks when Miki Keller told me to pack my bags for a European summer tour. Since my trips to Spain and Japan, I'd become wary of international cuisine. My standard diet consisted of Top Ramen, SweeTarts, Twizzlers, Nerds, and fizzy-sugary Zotz washed down with Coca-Cola. If it had a name like Zip Zap Zonker, it was a staple. And if I was feeling particularly health conscious, I'd drink orange Tang. In preparation for this trip I stuffed a huge Gotcha duffel bag with equal parts clothes and candy, plus two economy-sized plastic containers of powdered Tang mix.

The tour was multifaceted. We were to meet distributors, do autograph sessions at shops, and hit the Euro summer camps to show Morrow's presence. Morrow needed photos of new gear for the coming year's advertisements, so they hired Trevor Graves to come along and shoot me and a hot new kid named Jim Moran.

Humility in Norway

When we flew into Oslo, Norway, my knowledge of the country consisted of Vikings and pro snowboarders Terje Haakonsen and Ashild Loftus. I got off the plane and, though the skies were gray and rainy, every single girl I saw was a super model. I took this as a good omen, but things soon turned sour. That night I found out Jim Moran is the planet's loudest snorer, and thus the Euro trip from hell began.

First stop was a glacier near Stryn, which is a ten-hour drive into the middle of nowhere. That time of year in Norway, it never gets dark. Between the light and Jim snoring like a wounded elephant, I couldn't sleep the night before. I was whacked out of my skull with jet lag.

We got to the glacier base area, and I was surprised to find that I recognized a bunch of people from back home. Snowboarders are like moths to the flame. Transitions made of snow, like halfpipes and quarterpipes, are what attract them to these meetings in far-off places.

I was fired up to see Mike Ranquet flipping me off, a standard greeting for Ranky. He said, "Let's go look at this piece-of-crap U-Jump," and Jim and I followed him. We all thought we were hot shit, and out there in the middle of nowhere, we figured we were even hotter. The halfpipe was empty, but it looked pretty good. There were a few local kids hanging out around the top, looking timid and nervous. *Poor little guys,* I thought, feeling sorry for them. Ranquet verbalized my other thought, "All right, everybody," he yelled at the top of his lungs. "Have no fear, the American Super Pros have arrived!"

Ranquet dropped in and proceeded to eat shit on the first hit. I quickly dropped in to save face for our crew, and landed on my head. Moran followed and ate shit, too. It was creepy and didn't make sense. It was as though the pipe had sensed our cockiness and spanked us. The transitions were a little abrupt, we reasoned, out of self-defense. As we limped back up, the Scandinavians sent a wave of riders into the pipe. The three of us stopped to watch and our jaws dropped. The kids tore the living shit out of that pipe. All were spinning 720s, and they weren't just good; they were insanely good.

"Where'd all the fucking Terjes come from?" asked Ranquet, who was a super-progressive rider in his own right. He was landing backside 540s backward and stuff like that, but even he was amazed at the fever that had infected Scandinavia. That day we saw Sebu Kohlberg, Aleksi Vanninen, Oscar Norberg, Johanne Oloffson, and Daniel Franck ride. Other than a tiny section at the end of a Fall Line film that included Daniel and Terje, this was my first look at the Scandinavian riders who were about to hit North America. My first thought when I watched them was, *Holy shit. What am I going to have to learn next year?* My second was how I'd been humbled by a bunch of nice kids who demonstrated none of the attitude I'd had when I rolled up to the pipe.

TransWorld SNOWboarding was, at the same time, researching and compiling a story called "Scanners" that introduced the world to the next wave of freestyle talent: most of them from Norway. The article would aptly describe our humbling experience that day: "The American freestyle scene is being blown away by a quiet yet eager crew of Scandinavian kids." From then on out, every serious snowboard company sent talent scouts to those shores in search of the next Terje.

After a few more humbling days, we returned to Oslo. Just as we hit the city limits, I started patting my pockets for the passport I'd left in plain view on the night-stand at the Stryn hotel so I wouldn't forget it. Somebody at the hotel ran it to a train station, and it got to Oslo the next morning just in time for us to make our flight to what Miki called the "boot country." I had no idea she was talking about Italy, but acted as if I did.

Panic in Italy

Our stay in Italy consisted of signing autographs at snowboard shops, meeting our Italian distributor, and watching Miki fend off scores of Italian suitors who were trying to capture her heart. She wasn't impressed. I started to get a little claustrophobic (being confined to my little group of English speaking friends) and homesick. Some time before, Colorado pro Adam Merriman had versed me on the "panic button," an imaginary button snowboarders hit when they have to get the hell out of wherever they are. Several times on this trip, my finger was hovering over that small red panic button. As my career progressed there would be times when that button was the size of a manhole cover, and I wanted to pound it with my fist. But in Italy I managed to hang in there and complete the mission.

For a week, we toured warehouses, shook hands, and ate pasta. I couldn't find anyplace without cobblestones to skate and we didn't go snowboarding because it hadn't stopped pouring rain since we'd left Oslo.

Disaster in France

We took a short trip to Tigne, France, to snowboard a summer glacier. Our hotel rooms were on the fifth floor, and there was no elevator. Burton was making rolling board bags and duffels, but Morrow, like every other company, was two years behind. So I had to lug a hundred pounds of snowboard gear, clothes, and candy to each country. By the time we got to France, I was in serious need of a washing machine. All the sweating made me the world's most disgusting human. So I washed a T-shirt, a pair of socks, and underwear in the sink and hung them around the room to dry overnight, but it was so wet and humid that they never dried. Riding in the rain didn't help.

After two miserable days of riding I was in a bad mood, and as we packed to leave I was cursing the French for not having an elevator. With my bags packed, I looked out of my room to the parking lot below and told Trevor, "I'm not hauling my shit down five floors. I'm gonna bomb it off this balcony."

I hefted my duffel up and over the railing and watched it fall. When it hit the ground, all the seams blew out like an exploding banana. I ran outside and found that the Tang had mixed with the rain to create a huge orange puddle, which had permeated all my stinky, dirty clothes. Nobody had an extra duffel, and we were late for the train back to Italy, so I threw everything in a hotel trash bag and dragged my board bag behind me. Everything, including myself, was sticky and mildewy, and I had nothing clean to put on. I would call Tigne "Tang" in all future visits to France.

We were stuck in a smoking car on the train, so by the time we got back to the hotel late that afternoon, I'd added "ash tray" to my mildew, body odor, and Tang scent bomb. I showered first, then went to the front desk with a towel around my waist to ask where I could find a washing machine. All I knew was a little incoherent Spanish, but I figured, I'm a tourist, she'll tolerate my "el washing machino" attempt at conversation. The lady just looked at me and walked away.

The hotel was a step down from a Motel 6, but had a nice view of a lake. "Fuck it," I said, and lugged my clothes down to the water where I washed all my stuff with a bar of soap from the room—"old world" style. I laid everything out to dry on rocks

Method air at Stratton, 1990.

Alley-oop method at Les Diablerets, Switzerland, 2001.

Chillin' with my *Star Wars* collection.

There's nothing like a perfect jump with a perfect background and, of course, a perfect landing.

Tuck-knee invert at Zero-Gravity,
Nashua, New Hampshire, 1991.

Live at the 1997 U.S. Open.

Me and Lindsy at our Hawaiian wedding, just the three of us…

Cam and me, 2002.

On the beach with the Morrow Team—
my extended family for ten years.

Mom, Dad, and me after my fourth-place finish at the 1990 U.S. Open.

Snowboarding is just an excuse to suck at skateboarding.
Holding my own in Norway, 1992.

There's no crowd like the U.S. Open Crowd. Trying to give them a good show en route to my second Open win in 1997.

in the sun. In the room I shared with Trevor and Jim, their own collection of stinky clothes were hung up, with the heat turned on full-blast to dry them. It was like the most disgusting sauna in the world, and Trevor and Jim were actually asleep in it.

We finally got some good weather for snowboarding on the summer glaciers, and I felt like a beginner. I couldn't land anything. Jim Moran, on the other hand, was on it. Our Italian distributor joined us at the end of the day and took us out for some cappuccinos. He started gushing about Jim in a thick Italian accent, talking with his hands waving all over the place: "Ah, Jim-a Moran-a, So-a great-a. He's the next Craig Kelly, no?"

Trevor sensed a gap in the guy's incessant babble and stood up for me with, "What about Todd? He's one of Morrow's top riders."

"Sì, Todd is-a okay," the distributor said, "but Jim-a Moran-a is so-a young and so-a great-a. His style, it's-a bella, bella."

Great, I thought, looking at Miki. She knew I'd had a bad day riding, but she had to play it up with the distributor. She wasn't selling Todd Richards or Jim Moran. She was selling Morrow, and if the Italian distributor was happy, she was happy.

That moment freaked me out because I was only twenty-two years old, and I suddenly felt like the "old guy." When I was eighteen, nineteen, even twenty, I'd looked up to my "elders." Now I was being brushed off for a fifteen year old, and my career was just getting rolling. *I have to get back on my game,* I thought, even though my game had only been off for a day or two.

Heaven in Geneva

Our next major city was Geneva, Switzerland, and I loved it. The sun was out, there were skateboard parks, and the language barrier wasn't as gnarly as the other places we'd been to. We'd ride small glaciers at resorts outside the city all morning, and when we got back, I'd go skateboarding. I learned how to ollie into my airs on mini ramps and vert, a new technique I'd been trying to learn after watching recent H-Street skate videos.

As a result of those skate sessions in Geneva, my snowboarding got better, too. I continued to use skateboarding as a way to pull my head out of my ass every time snowboarding drove me crazy. My skateboarding outlet also helped when I felt younger riders were threatening to surpass me. Although I didn't know it at the time, Jim Moran, the Scanner kids, and later, riders like Shaun White and Danny Kass would light fires under me that kept me motivated. They would push me to perform, whether in contests or during photo shoots, and fresh new tricks were what kept things fun.

Getting My Spin On

The 1992/1993 season was a transitional year for me and for snowboarding as a whole. Suddenly, contests weren't as important for a rider's career because the magazines and videos started to hype freeriding and riding for fun, not just for competition. There were so many snowboarders that most resorts were forced to allow us on their slopes or go out of business. The ski industry was feeling the bite in their profits as crossover athletes sold their skis and picked up snowboards. More and more snowboarding companies popped up. Skate brands like Santa Cruz and Vision wanted a piece of the action and expanded their snowboard lines to attract the snowboarders who wanted the skateboarding-on-snow imagine. Virtually every ski company that had been dabbling in the snowboard market started advertising heavily in the magazines and offered full board lines to, hopefully, take back a bit of the pie they'd lost during the previous couple years.

Spinning was gaining popularity, and combining spinning with bonking (tapping inanimate objects, like fallen skiers, with the bottom of your board while ollieing over them) called for shorter boards. So Morrow, along with a lot of other companies, debuted boards that appealed to the Jib-o-Maniacs such as the Spoon Nose, which had a nose with a weird spoon shape that didn't catch on things like a traditional board did. It looked so much like its namesake that one of the early advertisements didn't show the board at all. Instead, it showed a tablespoon. I was accustomed to riding on boards that were about 165 centimeters long, and the Spoon was a 160. I thought, *Oh god, this thing's way too short,* but after a few days riding, I found that the length was indeed easier to spin.

Some jibbers began sawing the nose and tails off their longer boards to lighten the weight. Those boards were magic (or so we thought). Shorter lengths meant less "swing weight," which meant you could spin and land tricks easier. Brands like Joy Ride really capitalized on this theory, making ridiculously short boards that continued to fuel the progression in riding styles and board construction. K2 followed up with a really wide board for big-footed kids like Adam Merriman, who for years had been dealing with his toes and heels hanging off the sides of his boards. K2 called the board the Fat Bob, and its short and fat design became one of the most copied shapes in the industry.

As the worldwide jib movement continued to pick up speed that season, I continued to do whatever Morrow asked of me. We came to the mutual conclusion that I could get a lot of my "work" done by staying in Colorado, which saved them travel expenses and meant more money and more time in front of the cameras for me. It also allowed me to get into a practice schedule, so I wasn't always having to get used to new terrain. I could just get better and better on familiar terrain.

Photographers were more than happy to shoot photos while freeriding, which gave me a break from the halfpipe. In January 1993, photographer Gregg Adams

My first cover shot (February 1993 *TWS*). Freeriding (?!?) at A-Basin.

called me with some good news. He said that *TransWorld* had asked him about a freeriding photo of me he'd taken the previous spring at Arapahoe Basin, and he hinted that it might be a big shot, a full page or maybe a spread. A couple weeks later, Rob Morrow phoned to say, "How's it going, cover boy?" I had scored the cover of the February 1993 *TransWorld SNOWboarding*. My mom was just as proud of my self-bleached hair color as she was of the cover photo.

That season, resorts, including Vail and Breckenridge, began investing in halfpipe-shaping machines to build pipes with perfectly rounded transitions. They hired snow-boarders to oversee the construction of snowboard parks, which meant riders would finally have a place on the mountain where they could hit jumps and jib the hell out of man-made objects built to withstand abuse from steel edges and P-tex. The original reason for these parks was to separate the skiers from the snowboarders, but skiers snuck in to hit the best jumps on the mountain.

With all this fun stuff at the local resorts, why leave? I put more and more miles on the GTI making the one- to two-hour drive back and forth from Boulder to Summit County and Vail every day. Morrow, Gotcha, and Oakley (my new sunglass/goggle sponsor) were happy with my strategy for getting coverage in photos and film. It wasn't like I was completely bailing on the competition scene (even though it was becoming "cool" to boycott contests). I was just spacing out my contests so I could fill up my bag of tricks.

During this time, I also started freeriding Vail's back bowls with Zach Bingham, "Ninja" Jay Isaacs, Jason "J1" Gerardi, and Jason "J2" Rasmus. We never thought about how dangerous the mountains can be with avalanches, cliffs, and unmarked hazards. If it snowed two feet overnight, we'd head straight for the bowls and out-of-bounds gullies that were great for snowboarding but stupidly dangerous. Snowboard-ing hadn't really lost anybody to avalanches, so powder was only associated with fun. Freeriding pioneers like Tom Burt, Jim Zellers, and Craig Kelly had taken a moun-taineering approach to snowboarding and educated themselves about avalanche and backcountry safety. But for the most part, this type of awareness hadn't reached the snowboarding masses and could only be found in a few small magazine articles.

One day that season, a few of us followed Zach down a windblown ridgeline. It was the day after a storm—fast snow, clear blue sky. We were cutting down off the ridge, about to have an epic pow run, when Zach threw on the brakes, waving his hands for us to stop. We pulled up next to him, peered over a roller, and realized that we were perched on top of an eighty-foot cliff with no way down. Above us was an open slope, and it didn't take a rocket scientist to deduce that if the snow we were standing on slipped, we'd get swept off the cliff. Suddenly, we were shitting our pants. Very carefully, we took our snowboards off and hiked, as gently as possible, back up to the ridgeline.

The Temporary Tornado

Snowboarders who didn't compete proved their abilities through public opinion. Thus, being seen in videos and sequence photos in magazines was the only true documentation of someone's riding skills. Once upon a time, any trick people saw in a magazine was rad if it was tweaked out and captured at the right instant. Now, people were becoming suspicious of single photographs. The big question was, "Did he make it? It doesn't count if he didn't make it." In the magazines' start-to-finish sequence photos, riders could analyze a trick from take off to landing.

Tricks have never come easy for me. I've had to practice the hell out of everything I've ever learned. In 1993, I wanted to take the jib-spin style to the halfpipe, which meant I had to get comfortable in the air. The best way to get comfortable spinning, I reasoned, was to do it off the smallest jumps. The smaller the jump, the less airtime, the faster you have to spin. Then, as you graduate to bigger air, you have time to grab your board in different ways, slow down the rotations, and achieve that slow-motion Roach style.

Once I got it in my head that spinning was going to be my next thing, I'd spin off of every bump I could find. I'd ride with my friends from the Vegas crew and try all sorts of new tricks. I had no pros to impress when I rode with Balls and Geb, and their constant antics and insanity helped me overcome my self-consciousness. Taking yourself seriously around those guys was impossible. One day, Vail local and pro rider Adam Merriman saw me going from jump to jump to jump, spinning like a top. He joked that I couldn't make three turns without spinning off something, and he called me "Todd, the Temporary Tornado."

Hanging out with Balls and Geb also gave me the strength to break up with Carrie ("Just do it. What are you going to do, marry her?"). We were still living together, but we'd grown further and further apart as our careers progressed. We were too young to settle down with each other in the first place, but our mutual adventure to Colorado helped both of us grow. But as we grew, our personalities began to clash. That spring, I moved into Geb's house in Boulder, and that was that. I was twenty-three and single.

Over-the-Counter Chile Powder

I rode A-Basin until it closed in June, then I got invited to be a paid coach for a couple of sessions at High Cascade Snowboard Camp at Mount Hood. I got another raise from Morrow, Oakley was paying me a pretty good salary, and Gotcha (despite their bizarre color combos and multicolored vomit patterns) was hanging in there as my biggest monthly paycheck. Making rent wasn't as bad, and I only ate Ramen when I wanted to, not because I had to.

I went to Hood at the end of June and roomed with High Cascade's chef, Chris Owen, who, in addition to his fine culinary skills, was a good snowboarder and photographer. Our room at the High Cascade lodge was about the size of a closet.

Nowadays, every kid at a snowboard camp has an agenda and wants to be the next Terje. They're almost too serious. Back in 1993, they were just a bunch of out-of-control kids with a week-long pass away from their parents, and keeping them focused was the hardest trick I learned that year. In between coaching duties, I was able to concentrate on my own riding. Between the tornado spinning sessions at A-Basin and the summer at Hood, something happened to my riding—I learned all the tricks in the pipe I'd been thinking about all winter long.

It rained every other day that summer at Hood, which was perfect. It gave me time to go skating at Cal Skate Park in nearby Portland. I learned a bunch of revert tricks on the mini ramps—like two new ones each session—and the next day I'd be pumped up and ready to ride. All of a sudden, the learning curve wasn't nearly as steep as it had been in the past, thanks to the lack of pressure and the alternating skateboarding and snowboarding sessions. The snowboarding tricks I'd been gutting around on straight jumps were way easier in the halfpipe. I learned frontside 720s, frontside 900s, fakie 720s, and fakie 900s in a period of two weeks.

Since snowboard movies always premiered in the fall, there was always a bunch of filmers at Hood trying to get last-minute footage (footie) and document the most current tricks. Likewise, riders were always trying to get more footie to expand their segments. You could never have enough coverage. Tricks and logo shots you got published in magazines or included in films were used to negotiate your sponsorship contract for the following year. People who got both publicity and had good contest results were highly sought after by most of the companies. Still, a lot of riders were determined to wave the "contests are weak" flag.

I wanted to be in snowboard videos, but it was more about gaining respect from my friends. If a rider pulled a 900 and nobody saw it, he didn't want to run up and say, "Did you see that? Did you see that?" The videos did the talking for him. The name of the game was acting like you didn't give a shit, but I think everybody wants to get noticed when they pull off something big. Videos let us maintain that cool facade with minimal outward conceit.

I was pretty sure my filming was over for the year when Dave Seoane, a pro rider turned cinematographer who was helping Fall Line Films complete its sixth snowboarding movie, *Project Six,* asked if he could film me. He said he'd been watching my

900s and thought they were some of the more progressive tricks he'd seen that summer because I was landing them consistently. He invited me to go to Chile with him and some other riders, which was a huge honor because Fall Line Films was established and known for putting out good snowboarding movies. A week later I was on a plane to South America with Shaun Palmer, Jay Nelson, Jason Basarich, and Janna Meyen—the best girl rider I'd ever seen.

I sat next to Shaun Palmer on the flight and he gave me constant shit about not doing my handplant against Mike Jacoby three years earlier at the OP Pro at Copper Mountain. The flight attendant served us chicken potpies for dinner, and I noticed Palmer didn't touch his. When she came back and asked if she could take his tray, he told her he wasn't finished yet. I thought it was odd, but I fell asleep and didn't wake until we were landing in Santiago. While going through customs I kept smelling chicken potpie, but couldn't tell where it was coming from. Outside the airport, I pulled the hood of my sweatshirt over my head, and it felt kind of heavy. Seconds later, gooey chicken potpie juice began dripping down my neck. Palmer just looked at me and smiled.

We hired a driver with a minivan to haul us into the mountains. The resort, Valle Nevado, was getting hammered when we got there. It dumped about three feet, which made it possible to huck our carcasses off anything we wanted without fear of serious injury. I was spinning all over the place and going over the nose on a regular basis in the deep powder. According to Palmer, my crashes were a result of my "pussy-ass jib board."

"A submarine would perform better than that piece-of-crap Morrow," he told me. Mike Ranquet and the Palm are the kings of sarcasm, thrown down with brutal honesty when appropriate. If you're having a bad day, don't expect any mercy. But I took his advice, pulled out a longer board I'd brought along, and started sticking my landings.

After a week of riding at Valle Nevado, I felt good about the majority of my tricks, but couldn't imagine I had enough footage to make it into the movie. I chalked it up as a learning experience.

We returned to Santiago a few days before flying home. On the second afternoon, we all went to hang out in a cantina near the hotel. A couple big, tough looking guys wearing flannels and dark sunglasses walked in like they owned the place. They were Alaskan pro riders Jay Liska and Ritchie Fowler, notorious big mountain snowboarders who rode big boards, wore their sideburns long, and drank whiskey like water. They were in Chile getting filmed for another movie. Palmer welcomed them to our crew by calling them pussies and telling them to lose the sideburns.

We were drinking and having a good old time when Ritchie said, "Hey, did you know that you can buy Valium over the counter down here?" An hour later, we were all loitering outside of a pharmacy like it was an ice cream parlor. Both of the Alaskans came out shaking bottles full of valium like they were tambourines.

"We're saving these for the flight home," they said.

At the airport departure lounge the next morning, they doled out Valium to any takers.

"What does Valium do to you?" I asked.

"Oh, it'll help you sleep on the flight," Ritchie said. I figured, *What the hell,* and downed one.

An hour later, nobody was feeling tired, so we all took another pill. When our flight was finally called, I stood up and it hit me like a truck. The only prescription drugs I'd ever taken were antibiotics. I had to hold on to people I didn't even know in order to stay upright.

At one point, I realized I was leaning on Mark Gallup, a photographer who'd taken pictures of me at Wolf Creek in Colorado. It was bizarre. *What's he doing in Chile?* was the most coherent thought I remember having before things got increasingly hazy. Gallup smiled and patted me on the back in slow motion.

"Todddddd," he said with a big grin, "weeeeee got thaaaaaaaa coverrrrrr of *TransWorrrrrrrrld!*"

Ooooh, wow mannnnn, I thought, and followed him onto the plane. I didn't even remember seeing Gallup until the *TransWorld* issue came out the following December.

I found my seat in the last row and thanked god for having made it that far. I looked across the aisle, and there were Ritchie and Jay in their Blues Brothers dark sunglasses, tandem flannels, and matching grins behind unshaven faces. They stared at me for a second and then said, "Ah shit. Let's smoke!" Smoking was still 100 percent encouraged on foreign flights, and this wasn't a good thing for me as I can't stand cigarette smoke. My head started getting really, really heavy on my neck, so I just leaned over against the window and wham! Good night. They could have performed surgery on me and I wouldn't have felt a thing. The bits that faded in and out go like this:

Flash: I sit up suddenly and see the flight attendant next to me, obviously agitated and looking down at her feet because Palmer has used a blanket and pillow to make a little nest for himself in the aisle, and he won't budge. She starts kicking him in the head. Apparently it isn't okay to sleep on the floor.

Flash: I wake up briefly to see Ritchie in a heated argument with the same flight attendant. He is standing in the plane's galley, his pants pockets full of the little whiskey bottles he's swiped from the beverage cart. While he yells at the attendant, he passes the bottles back to Jay, who tucks them into the seat pouch.

Flash: We get into LAX at like nine at night, and my flight to Denver isn't until the next day. I have the vaguest recollection of someone who apparently knows me picking me up in front of the airport. I later learned it was Morrow's Southern California rep, who must have thought I was some slobbering drug addict.

Flash: We're sitting in some L.A. restaurant, and I look over to the next table and James Belushi's sitting there.

Flash: I wake up the next morning, and I'm in Manhattan Beach, in the condo of some guy who shapes surfboards.

When I finally got back home to Boulder around noon, I was still feeling pretty weird. I needed to do something familiar to get my head screwed on straight, so I asked Geb to go skating with me. A good vert session, I reasoned, would sweat the drugs out of my system.

I climbed up on top of the vert ramp at the Boulder skate park and dropped in. That's all I remember. Geb later told me that I made the drop no problem, but then it looked like I fell asleep in the flat bottom. I didn't even absorb the transition, just slammed full speed into the opposite wall. Not a hipper, but a head-on collision with steel. "You just slid down the wall like Jell-O," Geb told me after he'd gotten me home. The moral of this story, boys and girls, is that who-knows-how-many milligrams of self-prescribed Valium is not a good thing, even if it is—technically—legal in South America.

I flew to San Diego a couple weeks later for the annual Action Sports Retailer tradeshow, which was where most of the snowboarding movie premieres took place. I saw Ritchie in his standard *Northern Exposure* Hollywood style and a grizzly Alaskan beard to boot. I started to say, "Were you . . ." and he stole the end of my sentence, " . . . messed up for like five days? What was that shit?" I was like, "Yeah, jeez, that shit was fucked up," and we laughed. "You tried to kill me, you drug addicts!" I joked out loud as people walked past. "No shit," he said. "You were fucked up at the airport in Peru."

"Peru?" I had zero recollection of the two hours we apparently de-planed in Peru on the way back to Los Angeles. Scary.

_My first pro model takes flight on my first trip to New Zealand, 1994.

RIP, SPIN, AND WIN/
GETTING MY GAME ON

The magic of going to tradeshows lasted about one year. In 1993, it was already old, with different-colored snowboards, different Reef Girl models walking around in different-colored G-strings. Boobs everywhere. Yawn.

One day while on the tradeshow circuit, my friend Alexei Garrick introduced me to a girl named Christine Sperber, an aspiring pro who happened to live in Breckenridge. We hit it off and I invited her to the *Project Six* movie premiere party being held that night at a bowling alley in San Diego.

I was too into Christine to pay any attention to the movie. She and I were still talking after it was over, when a couple pros came over and shook my hand.

"Whoa, dude, nice segment. That was sick!" they said.

"What was sick?" I asked.

"Your segment in the movie. Didn't you see it?"

I hadn't expected to get anything out of that footage in Chile, but apparently it turned out okay. The Fall Line guys only had the original edited version with them, and I had to wait until the movie was released on video in November before I could pick it up at a snowboard shop in Colorado. My name was in the credits and everything. I'd seen homemade videos of my riding before, and I'd had sections in another video called *POW* that were too painful to watch. I was super-critical of myself, but in *Project Six*, I didn't look nearly as bad as I'd expected.

Two videos filmed at Vail Pass and A-Basin—*Big Jean Fantasy* and *Anthem*—came out soon after, and my sponsors were stoked on my coverage. Great timing, because I was about to renegotiate my contracts for the coming winter. Every company gave me a raise, and when I added up my salaries, I realized I was going to make about $50,000 dollars the next year—not including contest winnings or bonuses. I was rich!

A few months after the ASR show, I moved from Boulder (I was still couch surfing at Geb's place) into Christine's condo in Breckenridge. So much for being single. She was working at a restaurant called Pasta Jays and rooming with Wendy Powell and Matt Hale—both sponsored snowboarders. It was a snowboarding flophouse, with random riders constantly crashing there.

Christine and Wendy knew Ken Block, the psycho driver I'd met a couple years earlier in Breckenridge who was the founder of Eightball clothing. He and a couple of partners were now working on a new brand called DC Shoes and an underground snowboarding 'zine called *Blunt*. The *Blunt* formula was alcohol, party, party, party, oh, and snowboarding—essentially a snowboarding version of *Big Brother* skateboarding magazine. It was really popular among snowboarders and really unpopular among ski resorts, parents, and snowboarding companies because of its blatant disregard for authority. It also covered the most progressive snowboarders and turned down advertising from big companies like Burton and Morrow.

One night I got pumped full of margaritas and was interviewed for *Blunt*. It was in a way that fit the *Blunt* party formula. It wasn't necessarily inaccurate, but I wasn't too happy with how I was portrayed in the interview. My sponsors, especially Morrow, were kind of pissed off. My image and lifestyle didn't focus on drugs and alcohol, but that's the impression you got after reading the interview.

I complained to Ken Block, and he made it up to me by running another interview, which focused more on snowboarding, less on partying. What I didn't expect was that he'd run interviews of me in the next four issues of *Blunt*. One of the articles was titled "Exclusive Interview with World Champion Todd Richards," which I thought was funny. I couldn't imagine anyone taking it seriously: I'd never even won a major international contest, and I definitely wasn't a world champion.

A few weeks after the article came out, Ken got a phone call from the International Snowboard Federation, complaining that "Todd Richards can't be named a world champion because he isn't technically the world champion." The magazine ran a sarcastic retraction, and I became simply "The *Blunt* Magazine World Champion," a title Ken made up. Morrow calmed down after a couple issues because even though they weren't allowed to advertise in *Blunt* (Ken wanted to keep the magazine small and underground), I was getting more coverage than any other snowboarder.

Breaking the Third-Place Curse

I was ready to lay it all on the line during the 1993/1994 season. A year earlier, Jeff Brushie and Terje Haakonsen had consistently kicked my butt in the few contests I entered, and now I was ready to attack my limitations. Either I was going to win, or I was going to hurt myself trying.

The winning contest trick for both Terje and Brushie had been the fakie 720, which they could do huge and smooth. Nobody, however, did big combination moves like a frontside 720 to a backside 720. I woke up every morning, drove from Brek to Vail (which had the best pipe), and practiced from ten until two or three in the afternoon. If I missed a day, it was like I'd forgotten to take my medication. I was driven by endorphins, and hiking the pipe ate up all the stresses in my life, the biggest source of which was my personal goal to win contests.

In December, I took a break to fly back to Massachusetts and spend Christmas and my birthday with my mom. Two days after the holiday and one day shy of my twenty-fourth birthday, I cut the trip short. I had to get back to Colorado. In my mind, all that I had learned was at risk of being forgotten if I didn't get back in the pipe.

On January 11, 1994, I went to Snow Summit, California, for a PSTA event. This year, the PSTA tour was sponsored by Butterfinger and was being touted as the biggest contest circuit in America. From the minute I hit the snow, I didn't let anything sway me from my goal. If I fell trying a trick in practice, I'd get up and do it again. I told myself I was going to win, and for the first time the pressure I put on myself turned into confidence.

My first run was pretty much autopilot. I knew exactly what I wanted to do on every section of the pipe, and it all came together, including a big fakie 720. It sounds cocky, but I knew I had the contest won before I took my final run against my old pal, Jeff Brushie, who was my biggest competition there. I watched him do his final run and he sketched, just barely, on a couple of tricks that threw off his momentum. He opened himself up for the kill.

In the starting gate I told my dad, "I'm going to win this." The next thing I knew, I was sliding that final rail at the end of my run. My arms went up, and I screamed. I knew I'd won, but for the life of me, I couldn't remember what I'd just done. It was like someone else had been in my body. I had to watch the video to see what I'd done to break Brushie's winning streak over me.

Once a rider wins a big event, there's no turning back. From then on, it's expected of him. For the last few years, top three—or even top five—had been my safety zones. Now that I'd discovered I could let it all out and was capable of winning, I knew I would run with it.

You Don't Make Fifty Grand a Year

One afternoon at Brighton, Utah, I rode up the chairlift with a middle-aged skier. After a few minutes of silence he said, "So, snowboarder, huh?"

"Yep," I replied. "You tried it?"

"God, no," he said. We did the whole chairlift coffee-talk thing, with him asking, "What are you? In school?"

"No."

"What do you do for a living?"

"I snowboard for a living."

"Snowboard for a living?" he scoffed. "What does a snowboarder make? A couple hundred a month?"

I figured my income was between me, my accountant, and the IRS, but I felt obligated to stand up for myself and snowboarders in general, so I told him the truth. "No. This year, I'll make around fifty grand."

He lifted his goggles up, looked me in the eyes, and said, "You kidding me? I make fifty grand a year, and I'm twice your age. You don't make fifty grand a year."

I shrugged and said, "All right, I don't." We got off the lift, and I said, "Have a good one," but he didn't respond. I think he thought I was yanking his chain and was pissed about it.

Not too long after, I decided I needed a more dependable car. To be honest, I wanted something flashier. Something a skier would look at and say, "That's a nice car. I bet that kid makes fifty grand a year." I traded in my GTI for a shiny new Passat because I couldn't afford an Audi.

I competed in another Butterfinger Pro Tour event at Snowmass in Aspen a few weeks later, and the streak continued. I beat Brushie again, and people figured maybe it wasn't a fluke. Throughout the winter, we had a sort of dueling-tricks rivalry going on. If Brushie wasn't there, I was the favorite, and if he was there, results just depended on the day. We'd watch each other in practice and try to formulate our game plan for the contest runs. To me, it was all just practice for the U.S. Open.

During this era, a lot of snowboarders had their own pro models—a marketing ploy borrowed from skateboarding, which gave companies a way to support their pros by giving them royalties off board sales. Most of the great riders had their own models. But there were also a lot of not-so-great riders who got them. Nevertheless, it was a prestigious honor that every pro aimed for. After I beat Brushie, who had a well-deserved pro model, I asked Miki Keller, "Okay, when am I gonna get mine?" Morrow had purposely avoided giving out pro models for business purposes: All their boards could be marketed by all their pros, and it kept the price down. In addition, paying royalties meant more accounting for Morrow, and more money for the rider. She tried to brush me off, but I kept on her.

"No really. Give me a pro model. Don't I deserve it?"

She appeased me by saying, "We'll give you a pro model when you win the U.S. Open."

Fair enough.

This One's for My Dad

I went back east to Vermont in the spring for the 1994 U.S. Open.

There was a big buzz about Daniel Franck from Norway, Ingemar Backman from Sweden, Aleksi Vanninen from Finland, and the Americans: Jeff Brushie, Noah Salasnek, Lael Gregory, and me. For years, I had been content to take top three at the Open, but this year I didn't want to be in the top three unless I was number one. My family was there, and I was confident. My mom was my biggest fan. She went nuts at contests, blowing a whistle when her throat got too hoarse from screaming. The U.S. Open was her favorite because it drew the biggest crowds. She'd bring along my cousins and make it a family affair. The Clarks, the parents of my childhood friend Darryl, often joined her as well.

Stratton was special for another reason. It was the last place my dad had watched me compete. He was with me at every event, the last person I talked to before every winning contest run I'd had. He was the only one who knew about my secret weapon—the back-to-back 720s.

For weeks, I'd been practicing this combination trick at the Vail pipe. I wouldn't go home until I nailed both tricks clean, back-to-back. A few times I got so tired I was ready to leave at three in the afternoon, but I wouldn't leave until I nailed it or it got too dark to see. Some of my friends stopped driving with me because they knew if I got rolling with a trick and couldn't pull it, I'd stick it out forever.

It's funny to look back at both my secrecy and the sheer progressiveness of the back-to-back spin tricks. Today, kids with pacifiers in their mouths are pulling combo spins their second day in the pipe, but in 1994 it was a big deal—and risky, too.

When my qualifying run came up, I knew I could make finals with a single frontside 720, so that's what I did. During practice for the finals, I saw a lot more riders doing fakie 720s, especially the Scanners. Even a few girls were gutting around 540s, maybe a 720 here and there. Nobody, however, was sticking frontside 720s, and nobody thought about a frontside 720 to a backside 720 because the chances of falling were too great. I dropped into my first practice run and nailed back-to-back 720s and, as Andy Coghlan would later tell me, "It caused a scramble."

Coghlan and company had set up serious betting on the slopes of Stratton. The Boarding House had gone out of business, but the riders who used to hang out there remained friends, and they were running a gambling ring for the Open. Going into the contest, Brushie was the hometown favorite to win. Bets had to be made before the qualifying runs began. Then followed another round of bets on the finalists that had to be placed before the finals began.

With my trick unveiled, the odds shifted to me. More important, getting that first public one out of the way without falling was a huge weight off my chest. I might have lost my momentum if it hadn't come together.

At the moment of truth, I stood in the starting gate, asked my dad to help me out, and heard my mom, who was near the top of the pipe, screaming her brains out and blowing her whistle. Nobody came close to beating me.

It's impossible to convey the feeling I had, but suffice it to say, it was one of the most emotional moments of my life. The mainstream media were taking more interest in snowboarding, and as I stood there on the podium with all these cameras around me, it didn't seem real. I kept wanting to look behind me to see who the cameras were pointing at. My mom had a perma-grin on her face and I was high-fiving and hugging other competitors as it got darker and darker. When the last interview was finally over, I came back to earth. I knew I had it in me to win, but I'd battled self-doubt my whole life. When I did win and people recognized me for it—which was way more important than the prize money or the trophy—the biggest thing I felt was relief that it was over.

My mom, who had stayed proudly off to the side during the media blitz, finally got to give me a hug. As we walked side by side through the snow, she whispered, "Your dad was here with you."

"I know," I said, holding up the trophy. "This is for him."

Now about That Pro Model

Back at my hotel, Miki threw a big party with pizza, drinks, and my extended family— the Morrows, the team, and various friends from the industry. We popped champagne, and Miki said, "Well, I guess we're going to have to talk about that pro model."

The significance of getting my own model didn't hit until I was flying home to Colorado the next day. A lot of pros had models, but I felt like I'd earned mine, and it was a huge accomplishment. At the same time I thought, *Oh, shit,* because with that pro model came a lot of responsibility. I didn't want to be a rider who people thought wasn't deserving. Although getting a pro model was the pinnacle of a snowboarder's success, I didn't feel any sense of relief. On the contrary, I was stressed out. Now I had to both maintain and improve upon those high standards. I'd won the U.S. Open and was named the North American Halfpipe Champion, but there were tons of motivated younger riders who were chomping at the bit to knock me off my pedestal.

In June 1994 I went to Morrow's headquarters in Salem to work on my pro model. I'd been riding a Morrow Revert, a 151-centimeter board with a centered

Winning the 1994 U.S. Open still stands out
as a high point of my career.

stance and stiff flex—all the things I'd hated a few years earlier. Now I loved it and thought, why design a whole new board if I was happy with something already in production? Morrow liked the idea because it helped them keep production costs down. The only thing I had to deal with were the graphics.

I wanted something that represented me and would appeal to younger snowboarders. I'd read Michael Crichton's *Jurassic Park* a couple years earlier, which had rekindled my interest in dinosaurs. The movie was just being released on video, so I figured I could capitalize on the dinosaur craze and stay true to my personality at the same time. I drew my favorite dinosaur, the velociraptor, and gave the illustration to Scott Clum, Morrow's art director. He digitized it, and a few days later the dinosaur was on the bottom of my first pro model.

Year of the Raptor

Snowboarding blew up in the winter of 1994/1995. Those of us who thought there had been too many companies when thirty snowboard brands showed up in magazines' buyers guides couldn't believe it when more than a hundred snowboard companies popped up out of nowhere. Someone once told me that the health of an industry can be measured by the thickness of the magazines surviving off that industry's advertising dollars. The first glossy issue of *International Snowboard Magazine,* which came out in 1986 and had newsprint pages inside, was thirty-three pages long and had twelve advertisers. The first *TransWorld SNOWboarding* issue of the 1994/1995 season had 360 pages and more than 250 advertisers.

Coincidentally, I received some sound negotiating advice from an attorney as I was heading into the season, and signed new contracts with my sponsors. If my board sold well and I continued to win contests, I could top six figures, which might as well have been a million dollars. I was still renting a room with Christine, most of my life was spent on the road and expensed by my sponsors, and I'd paid cash for my car. My mom told me I needed to invest my money in something like a house or at least some mutual funds. I brushed her off and kept depositing money into my checking account, which made 1 percent interest.

Hey, Mom, I'm a Janitor Now!

There was a lot of money floating around the snowboarding industry. Why not start a new snowboarding magazine? How hard could it be? We just needed a name and

Grabbing tail at Snow Summit, 1994, where
I finally broke Brushie's winning streak.

some writers and photographers. *Blunt* had already proven that you didn't have to know how to spell or write complete sentences to have a popular magazine.

Christine and I formed a corporation and called it Three-Legged Dog Publishing. We named the magazine *Drift*, worked out of our home, and made a pact to never work on powder days. She was the publisher and a couple writer/photographer/designers (Michael Burnett and Tyler Adair) offered their talents. We were on a mission to attract as many new people to the sport as possible, so we included an inviting warning on the first page of the premiere issue: "The activities shown in this magazine are some of the most dangerous things you could ever imagine doing. The individuals shown doing them are some of the most experienced and well-trained athletes on the planet. You should never attempt anything you see in this magazine and, in fact, why not consider collecting stamps instead? Stamp collecting can be a fun and exciting hobby the whole family can enjoy."

We were amazed when more than a dozen advertisers took us seriously. They almost covered the printing and production costs, and the ad revenue nearly let us pay some of the people part of what we had sort of promised them. Real advertisers empowered our talented slacker friends to use fancy titles like publisher, editor, art director, writer, advertising sales representative, and janitor (my personal title) on future résumés.

What I learned: Magazine publishing is loads of fun for about one issue, and then it becomes hard work. *Drift* magazine existed for three issues before dying a quiet death with absolutely no profits, but only minimal damage to my checking account. Nobody seemed to notice it was gone, and besides, it was kind of a hobby, not a serious business venture.

Five years later, somebody came up to me and asked, "Hey, whatever happened to your magazine?" It made my day knowing that *Drift* magazine had such an impact on the world of snowboarding.

Now that snowboarding was an ancient sport, a lot of veteran riders were beat up, burnt out, and looking for new careers. Some of the more successful and/or older riders had started their own companies, while others had moved on to work in the industry as sales representatives, marketing guys, PR girls, photographers, cinematographers, and any other job that could keep them involved with the lifestyle.

Team managers became a sort of purgatory for pro snowboarders transitioning out of their careers as athletes. Team managers didn't get paid enough money for the difficult jobs they did, continually playing good cop/bad cop between pro snowboarders and the business people who set budgets.

Matt Schlingman was a Morrow pro from Summit County who came on board as team manager when Miki decided handling the marketing and the team was too much for one person. It was weird because Miki had been the only team manager I'd ever had. Schlingman knew all the shit we'd pull on the road because he'd been there himself, and I resented him for it. At times I thought that he still wished he was a pro himself. We were cordial with each other, but I never got used to the way Schlingman referred to himself in the third person. "Oh, looks like the Schling is going to be running late," he'd say, or, "Schlingzie's going riding with the team today." He could have filled a dictionary with Schling-isms.

Eventually, Schlinger moved up the ladder, and the manager slot was up for grabs. My old pal Chris Owen (the chef from High Cascade) knew the entire team, plus his photography was getting published in magazines. He was even known around Morrow as "Ovens," because he'd bake cookies for the marketing department whenever they sent him free stuff. He seemed like a good choice, and the team got behind me in recommending him for the job. He took over Schlinger's position two seasons later.

Oh Yeah, I'm Big in Japan

Owning a Passat hadn't cooled my infatuation with German cars; I started dreaming about Audis. At the end of 1994, I went home for the holidays and jokingly asked my mom for one as a Christmas present—or better yet, a twenty-fifth birthday present. She told me to use my money to buy a house instead.

I had about fifty grand burning a hole in my checking account and ignored my mom's advise. Morrow was sending me to Japan for the Nippon Open, so I bought all the car magazines I could find to read on the flight.

In Tokyo, I met Morrow's distributor who had with him a Japanese kid I'd seen around Breckenridge. The kid's name was Nobu, and he was dressed in pure gangsta attire. You could barely see his eyes from underneath the red bandanna on his forehead. He looked like a mini–Tarquin Robbins, an American pro who epitomized ghetto-on-snow fashion.

"Hey, Nobu, what's up?" I said.

"Ahhh mannnn," he rolled out. "I'm just heeere to help out."

Soon enough, I found out that Nobu and this other Japanese rider who spoke zero English were going to be my escorts. The Nippon Open had become a big annual contest in Japan, and I was stoked to be hanging out with locals until I realized that everything Nobu said was preceded by the word "so," which he drew out to "sooooooooooo" and finished with some equally drawn-out adjective.

They took me to Electric Town where I bought a mini-disc player and Nobu said, "Sooooooooo raaaaaaaaaad." Then I picked up a Godzilla with blinking red eyes and he said, "Soooooooo coooooooool." I bought something else, and he said, "That's sooooooooo sooooooooomething." Literally.

At the contest, I discovered that the entire Japanese snowboarding community had adopted the gangsta look. There were so many chains hanging down to peoples' knees, it was hazardous to hike the halfpipe because you could get whipped in the forehead when somebody threw down a spin.

I was supposed to compete in a big contest—The North American Championships—coming up the following Saturday. I wanted to do well, so I wasn't into destroying the hotel like most of the other visiting pros. Vending machine beer didn't appeal to me this trip, and I was soooooooo over the Japanese version of ghetto speak that at night, I avoided everybody and chilled in the hotel room. I got back to Colorado on a Thursday and went to the Audi dealer in Boulder the next day. The test drive made my Passat an unbearable P.O.S.

It had been a banner year for me with contests, and I stood to take home another ten thousand dollars if I won the NAC contest in Vail. So I went ahead and tapped my checking account, dropping it on my first Audi, a 90S Sport Quatro in red—the highest performance snow car on the planet as far as I was concerned. Booyah.

I left the dealership thinking, *Oh my god, what did I just do?* The car cost like thirty-five grand, way more money than I'd ever committed to anything in my life—but I had to do it. All I could think about that night was, *I have to win the contest so I can pay for the tax, license, and registration when I pick it up on Monday.*

Early Saturday morning, Mike Cruckshank, my Gotcha team captain, called me just as I was leaving to check out the Vail pipe for the contest.

"Todd," he said, "I need you to go to Japan on Monday."

"This Monday, as in two days from now?" I asked.

He confirmed, and when I asked for how long, he said, "About four hours, just to show face at a tradeshow." Damn, it would be another two days before I could pick up my Audi.

Later that day in the Vail pipe, I felt confident rolling up and practicing a few runs, and I got pretty cocky. I actually told some of my friends that I had to win to pay for the car I'd just bought, flaunting it like an idiot and testing myself under the pressure. Luckily, I was on my game, and I did win. After the contest ended on Sunday, Oakley threw a huge party at Garton's Bar in Vail, with Perry Ferrel from Porno For Pyros as the main act. Pros Billy Anderson and Janna Meyen stopped by my place in Brek to change for the festivities. Billy was around eighteen and looked about twelve, but he was determined to get into the bar one way or another. He left the house in a blue prom dress.

Somehow it worked. Billy slid past the bouncer and wormed his way into the thick of the crowd without being detected. The bar was packed to capacity, and the floor was rolling like an earthquake. Standing at the bar in his prom dress drinking a beer someone had bought him, Billy couldn't keep his eyes off six-foot-three pro volleyball babe Gabrielle Reece, who was covering the event for MTV and wearing some sexy thang. When she came within range, Billy casually reached out and grabbed her ass. Not just a subtle little, "Oops, I touched your butt," but a full-on honker. She spun around and nobody was there. Then she glanced down and saw Billy in his little blue number. He pointed to some random guy and said, "He said he'd buy me a beer if I grabbed your ass." Gabrielle stared at him for a minute. She could have kicked his ass, but she only said, "Oh, all right," winked at him, and walked away.

Since Oakley had brought along Perry Ferrel, I got to go up and meet him—the backstage treatment. As I was standing next to him, somebody said something funny and both Perry Ferrel and I started laughing. Trevor Graves, the ever-present paparazzi, took a picture that ended up in *Snowboarder*. In the photo, I look like I'm totally broing down with the rock star. In reality, I don't think I said anything more than, "Hi, I'm Todd," to which Perry responded with, "What?" So, me and Perry, we're pretty tight.

Kickin' it with Perry Farrell in Vail, 1995.

At five the next morning, I flew out of Denver's Stapleton International Airport on its last day before closing forever. I got into Tokyo, drove straight to the tradeshow, and found Gotcha's distributor booth, which was also selling Ocean Pacific snowboard gear. Damian Sanders, who had intimidated me so badly, at the 1990 Vision Pro in the Snow at Tahoe, was showing face for Ocean Pacific. He had injured his knee pretty badly, but was holding on to his image as a pro. He had always been a great self-marketer. At this tradeshow, his canine teeth had been filed into vampire fangs. He was dressed entirely in black leather and was hanging out with a hot dominatrix-looking stripper who made me nervous.

I wandered around the booth for an hour, signed some posters, shook some hands, bowed to a lot of Japanese business people, then went and had dinner with my distributor and Damian, who ended up being a pretty normal, down-to-earth guy, despite his teeth and dominatrix sidekick. I jumped on another plane and flew home in time to land at Denver International Airport on its grand opening day, Tuesday, February 28, 1995. While other travelers dealt with the baggage system from hell, I grabbed my carry-on, caught a shuttle to the Audi dealer in Boulder, and drove back to Breckenridge in my new whip.

Everything Is Extreme

During the summer of 1995, ESPN put on the first Extreme Games, the brainchild of ESPN director of programming Ron Semiao, who had seen the writing on the wall back in 1993. He recognized skateboarders, snowboarders, BMX freestylers, and the like as more than a bunch of kids having a good time; they were athletes with real abilities. But there was no Monday Night Snowboarding or Skateboarding Super Bowl, and none of these so-called alternative sports were part of the most respected athletic competition in the world: the Olympics.

I don't know who first coined the phrase "extreme sports," but for years skiers and climbers had used the word "extreme" when referring to dangerous terrain. It was considered "extreme" if it was so exposed (to cliffs, crevasses, etc.) that if you fell, you died. Someone at the Associated Press must have put the word out on the wire, because all of a sudden everything was extreme: skateboarding, surfing, skydiving, snowboarding, bungee jumping.

More than 100,000 spectators showed up for the first Summer Extreme Games in Rhode Island. The programming reached 720,000 households and was nominated for more Sports Emmy awards than any other ESPN broadcast. Research showed that the Extreme Games were the most watched sporting event of the year by U.S. males between the ages of twelve and thirty-four.

I had another banner year of halfpipe contest results in the winter of 1995/1996, and because of my winning season, ESPN thought I might be a good representative for freestyle snowboarding. Ron Semiao invited me to Newport, Rhode Island, for the second annual Summer Extreme Games to be a mouthpiece at a press conference in which ESPN introduced the idea of the Winter Extreme Games. I answered questions from the press about snowboarding, and in a private meeting told ESPN how I thought the snowboarding events should go down.

By 1996, Ron and ESPN had dropped the word "extreme" after getting a lot of shit for it, but people still heckled them. When Ron was invited to be a speaker at an annual snowboarding industry conference put on by *TransWorld SNOWboarding*, someone tried to put him on the spot by asking what the "X" stood for. Ron replied, "It stands for the unknown."

Regardless of where that X really came from, it turned out that Ron's description was pretty accurate. ESPN had proven itself by accepting and nurturing the most bizarre athletes and the most unusual sports. The producers had no idea what might come up in the future.

The first Winter X Games were scheduled for January and February of 1997 at Snow Summit in Southern California. They were to feature a strange collection of events, including snowboarding, ice climbing, super-modified shovel racing, and snow-mountain-bike racing. With the games on the not too distant horizon, everyone in snowboarding wondered if ESPN would make a mockery of our sport.

That same season, the snowboarding industry saw an even more insane increase in companies. *TransWorld SNOWboarding* topped 500 pages, so the industry was booming—or at least the magazines boomed while the companies battled it out to sell product to the growing number of snowboarding participants. My sponsors kept giving me raises. Airwalk snowboard boots (who had sponsored me for a couple of years) started making outerwear, and Gotcha and I shook hands and went our separate ways. My pro model was doing okay. We hadn't marketed it a whole lot, and just by word of mouth, about 1,000 boards had sold. My royalty deal was ten dollars per board—a nice bonus. Contests were attracting bigger and bigger corporate sponsors and that meant bigger prize money purses. All of a sudden, snowboarding for a living seemed like something I could bank on as long as I stayed healthy.

Rage Phase

It would be criminal if I didn't convey the shocking truth about snowboarders' use of alcohol as a performance-enhancing drug off the mountain.

I don't go anywhere without my big-ass headphones.

No snowboarding movie documents this better than *Whiskey,* a 1996 Boozey the Clown production that made a valiant effort to scare off the mainstream consumers and parents ESPN was trying to attract. In it, Canadian super-pros Sean Kearns and Sean Johnson, American pro Jimmy Halopoff, and a bunch of other freedom fighters spend a winter getting as numb as possible (on alcohol), then bust empty beer bottles over their own heads. It was an instant hit among the PG-13 audiences. I can't remember any of the snowboarding, though I hear it is pretty good, too. There were three sequels, but sadly, I wasn't involved with any of them.

Other less-publicized acts of genius are worthy of mention, including the following punishment for anybody stupid enough to pass out drunk in a room full of creative, artistic snowboarders.

There were always prospective victims at the U.S. Open. The secret was to pick the weakest animal in the herd and then patiently wait for him to drink himself to oblivion. After he passed out, someone would generally say a prayer to the effect of, "God help him," then we would move in like hyenas, with magic markers, honey, duct tape, and anything else that was handy.

It would begin innocently enough, with a large "idiot" written on the forehead. A moustache would be added, then a big red penis on the cheek with the business end aimed right at the ol' kisser. Empty beer cans and beer bottles would be shoved ceremoniously down the victim's pants, honey massaged into his hair, and by the time we'd finished, his entire face, eyebrows, neck, and other exposed skin would be covered in "non-toxic" ink.

The coup de grace was duct-taping beer bottles onto both hands. Not like he's holding the bottles, but with the bottles pointing in the same direction as his outstretched fingers. When he'd go to scratch himself, hopefully on the head or the balls, it would be with a thunk. It's nearly impossible to free yourself from this predicament without assistance. I'm continually fascinated by the subtle genius of duct-taping bottles to a person's hands. Bravo to whoever thought of it first.

And if a passed-out victim wasn't available, snowboarders often improvised with other props, the most memorable example of which I witnessed outside Tommy

Chris Owen was impressed with Swiss culture, St. Moritz, 1997.

Africa's nightclub in Whistler. I had just won the 1996 Westbeach Classic and was making a call on my cell phone when I witnessed a jailbreak.

Someone I couldn't identify without reasonable doubt—but who resembled a major player in the *Whiskey* movies—was escorted out of the notorious Whistler club in shiny silver handcuffs. The police officer placed him in the backseat of his car, then rushed back inside with a second set of handcuffs at the ready. A moment later, a locally famous Whistler party regular staggered out the front door, saw the pro snowboarder in the backseat of the cop car with his mug smashed up against the window doing the blowfish thing. The party guy walked up to the cop car, opened the back door, and said, "Hey man, what are you doing in there?"

The said snowboarder looked both ways and bolted into the darkness, leaving party guy standing there looking confused. I thought it best to vacate the premises as quickly as possible.

I imagine the snowboarder was able to saw through the chain binding his wrists, but he must have had a heck of a time getting the actual cuffs off. If he had to ride in a contest the next day, I guess he wore them like bracelets under his gloves and jacket. I'm sure he got them off eventually, but his souvenirs no doubt made for interesting conversation pieces until he did.

Sponsor Me, I Rip

Outside of my mom, Palmer "Balls" Brown and Mark Gebhardt were probably my second favorite fans because they kept me grounded, especially as I got better and better. They'd seen me transform from an insecure dork who couldn't win a contest and was trying to fit in and impress everyone, to a confident dork who won lots of contests but was still trying to fit in and impress everyone.

Balls and Geb had a "milk it while its lactating" mind-set and advised me accordingly. My mom had stepped down from her management duties and only interjected casual advice on a weekly basis, usually, "You really should buy a house." Other than that, I was flying solo concerning business matters.

In March 1996, I went to the annual Ski Industries America tradeshow in Las Vegas with Balls. For years the ski industry had ruled the Strip, but what with the walking canes, wheelchairs, and generally elderly skiing crowd, the Las Vegas convention center had been on a spiraling nose dive toward Mount Boredom. The increase in snowboarding companies breathed new life into the ski industry, although at the SIA show, snowboarding manufacturers were kept separate in an area known as the Ghetto. The Ghetto was the place to party, party, party, and "discreetly" do business, acting as if we didn't care about money. Keg get-togethers, strippers, and stand-up comedians were invited to different company booths at the end of each day, and things sometimes got out of hand. One company got busted when a cloud of smoke betrayed their impromptu meeting one morning. An SIA representative investigated to find a bong being passed around a group of sales reps. The company later called the stunt an exercise in corporate team building. To some, they were idiots, to others, heroes.

The Ghetto had so many companies in it people began to speculate that any idiot could get sponsored as a pro snowboarder. Balls thought he'd conduct an experiment. You have to understand that Balls absolutely sucked at snowboarding. He could get off the chairlift no problem, but his style ended there. At SIA, Balls walked over to the booth of a new snowboard company, introduced himself, and told them that he ripped. He threw out my name as a reference and left the tradeshow with new board and binding sponsors.

Since Balls was now pro, he figured he better go to Mount Hood over the summer because that's where pro snowboarders go. His sponsors needed photos of him in the pipe, so I taught him how to do a mute stiffy, an outdated trick that we announced he was "bringing back." Balls is a pretty tall guy, and his snowboarding pants always look like high-waters. In mid–mute stiffy grab, they hiked all the way up to the tops of his boots. Regardless, he actually got an advertisement placed in a magazine.

Balls' reign as a pro snowboarder only lasted a few months. Eventually, one of his sponsors saw him ride in person and realized they'd been had. Balls was asked to hand back his gear and he retired, but we agreed that it was a good run while it lasted.

Frontside air at the Vans Sierra at Tahoe competition in 1997.

RAMEN NOT REQUIRED/
THE SALAD DAYS OF SNOWBOARDING

By the time the 1996 season rolled around, pros were buying sports cars and houses and living larger than they ever had before. My second pro model, which also played on the dinosaur theme, was being sold in a few different sizes. My idea for the graphics was that a dinosaur claw had ripped the graphics off my old board, leaving most of the base white. I thought it was cool. Nobody else seemed to get it, but that didn't seem to matter because sales had skyrocketed to almost 20,000 boards. Amazing, considering the number of models available and the fact that Morrow wasn't a huge company. Terje's model, by the way, was rumored to be selling close to 100,000 boards.

I was still sharing a rental condo with Christine and putting every paycheck into my low-interest checking account. I knew my mom was going to strangle me if I didn't do something about the six figures rotting away. The right house jumped out at me after a few days of searching—wood floors, big windows, a spa on the deck, a sauna, and a couple extra bedrooms for visiting friends and family. My mom was ecstatic that I had finally made a wise investment. I took possession of my first home on December 28, 1996. Happy birthday to me.

Within a month, I also picked up a roommate, Buff, to keep watch on the house while I was traveling and to help with the mortgage. A few days later, I hosted my first house guests: Alexei Garrick and Joel Muzzey, who had come out to interview me for *Eastern Edge,* a well-known East Coast snowboarding 'zine. Within a week, I was back on the road and my houseguests stayed to ride Brek.

I was in Japan when Alexei left the sauna on overnight. It melted the snow around that side of the house, which flowed under the house, froze, and burst the water pipes. I got an urgent call from Buff, saying, "Dude, there's something seriously wrong. There's no water pressure in the house." I was lacing up my boots to go and compete in a snowboard contest, and at the same time had to locate a plumber in Breckenridge. Between practice runs in the halfpipe, I called the plumber on my cell phone, and during the finals I okayed his estimate. Welcome to adulthood.

"X" Stands for the Unknown

At the end of January 1997, I arrived at Snow Summit in Big Bear, California, for the debut Winter X Games, expecting the same turnout as the U.S. Open, which usually drew a few thousand people. Thirty-eight thousand spectators were there to watch the various events. The games were being televised to 198 countries in twenty-one different languages. I couldn't believe snowboarding was getting this sort of reception. It was a little overwhelming when I thought about all the eyes that would be on me. Crazier, still, was the growth explosion of the sport. Seven years before, hardly anybody even knew what snowboarding was.

The X Games executives had taken the riders' advice and had a best of two runs format that really let us hang it out there. The first round, I got the highest score with a big McTwist, an inverted 720, and some "filler" jumps in between. It was enough to edge out Daniel Franck, Rob Kingwell, Ross Powers, and Frank Wells. In the second round, Daniel Franck had a smoking run with some killer back-to-back spins and edged me out of first. I got to go last, so I repeated my first run with another McTwist and inverted 720, but I knew that wasn't enough to beat Daniel, so at the last second I decided to try a 900. The wall wasn't right for the trick, but somehow I landed it. It was complete luck. That trick edged out Daniel, and I took home the gold medal for the halfpipe event. Suddenly, the world's eye was focused on alternative sports.

Plenty of naysayers accused ESPN of cashing in on what we'd built up purely on the love of the sport (although many of those same naysayers were busy flaunting their medals and happily cashing their paychecks). I was wary at first, too, but I tried to look at the big picture. The more I thought about it the more it seemed to be a win-win situation for everybody involved. There was no reason to be bummed about the way we were portrayed. We were treated like legitimate athletes, which was kind of weird, but we were also fired up about being in the spotlight with microphones shoved in our faces.

The X Games marked the end of one era but simultaneously gave birth to a whole new world of possibilities. It was sort of sad to say good-bye to being a bunch of misunderstood outcasts. A lot of joy was derived from that punk-rock spirit, and once the masses join your ranks, it's over. That image had already begun to change, but the X Games put the icing on the mainstream cake.

I was by no means a snowboarding pioneer, but I was around near its beginning, and that could never be taken away. I was mostly a spectator for the Coghlan/Kidwell/Kelly/Palmer reign, the first modern era of snowboarding. I was a part of the second wave of freestylers, including Jeff Brushie, Jason Ford, Noah Brandon, Chris Roach, and Terje Haakonsen, who saw the sport through to the X Games era. We were determined to continue the progression of ourselves and the sport.

I no longer had any older riders to look up to, since most of them weren't riding pipe anymore. So I started keeping my eye on the younger kids. One who stood out was Billy Anderson's little brother, Jeff. Billy was part of the Morrow team and Jeff was sponsored by Burton, which was renowned for nurturing younger riders like Shaun White. Jeff was around twelve years old when I first saw him ride, and he reminded me of my old mentor Chris Roach, only in miniature. His style was smooth and the air he was catching was beyond anything you could imagine for his stature. He looked like he was supposed to be snowboarding and that fired me up more than anything else.

The King and I: Terje and me back in 1992.

The Raptor and the Cat

Kids like Jeff Anderson were making waves in the sport, but Terje was still considered the halfpipe god of the universe, and I still hadn't beaten him. I guess there was a sort of masked rivalry between Terje and me, but I felt as much reverence for him as I did rivalry between us. I wanted to beat him, but I respected him more than any other pipe rider.

With all this in mind, I headed back into the pro tour with a vengeance. Competition is all about momentum. Once I got it rolling, I did everything possible to keep it going. I thought the socks I wore at the X Games had had something to do with winning, so I wore them every single day for the rest of the season without washing them. I also told myself at every event, just as I'd done at the X Games, "I'm going to win this contest."

The ISF Vans World Championships were held at Heavenly in Tahoe, on February 20, 1997. I rolled out of bed the morning of the halfpipe event determined to beat Terje. I put on my lucky socks, geared up, made sure my stickers looked all right on my board, and headed to the pipe. By the end of the day, Terje had me beat by a tenth of a point. I'd forgotten to tell myself, "I'm going to win this contest," and I was pissed.

Two weeks later, at the fifteenth annual U.S. Open, my socks stunk so badly I had to keep them and my snowboard boots in the hallway outside the hotel room. But on the morning of the halfpipe finals, I held my breath, laced up my boots, and told myself I was

The sweet results of the 1997 U.S. Open.

going to win this contest. I dropped in on my final run, everything went silent, and I knew at the bottom that I'd won. I'd beaten Terje for the first time ever in front of the Open's biggest crowd to date, 10,000 spectators. Besting Terje at Stratton was the ultimate achievement thus far, so forgive me if I admit that I thought I was the shit for about a week.

Welcome to FIS Country

The 1997 Winter X Games had gotten snowboarders into the gold, silver, and bronze medal mentality. When we got word that snowboarding would be an official event at the 1998 Olympics in Nagano, Japan, the competitive blood really got boiling.

While the Fédération Internationale de Ski (FIS) and International Snowboard Federation (ISF) battled it out for the right to be the governing body for Olympic snowboarding, riders kept doing what we always did. We went snowboarding and acted like it didn't matter. But I'd be a liar if I said the thought of being on the first U.S. Olympic Snowboard team didn't fire me up. Wheaties boxes, international prestige, the best half-pipe in the world—and let's not forget the cold hard cash that goes with it all.

Eventually, the FIS won the battle over ISF for the right to be the governing body in Nagano. The '98 Games were still a year away, but we had to compete in a certain number of FIS events in order to gain the necessary amount of points to qualify. Many snowboarders worldwide had been competing in the ISF system, but those points didn't count toward official Olympic teams. It's confusing as hell, but basically, each country's snowboarders had to have a certain amount of FIS points in order to justify the size of the team that would represent that country in the Olympics. Theoretically, if no U.S. riders rode in FIS events, America would have no Olympic Snowboard team. Blackmail? Yes. Terje boycotted the Olympics for this very reason. The fact that the FIS had not supported snowboarding since the beginning didn't help either.

There was another reason for these qualifier events, and that was to introduce us to a brand-new practice called drug testing. The moment I finished my winning run at my first pre-Olympic qualifier in Aspen, I was joined at the hip to a Snowmass ski school instructor/FIS anti-doping-committee thug. It was Big Brother's job to deliver me to the official-Olympic-piss-test room at a Snowmass hotel.

I've always been a nervous competitor and have to trick myself into being confident. I probably pee two or three times before a contest run, and that's after I've forced down a glass of water in the morning because that's all my stomach can take. I also have a problem peeing in public; a wall of urinals horrifies me. Clearly this was going to be a problem.

Ross Powers, Frank Wells, myself, and a few other riders were brought to a room that had stacks of Mountain Dew, bottled water, and Gatorade. An hour later, my stomach was ready to explode, and yet I still had no urge to piss. I was like the last kid trying to finish a test while the teacher is sitting there tapping her pencil. Finally, I felt the urge and walked into the "little room," which contained a toilet and a guy with a rubber glove holding a tiny specimen cup. He handed me the cup, then bent over and stared at my wiener. It was a pretty small cup, and therefore required Olympic-caliber aim with my super-soaker. Guaranteed that guy never stood that close to the hose again.

After the pee test, we got a list of things we couldn't ingest, like cough syrup and poppy seed bagels. For the most part, everyone vying for a spot on the Olympic team was squeaky clean. Some snowboarders smoke weed, but nobody thought of hippie hay as a performance-enhancing drug. We were just a bunch of guys who rode pipe obsessively, not he-men competitors hyped up on amphetamines or steroids. Of course, the IOC didn't see it that way. Welcome to the world of international Olympic competition. Did I sign up for this?

I ended the season in Whistler at the West Beach Classic. Despite their skeletal appearance, my lucky socks had held out, and I won the event. It was gratifying to see all the endless hours in and hiking the pipe really paying off. To work that hard and then pull it off consistently in contests was an emotional release. It was like I'd been holding my breath for the past three months and now I could finally exhale.

One slushy day in April at Loveland Pass, Colorado, I found a big jump that was perfect for something I'd been visualizing but hadn't had the balls to attempt. Now, with the season over, I wasn't too worried about wrecking myself, so I threw down a frontside 540 corkscrew to fakie, and miraculously didn't kill myself. The landing was almost perfect—barely on my tail—and it was smooth as butter riding away.

That trick was my version of the rodeo flips a lot of guys were doing. I couldn't bring myself to do rodeo flips because I was too scared to throw it over my shoulder, so I learned it the other way, flipping inward. People were patting me on the back like I'd invented something gnarly, when really I'd just been too scared to do a rodeo. Fall Line Films was completing their latest release, *Ticket to Ride,* and needed footage for my part. I pulled my new trick clean for the camera and was so stoked, I turned around and nailed a frontside 720 corkscrew a few minutes later. To have a new trick documented on film was the capper of my season.

On the downside of that winter, a breakup was brewing, and breakups always suck. Christine and I had been experiencing some drastic ups and downs with our relationship. Her friends didn't like me, and my Vegas friends in Boulder were doing the same thing they'd done with Carrie, "Lose the baggage. Drop the anchor." Friends, I've found, are a good sounding board when it comes to relationships, although you always know what's right inside. In the end, Christine and I agreed that our personalities probably weren't matched for the long haul, and we parted ways in the spring. She headed back to Hood as the manager for High Cascade Snowboard camp and, to give us some space, I decided that would be my first summer in five years that I didn't live full-time on a glacier.

I knew that meant missing an Olympic Training Camp that was scheduled to take place that summer at Hood, but I'd never used a coach in my life. I had been riding nearly three hundred days a year for seven years in a row. I was super-confident in my bag of tricks, so I figured I'd let everybody else spend the summer practicing, and if I heard about any tricks I needed to be worried about, I'd have time before the Olympics to better them. I was cocky about it, which was another reason I needed a break. It was time for me to find my stoke again, to be humbled.

It was time to skate.

Refueling in Boulder

The Colorado Rockies in the summer are beautiful, no matter where you are, but I couldn't get into the Breckenridge summer scene. It seemed like there were nothing but couples all over the place—mountain biking together, holding hands on the street—and it wasn't working for me as a newly single guy because there weren't enough fish in the dating pool. I needed a change of scenery. Geb sensed I was being a weepy, sensitive type and got my ass back to Boulder, where a large number of per-spective bachelorettes walked around without boyfriends.

I rented my Brek house out for the summer and moved into a place in Boulder that Balls had bought and was sharing with Geb and a guy named Chris McNally. Chris was High Fashion Man; he wore tight shirts and did 500 sit-ups a day. Geb had gotten into pumping iron so he was Mr. Steak Neck. Being the impressionable guy I was, I started pumping iron too, and before you knew it I had bought a few tight shirts and was attempting to be Suave Guy at the bars. Every night we went to this bar called the Rio—famous for its five-shot margaritas. There was a limit of three mar-garitas per customer; any more and you'd be legally blind. I loved the drinks because they gave me liquid courage, which in turn helped me slur out pick-up lines.

All my friends worked real jobs and/or went to school, so I had to find a way to fill the time between hitting the snooze button and ordering the first round of drinks at the Rio. On an average day, I woke up around ten, rode my bike to Wild Oats Market for a break-fast burrito, went home, played video games till my burrito settled, then pumped iron. From three until six, I'd kick it at the skate park. Then I'd shower, gel up my hair, throw on a shirt that would fit a fifth grader, and head to the Rio to meet Geb and the boys.

As the summer went by, we decided that Balls's house needed a little help if we were going to be able to impress the ladies we brought home. Since I had become Todd Richards, Pro Snowboarder with a Huge Disposable Income, it was decided that I would be the one to purchase a pool table and a new couch. I also bought a bedroom set for me, just in case. Now we had the stylin' bachelor pad, and just in time because I'd met this insane girl I'll call Rebounda at the Rio. And, yes, she was literally insane. I was on the rebound and looking for someone to cling to, so I chased her around like a puppy with a leg-humping fetish. Sometimes, Rebounda would turn off the switch and become the ice queen, and I couldn't understand what I'd done wrong. The next day, she'd turn it back on. I was really confused.

One day Geb introduced me to a beautiful friend of his from school. Her name was Lindsy Lozano. She was studying art and photography and had a pro skateboarder soon-to-be-ex boyfriend whom I recognized from the skate mags.

Lindsy became my go-to friend when I was bummed about Rebounda and needed to talk to someone. Her friends knew my friends, and we all started hanging out and partying at the Rio more and more. Something weird was going on between Lindsy and me. We had this top-secret but unrequited romance. Nothing ever happened between us, but I really dug her even though she had a boyfriend and I had Rebounda. For a while I thought her boyfriend wanted to kick my ass. I think he thought Lindsy and I had taken things to the next level, which we hadn't. It was the perfect premise for a WB action sports soap opera for a while, but eventually, he got over it.

That summer I had gotten a frat boy haircut and cleaned up my image with the theory that I'd get more chicks that way. Lindsy was an avid snowboarder and knew who I was before we met. In fact, I thought I was one of her heroes until one night, she said, "I didn't realize you were such a jock. I thought you'd be different." It was like a slap in the face. I stopped working out immediately and filled my time with more skateboarding.

By the end of the summer, Lindsy's relationship was on the rocks and she had moved to Los Angeles. I moved back to Breckenridge and was totally depressed because I couldn't see her anymore. The minute I heard she'd broken up with her boyfriend, I was on a plane to Los Angeles.

Lindsy eventually told me that the first time she saw me she had a crazy déjà vu, like a warm familiarity. I told her she was whacked, but deep down, I liked hearing that. She wasn't afraid to speak her mind, and I dug the fact that she was an intuitive person who thought about things like destiny. I kept it to myself, but in the back of my mind, I was thinking that she was "the one."

I loved hanging out with Lindsy because it was like chilling with one of the guys.

How could I not fall in love? Lindsy in 1997.

It was like I was dating a bro. Wait a minute. Did I say that? Anyway, she snow-boarded, skated, liked the same music, and most important, could sling shit in a respectable manner. (I often gauge a person's intelligence by the speed and creativity of their wit.) All of this while having the looks of a supermodel. Talk about a catch.

_Jumbo hype and jumbo reaction after a run
in the rain at the Olympics, Nagano, 1998.

THE OLYMPIC HYPE MACHINE/
THE LONGEST WINTER

The winter of 1997/1998 began with a frustrating lack of snow, and I really needed to go snowboarding so I could burn off the Lindsy withdrawals I was experiencing. It was the year of the Olympics, and here I was falling in love. Perfect timing.

To add to that stress, I'd been interviewed by a bunch of different magazines over the summer—*Newsweek, Sports Illustrated, GQ, Outside.* Publications that hadn't given a shit about snowboarding before the Olympics now were pulling me out of the hat as "America's Great Halfpipe Hope." Writers were asking me questions like, "No pressure, Todd, but you will win a gold medal in Nagano, right?" Didn't he say, "No pressure?"

In late November, I was invited to Salt Lake City for my first Olympic press junket. I had headshots taken for the Associated Press and taped mini segments for television stations like, "Hi, this is Todd Richards and you're watching the Olympics on CBS." At the press conference, some of the reporters asked about my background as a skateboarder and implied that it must be difficult for me to stay focused as an athlete because of this "free spirited" background. I responded with a question of my own:

"Why do you think skateboarding isn't in the Olympics? It's a hundred times harder than snowboarding, so maybe it has something to do with the politics of the IOC. What do you think? Any ideas?"

I must have scared them because nobody answered.

My sponsors were really excited. They knew what the Olympics could do for marketing, and huge numbers were being thrown around. My contracts were up in December, which was a big "meeting" month for me (I still didn't have an agent or anything). It was also a busy contest month as I geared up for Nagano in February.

But I had to get my contracts settled first, and I knew I was in for a battle with Morrow. Back in 1995, Rob Morrow had stepped down from his role as president of the company and the family vibe of the company had gone with him. Shortly there-after, Morrow became the second snowboard company to go public. It was in Mor-row's best interest to have one of their snowboarders on the winner's podium on Wall Street—I mean, in Nagano. Morrow was a money-making machine that, unbe-knownst to me, was hemorrhaging cash. The company had gone through a couple CEOs, and the one at the helm in December 1997 was a jerk.

For a few months, Mr. Jerk had been dropping hints to me about the company's budget and how I needed to be a team player, obviously trying to soften me up for the negotiating table. I was thinking, *Screw you. You just sold 30,000 boards with my name on them. I've been with this company for nine years. The Olympics are a once-in-a-lifetime opportunity, and if you want me to flash the Morrow logo around the world, you need to pay me!* And that's what I intended to tell him as the big sit-down approached.

But I had an ace up my sleeve. Tim Swart, my friend and the team captain at Air-walk, told me that Airwalk was going to start making snowboards and outerwear. They wanted to sponsor me when my contract with Morrow ran out—a million-dollar deal over three years, with additional bonuses if I medaled in Nagano. As far as I knew, this was the biggest deal any snowboarder with the exception of Terje had ever been offered. With this in mind, I retained the services of an attorney. The Olympic hype machine had just made the jump to light speed.

Morrow's negotiating team flew to Colorado, and we met at B.J.'s restaurant in Boulder. To calm down before the meeting, I threw back two big shots of tequila and then settled into a booth with Rob Morrow (who was still a company figurehead, but had no real power), team manager Chris Owen, and Mr. Jerk the CEO. Rob and Chris looked almost embarrassed as the corporate money guy tried to lowball me. My dilemma was that I really liked the Morrow team and the company. My alternative, Airwalk, wasn't as cool and also wasn't proven as a board manufacturer.

It amazed me how a meeting about one basic issue could drag on for hours. The point was, I wanted a three-year one-million-dollar contract. Period. I was getting pretty pissed off that Morrow wasn't stepping up to the plate, and Rob and Chris were unable to interject anything because it was a money issue. I was just about to say, "Pay me, or I'm riding for Airwalk, period," when Mr. Jerk spoke up.

"You know what, Todd?" he said. "We want you to ride Morrow at the Olympics. And we want to thank you for all these years. We're going to give you what you want."

I went nuts inside. I was shitting my pants, but I tried to play smug, like, *Damn right, you are.* Basically, Mr. Jerk had the ability to pay the amount the whole time, but he wanted me to crumble and take less. When I didn't give in, he had no choice but to agree to the million-dollar contract.

Lindsy, who had been hanging in Boulder to give me emotional support, met up with me after the meeting, and we partied our asses off.

I picked up two more sponsors, Nixon Watches and Special Blend Outerwear, both of which offered me a nice bonus if I won a medal in Nagano. My mom was already asking about making reservations for Japan, and *Time* magazine interviewed me, asking, "Who else will be on the team with you for Nagano?" I tricked myself into downplaying the whole thing like, "The Olympics are no big deal. It'll be fun. Whatever."

The next FIS World Cup event was in Whistler. The day before the event, I asked a journalist what time practice would be the next day. She checked her schedule, and gave me the wrong information by accident. When I showed up to practice, there were a lot more people than I'd expected, a serious crowd, really. If I hadn't known better I would have thought the contest was already in progress.

While on a chairlift to the top of the pipe, I heard crowd noises and began to think that maybe it *was* in progress. I slid down to the top of the pipe and asked one of my bros, "Did they change practice time?"

"Nope," he said. "It was two hours ago."

Just then I heard my name over the loud speaker: "Next up, Todd Richards." *Fuck!* I scrambled to get my competitor's bib on and barely had enough time to watch the guy before me take his run. I hadn't even looked at the halfpipe yet, much less ridden it.

"Little help here, Dad," I said, and dropped in. The run was pretty tame. I stuck with the tricks I had on lockdown—a frontside 900 and an inverted frontside 720 were my money moves that hardly anybody else was doing—and finished it off with a McTwist. I won the contest without a practice run, which told me that I was on my game.

Grand Prix Number One

The Grand Prix Olympic Qualifiers consisted of three contests held in December, January, and early February. It was a tight schedule since the Olympics began only a few days after the final Grand Prix event. Scores for the events would combine two runs, instead of taking the better of two runs. We were used to the latter format, which allowed you to really go for it on one run because you knew you had a second chance if you screwed up. Theoretically, I could get third-place finishes in all three events and still not make the team, even though I'd won most of the major contests in America over the past year. It was the bureaucracy of the Olympics, but I wasn't worried.

This is going to be a piece of cake, I thought.

I rolled up to the first qualifier at Sugarloaf, Maine, thinking I'd go, boom, boom, take first, and then only have to worry about taking a top-three in the next two events in order to make the team. My first run was flawless, but then I got cocky and fell on an inverted 720. I was left scrambling for excuses about the time of day, etc. I didn't want to put the blame on myself, but I was rip-shit pissed beyond belief. Ron Chiodi won and all but secured a spot on the team.

I flew to my mom's new house in Cape Cod for Christmas. Everything was decorated and festive but I was in full self-destruct mode. On Christmas Eve, I replayed the run over and over again in my mind, obsessing about it through the night. I woke up the next day, called Lindsy, who was with her family in San Francisco, and snapped at her when she tried to cheer me up. Same with my mom—I was a whiny, pissed-off drama queen. It was affecting me like no contest ever had before, and I realized I had to pull my head out of my butt quickly, which meant I had to get back to a halfpipe. I apologized to my mom and family and left around one on Christmas day, four days earlier than I'd originally planned. I got on a plane and repeated, "I suck," the entire way back to Denver. In Breckenridge the next day, I rode the pipe alone.

I needed Lindsy. She was going to be in Tahoe with her family, so I hopped on a plane to try and redeem myself as a reasonable boyfriend. Seeing her had a calming effect, but it only lasted about a half hour. I had to find a halfpipe.

Tahoe is a great zone for freeriding, but since 1992, its halfpipe reputation had gone downhill. I called every resort and finally located a pipe at Alpine Meadows. It was puking snow, so Lindsy tried to get me to go ride powder with her. But my head spun around a few times, and she realized I needed a little couch time with Doctor Halfpipe. I plowed through waist-deep powder and found what might have been considered a halfpipe back in 1985. It was more like a single-hit shoulder-high quarter-pipe with a berm to land on. I hiked that single hit all day long like a man possessed.

Who Am I? What Am I Doing Here?

The next Grand Prix wasn't until mid-January, so I had a little time to get my head on straight. Lindsy and Chris Owen traveled with me to Gerlos, Austria, for the Seiben Grand Slam of Snowboarding, known to pros as "The Hundred Grand Huck for Bucks." All the heavies were there—Scanners, Euros, Americans. I thought it would be cool to regain my confidence and bring home thirty grand. I made the finals without too much trouble, but on my last run, I locked up on a simple backside air, hooked my board on the top of the pipe, and became a human flyswatter. I bashed my head—hard—on the icy bottom of the pipe. Apparently, I got up, rode to the end, fell over, and passed out.

When I came to, a bunch of ski patrollers were around me speaking German. I had no idea where I was, and I totally freaked out. I started screaming, "Where am I? What happened?" Everything came back to me when I saw Lindsy and Chris, but I couldn't stop shaking. It was scary.

We went straight to our hotel, packed our stuff into the rental car, and headed to the airport, stopping en route at a roadside pizzeria. Chris and Lindsy went inside to order while I put my shoes on. When I tried to get out of the car, the doors wouldn't open and I couldn't figure out how to unlock them. I could not find the unlock button, and the release handle wouldn't engage because they'd set the alarm. I was trapped. Claustrophobia set in. I started getting delirious and was just about ready to break a window when Lindsy walked out and said, "What in the hell is taking so long?" I just sat there, shaking my head, "I can't get out of the fricking car!" She went and got the keys from Chris, hit the unlock button, and I was free.

I convinced myself I was jinxed, and I had to find some new magic socks or something—anything. I felt like I had the weight of the entire country on my shoulders, not to mention the expectations of the sponsors I'd tricked into paying me ridiculous salaries because I was supposed to be consistent and able to overcome pressure. When I got home, a Morrow press release was waiting on my fax machine:

MORROW TEAM RIDER, TODD RICHARDS, OLYMPIC HALFPIPE FAVORITE

I wanted to cry and scream at the same time.

Grand Prix Number Two

Earlier in the year, Lindsy gave me a good-luck rock she'd found on a recent trip to Alaska. I'd been carrying it in my pocket as part of a master plan that would get me on the Olympic team.

On the way to Mount Bachelor for the second Grand Prix event, Lindsy and I stopped at the top of a mountain pass I knew well. I wanted to spend a little time at a small lake where I intended to say a few words to my dad and skip Lindsy's lucky rock a zillion times across its surface, setting me free from all my constricting doubts.

Once there I had this deep moment with myself. I visualized the stone skipping across the open water of the lake and setting me free. Everything would be great again. I smiled with utter confidence and side-armed the stone with all my strength. The setup was perfect, and the disc-shaped rock hovered just above the surface, sliding in closer and closer and then . . . plop. No skips. Nada. I stared in disbelief at the water and screamed at the top of my lungs. After a couple minutes of hyperventilating, I walked as calmly as possible back to the car, got inside, and drove down the pass. Lindsy didn't say a thing.

When we got to Mount Bachelor the day before the Olympic qualifier, it was northwesting (translation: pouring rain). The few people getting on the lifts were wearing trash bags and looking grim. The whole "super pipe" phenomenon was beginning around this time, and this meant bigger transitions, walls, and decks, all of which were supposed to equate to bigger airs and more "extreme excitement!" This pipe was more like a semi-super pipe, and it was empty except for a few diehards. Usually, shit weather meant I was going to ride shitty, but apparently I'd exorcised my demons in spite of the unlucky rock-skipping incident. I rode well, thank god.

The next day the storm was gone, but despite a good session at the pipe my mind was still whacked. I'd never experienced nerves like this before. My MO had always been to turn the heat on during the qualifying rounds of contests knowing I'd make top five and be in the main event. That relative lack of pressure helped me win qualifiers, and I'd just try and carry the momentum through the finals.

But the Grand Prix was a whole new ballgame. If I won the qualifier, I still had two combined runs that would be scored. If I messed up on either run, I was screwed.

The snow was perfect: soft, but not too soft. I made the finals and started getting fired up. I have no idea what I did on my run, but it probably was a bunch of upside-down shit where I spun around and landed everything. When I finished, I looked at the score and realized it was high enough to win if I could pull off my second run.

I transformed into a machine at this point. I was on autopilot and everything was like strobe flashes. Suddenly, I was in the gate again, but I didn't remember going back to the top of the pipe. The crowd was screaming, but I couldn't hear anything. I dropped in, hit one big frontside air, and for a vivid second, I looked at this kid who was a spectator at the edge of the pipe. His eyes met mine, and we locked on to each other. It was less than a second, but it was like the world froze for a minute. Then I landed, hit the next wall, and without consciously planning it, launched into a 900.

I put up the highest combined score of the day. That was when the euphoria hit me. I couldn't say anything; it was like my throat locked up. I found Lindsy, and she was crying. She knew what this meant to me.

Grand Prix Number Three

At the Mammoth Grand Prix, I went to pick up my credentials and saw Pete Del Giudice, who'd been chosen to be the halfpipe team coach for the Olympics. He began to tell me what I could expect at the team briefings for Nagano, and I tried to remind him that I hadn't made the team yet.

"Don't worry about it," he said. "You'll make it."

The day before the qualifier, we were told that the Olympic Snowboard team had fourteen openings for men and women in two events: halfpipe and giant slalom racing. This meant there would be three or four people for each discipline, but nobody knew which discipline or gender would get four slots or three. I had to get a top three to be guaranteed a spot on the team. On top of it all, there was a blizzard in progress. It was snowing sideways and was bitter cold, with zero visibility. Standing at the bottom of the run, I could barely see the top of the halfpipe.

While everybody else was riding powder, those of us who were serious about the Olympics—like Ross Powers, Rob Kingwill, Jamil Khan, Tommy Czeschin, Ron Chiodi, Barrett Christy, Cara-Beth Burnside, and me—hiked the pipe to practice our runs. After practice, I couldn't sit still, and media people were lurking everywhere. Billy and Jeff Anderson let me hide out in their house, where I escaped into the video-game world of Resident Evil. Nothing like shooting a few zombies to forget about your troubles for a few hours. Back at my hotel, fellow Morrow teammate Tyler Lepore called to tell me that former MTV personality Kennedy had been talking about me on *Late Night with David Letterman,* saying to the world, "My money's on Todd Richards for a gold medal."

The day of the qualifier, I really began second-guessing my deal with Morrow, hoping there wasn't some clause that rendered my million-dollar contract null and void if I didn't make the Olympic team. But I put it out of my mind and pulled a first place out of my ass for the qualifying run.

In the finals, Ross, who'd qualified right behind me, busted out and went even higher than he had in practice or the previous run. I turned the awe I was feeling about how fricking high he was going into, "Yeah, well, I'll beat you at your own game." I did back-to-back 720s—not as high as Ross—and nailed a frontside 900, along with the basic straight airs and a McTwist. It wasn't enough to beat Ross, but I took second. A ripping kid named BJ Leines, who had impressed everybody with his recent Grand Prix runs, took third, and Ron Chiodi finished fourth. The men's Olympic halfpipe team appeared to be set: Ross, Ron, and me, with BJ as the wild card. After the scores were announced, somebody came up to BJ and said, "You're going to the Olympics!" I was so stoked to see BJ in there, I zoned before realizing, *Holy shit, I'm going to the Olympics, too!*

A ton of media had gathered in Mammoth to introduce the world to the first American Olympic Snowboard team. During the frenzy of cameras and microphones that took place at the bottom of the pipe, I just stood there with my cell phone and called everyone I knew.

Within hours, a power meeting was in progress at the Mammoth Mountain Inn. Sixteen snowboarders milled around looking confused until the Olympic snowboard team coaches, Peter Foley and Pete Del Giudice, walked out with some pretty somber faces. They took BJ Leines and a racer named Rob Berney aside to break the news they would not be on the team. Due to some executive decisions, two other riders who had slightly lower Grand Prix scores but had ridden more consistently at high-profile events, would take their places.

It wouldn't have been such a horrible, heartbreaking moment if BJ hadn't been led to believe he was on the team. BJ had already called his parents, friends, and sponsors with the happy news. I felt really bad for him.

To Nagano, with Love

We were supposed to be on a plane to Nagano two days later, but first we had to be welcomed as Olympians by the official Games Preparation Committee representative, who greased us up with a speech that sounded more canned than sincere:

"This is the first day of your new lives! You are now Olympic athletes representing the United States, and no one will ever be able to take that away from you!"

After that, massive stacks of paperwork kept landing in front of me, all of which had to be "completed in full" before I left the room. As I wrote my name and address over and over again, I'd tune in and out of the seemingly endless speech:

"You are elite athletes, and your country thanks you."

Plop, another stack of papers.

"If you ever need help with job placement or legal counsel after your Olympic careers are over . . ."

Plop. This military processing had everything but the rubber glove. I felt like I'd signed up for the French Foreign Legion.

"In and around the Olympic village, you will only be allowed to wear Official Olympic Sponsored clothing, from head to toe."

Don't get me wrong. I was honored to be part of the Olympics, but it was not the flag-waving stoke I'd envisioned during my first few hours as an Olympian.

Next came the press conference. I guess I'd been dubbed the skater kid, because I had to field questions like, "You come from a derelict skateboarding background, how does all this organized competition sit with you?" As in Salt Lake City, I tried to explain:

"There's no good reason skateboarders aren't in the Olympics. They've been at it longer than we have and their sport is a lot harder. The only reason we're here is because there is more money in the snowboarding and ski resort industries. That's why the IOC has finally allowed us in."

After I'd paid my respects to skateboarding, I relaxed a little and had fun with it. I mean, how often do you have reporters from *Newsweek,* the *Los Angeles Times,* and the *Backwater Bayou Gazette* all interested in what you have to say?

Most of the media were clueless, and it was gratifying to see somebody like Billy Miller, a snowboarding writer for speck-on-the-newsstand *TransWorld SNOWboarding,* formulate more eloquent and informed questions than the correspondent from *USA Today.* After the interview, reporters swarmed snowboard writers like Billy and Lee Crane to ask questions like, "Did he say McTwister? How do you spell that? Is that a new Happy Meal dessert?"

The highlight of the whole "making the team" experience came the next morning. It was a box full of red, white, and blue cookies that Lindsy's mom and aunt Mary had baked in anticipation of the celebration and FedExed to my hotel room. When you're living out of a duffel, these things matter the most.

That afternoon, the entire Olympic snowboard team was to drive to San Francisco to catch a plane. My standard 400-pound pro snowboarder travel kit was packed and ready to go: three snowboards, bindings, boots, street clothes, emergency food rations, and PlayStation with international outlet adapter and assorted games. I was explaining these contents to the reporter who was interviewing me for MTV's *X-Today* show when a knock on the door announced the completely unexpected arrival of my Official Olympic Duffel Bag. While on camera I sorted through all the neat stuff I had to carry as well, like my Official Hairdryer of the Olympics, Official Bathrobe of the Olympics, Official Shampoo of the Olympics, and Official Dental Floss of the Olympics. The real beaute was a Western-style denim jacket with a huge Olympic Team Member logo on the back. An extra hundred pounds of stuff I really would rather not use—except the bathrobe. That was tight.

I got to San Francisco with just enough time to kiss Lindsy good-bye as she caught her own flight to Japan.

I'm Officially Official

The snowboard team flew together, coach, on a regular airline. We shared the plane with a bunch of business people. So much for my dreams of a private jet. We landed in Osaka, Japan, and headed right to the Official Debriefing Hotel. We had dinner at the Official Dining Hall, and then it was off to the Official Processing Room, where we were stripped of our unofficial clothing and dressed in Official Olympic Clothing.

We'd all signed an agreement not to wear anything but official gear. It was bad enough that I had on Reeboks—the Official Sponsor of the Olympic Team—but I couldn't even put a sticker for my new clothing sponsor, Special Blend, on my board.

Could I possibly be any more
official?

No stickers allowed—soooooooooooo not snowboarding. Morrow had to make con-
cessions as well. Team riders always ride on snowboards with the following winter's
graphics so photos run in the magazine at the same time the boards are available in
shops. An IOC clause, however, said that boards ridden by Olympic athletes must be
available to the public by the time of the broadcast. To remedy this, Morrow pumped
out a certain number of boards in time for the Games and placed them in shops in
Japan and the United States. The IOC actually followed up with the shops to confirm.

We were blown away by the Olympic Machine. There was a massive convention hall
where we pushed shopping carts along a red line, stopping at every station to pick up
slippers, socks, pants, leather jackets, neck gaiters. Once we were finally geared up, it
was one in the morning. We took photos of one another because we looked so goofy.
We weren't allowed to customize our stuff at all, and every time we went out in public
we were required to display at least one Olympic logo. We were walking billboards.

On day two, we had to have physicals and give urine samples. We wrote down all the medications we had taken during the past six months and, after the doc signed us off, headed into a big auditorium where a guy stood up at a microphone and started in with another "This is the first day of your new lives!" speech. Before moving on to the next stage of processing, we had to get an Official Olympic Identification Computer Chip implanted in our foreheads. Okay, not really, but I'm sure that's coming in 2006.

Anyway, after the medical procedures, the entire U.S. Olympic Team, from ice dancers to lugers, got on a plane to Nagano. We were met there by a crowd of Japanese kids waving American flags, which was really cool—much more like the Olympics I'd pictured. I was herded onto a bus with mogul skiers, figure skaters, biathletes, and a bunch of other athletes I didn't recognize. Shannon Dunn sat next to me and pointed out different people. "There's Tara Lipinski and that's Todd Eldredge and . . ."

I didn't know it then, but Todd Eldredge was considered the best hope for a figure skating medal among the American men. At twenty-six, he was two years younger than me and a five-time U.S. national champion. Apparently, he had been getting all sorts of media play.

When the buses stopped at the Olympic Village, there was crazy security everywhere and a bunch of television cameras lined up along one side of the walkway. When I stepped onto the cement behind fifteen-year-old Tara Lipinski, who was all smiles like she was off-loading for Disneyland, somebody yelled, "Todd! Todd!" I looked around, thinking it was Ross Powers or Ron Chiodi, but I didn't see anyone I knew and kept walking.

"Todd! Todd, can we talk to you for a minute please?" I heard again, and this time I noticed a reporter with a news camera looking right at me. So I started heading toward him, but Todd Eldridge pushed me aside with his shoulder, stepped in front of me, flashed his pearly whites, and said something like, "Sure. Here I am, Mr. Superstar."

The reporter looked at him and said, "No, not you. That Todd," pointing at me.

That was about the raddest feeling ever, getting to step back in front of Todd Eldredge after he'd shoved me aside. As far as interview and media moments go, that was the highlight of my career. I was thinking to myself, *Eat a poo, ice dancer!*

Inside the Village, different teams were scattered around, keeping their distance from other countries' teams. I was standing with a tiny group of American snowboarders when I saw Babs Charlet from France and ran over to say "What's up?" I got stink-eye from the Austrians as I passed them and suspicious stares from the other French athletes as I high-fived Babs and gave him a hug. Suddenly, snowboarders were coming out of the woodwork, emerging from the different clusters of people. Hockey players and skiers with giant thighs were looking at us like we were spies infiltrating their lines, but it didn't matter. Suddenly, it was anarchy: American, Japanese, French, Norwegian snowboarders, all just hanging together having a grand old time.

Media Feeding Frenzy

We refueled at the official cafeteria, a gigantic food court with every fast-food place on the planet. It was fun to watch all these supposedly healthy-minded athletes ordering up stacks of Big Macs with supersized french fries and Cokes. Then the American Olympic Snowboard team attended another press conference. We sat at a long table, microphones in front of us, fielding questions from a huge crowd of reporters, their flashes going off and cameras rolling.

We were nervous, jet-lagged, and well aware that snowboarders were considered the clowns of the Olympics, young idiots unschooled in media etiquette. Ross broke the ice for all of us. He was asked if he had any major rivalries going into the Games, and he just could not spit out the word "rivalry."

"I don't think there's any rav, I don't thing there's any rivo, I don't . . . ahhhh, fuck it!" he said and slapped the microphone in frustration.

I leaned into my microphone and said, "Well put, Ross," which the reporters seemed to think was pretty funny. Unfortunately, my comment was construed as sarcasm (which it was), meant in a malicious way (which it wasn't). Some reporters attributed it to the rivalry between Ross and me, but that was all just a figment of the media's imagination anyway.

The follow-up question to this was from Billy Miller, the *TransWorld* writer who had scored a coveted Olympic press badge. He asked me, "So, Todd, how's all this media attention? How do you handle the stress?"

My response was, "I'm just imagining all of you are naked right now." The crowd cracked up and I apparently got pegged as the "funny guy" because after the open forum, we went into a big auditorium for individual interviews, and I had a gazillion requests. Each of us had an Olympic media liaison attached to our sides. Mine dragged me around from reporter to reporter to reporter from all different countries with interpreters running around everywhere. We'd finish an interview and the liaison would say into her two-way radio, "Yeah, Todd Richards is done here, over? Great, I'll trade you Shannon Dunn at *The New York Times,* over."

AT&T did one of the best things at the Olympics. They set up a welcome center where you could meet up with your family or friends and gave out free local cell phones to athletes and their families. When I finally got to go to the center, my mom was there with her boyfriend, John, and Lindsy was there with Trevor Graves, Chris

Ross and me a split second after he said, "Fuck it" to the international press, Nagano, 1998.

The Olympic media machine started early and never stopped.

Owen, and his wife, Amber. I was still in the head-over-heels stage with Lindsy and I really needed her for emotional support, but we had zero time alone. Television crews followed the snowboard team around at all times, so I walked around with Lindsy, my mom, and our traveling camera crew for an hour before it was time to go.

The Opening Ceremony

Just getting everybody to the opening ceremony was a logistical masterpiece. The different countries' teams were herded from hotel rooms to buses to holding pen to holding pen to auditorium and finally to the stadium. The line was miles long.

Some countries, like Mongolia and Russia, had these unbelievable costumes with traditional furry coats and funky hats. And there we were in our Western-wear dusters and cowboy hats. We were the snow buckaroos. Everyone had digital cameras, and we ran around posing with the craziest costumes until the Olympic police herded us back into position.

As the American team neared the Olympic stadium, groups of athletes began jockeying for position. The U.S. team was so massive, you'd get swallowed up in the crowd if you weren't at the front or back, so the snowboarders tried to lag behind. The women's hockey team and the men's curling team were in fierce competition for the caboose position. I tried to distract one of the curlers by asking him if he considered brushing his teeth a training exercise, but in the end, we let the women's hockey team take the rear because we didn't want to get cross-checked or high-stitched.

Then we entered the Olympic stadium in Nagano, Japan.

Nothing could have prepared me for that moment. I was totally screwing around, not taking anything seriously, but when I walked into that arena, it just gripped me in so many ways. I was overwhelmed with American pride. I saw the flag at the front of the line of the American team, and the crowd was roaring like nothing I'd ever heard. Every nationality and every country I've ever heard of was there—we felt like we were all one big team. The camaraderie got me right in the throat. Borders and politics melted away. North Korea and South Korea walked out together. I forgot about who was warring with whom. I forgot about all the bad in the world.

Then the speeches began, first in Japanese and then French and English. I hung on to every single word, even the ones I didn't understand. A hypnotic numbness set in: I realized I was on the inside of the Olympics, not on the outside looking in. Then, as it went on, I forgot about my nationality. I forgot about the competition and that I was a favorite to win the halfpipe event for the first American Olympic Snowboard team. I even forgot that I was a snowboarder. For a few minutes, I was just a human being and part of something so much bigger.

Back to Reality—Sort Of

By the time we got out of the Olympic Stadium, I was squirming in my cowboy outfit. American pride aside, I am a snowboarder, and a cowboy hat made me feel ridiculous. Just when I thought I was about to escape without seeing anybody I knew, there were Lindsy, my mom, and Trevor. My mom was beaming with pride, pointing me out to all the people she had met in the stands and no doubt telling them how handsome I looked. Trevor and Lindsy were laughing and taking pictures as fast as possible.

During the ceremony our bags had been transported by the mysterious Olympic machine to our final athlete quarters. We piled onto a bus in order to get to "shit camp," as it became known. Everybody on the bus was sick. People were hacking up lungs, sweating with fevers, and blowing their noses. At our new hotel, Ross Powers, Ron Chiodi, and I—and all of our board bags—were packed like sardines into a ten-foot-by-ten-foot room. They were both sick, and we were all claustrophobic.

My thumb was twitching above the panic button. My inner monologue went like, *I can't handle this. Yeah, I don't really like this. God, this freaking sucks. Oh my god, I'm gonna get the flu. I gotta get the hell out of here.*

We headed to the dining area at the top of the hotel and I said to everyone I saw, "God, can you believe these accommodations?" The Western version of the food

Official Olympic Cowboy outfit. Yea-haw!

they served was disgusting. I thought the pasta would be fairly safe, but it was spaghetti with "secret" clams—not just clams, but the entire shell—along with a host of other sea creatures, sand, seaweed, and everything else that could be scooped out of a tide pool, boiled, and served with tomato sauce.

I went over to our coach and said, "Pete, I can't handle it here. I gotta get out of here."

"You serious?" he asked, and when he saw I was, he said, "You gotta do what you gotta do to compete. We want you to get a medal."

Three hours later I was with Lindsy in her hotel room, which wasn't exactly IOC approved accommodations. The next morning, her hotel's breakfast (bulging fish eyeballs and carcass over sticky rice) was even sketchier than the meal of the night before. I drank some tea, and Lindsy and I found a convenience store down the street. After a sticky white-bean-paste dumpling breakfast washed down with an energy drink, I was ready to ride.

The Olympic halfpipe venue was tucked away at a little ma and pa resort near Nagano. It had one lift, which only athletes were allowed to use, and not-so-grand stands that wouldn't have handled half a U.S. Open crowd.

The pipe itself was in really good shape and super steep. Giant airs were possible with minimal speed. After three practice runs, I was having fun. It was sunny and clear, the snow was soft, and I started working out my Olympic run in my head. For the next three days, I practiced it: a frontside air to a McTwist to a frontside 720 to an inverted 720 to another air and another air (whatever felt good) and end with an inverted 720.

International Snowboard Federation competitions had always placed more importance on overall impression, giving snowboarders more freedom to experiment with their runs. The FIS judging, on the other hand, gave us a number of tricks that were mandatory. As such, you could do rotational inverted spinning tricks back-to-back all the way down the pipe and still lose, even though those are the hardest, most progressive tricks in snowboarding. FIS required a certain amount of straight airs (methods, Indies, etc.) and rotational tricks (360s, 720s, etc.), and there were different judges for amplitude (height) and overall impression.

The FIS thinks this type of judging scores riders on well-rounded runs. I could bore you for pages about why I think this judging slows down the sport's progression, but I'll just say this: Judging should be based on the best runs using the most progressive tricks, as it is done in skateboarding. Why make a "straight air" mandatory if it's easier to do? To make a long story short: FIS halfpipe judging really sucked—not the judges themselves, just the criteria to which they were forced to adhere.

Regardless of the FIS rules, I was on my game and pulled some of the biggest McTwists of my life—ten or fifteen feet out of the pipe. Ross and Chiodi told me

In the Olympic pipe, I was doing some of the biggest McTwists of my life—the day before the competition.

they'd never seen me go so big. I was skipping around thinking, *It's sunny, I'm ripping, I'm gonna do good in the Olympics! Yippee!* Then I started envisioning myself on a box of cereal, in an Audi commercial, on the cover of magazines, on *The Tonight Show,* rolling in cash. I figured it was good confidence building so I let my mind go. Why not? I'd worked really hard to get here.

After the second day of practice (one day before the halfpipe event), I walked off the mountain and a camera crew from CBS ambushed me. *Well,* I thought, *they must have seen me practicing those fifteen-foot-tall McTwists.*

"Hi Todd," said the reporter. "We're live. Can I ask you a few questions?" I told myself to sound humble and low-key about how hard I'd been ripping, but he said, "What do you think about Ross Rebagliati getting his medal taken away for drugs?" I was just, "Huh?" I hadn't even heard about this.

They cut the cameras and I interviewed the reporter until I'd heard the whole story about Ross, a Canadian snowboarder, testing positive for marijuana and having his gold medal in the previous day's giant slalom stripped. Then the CBS crew went back on live and asked me the same question about Ross.

My response was, "No comment. I don't know anything about it." The guy sighed and scampered off to find somebody who would have something juicy to say.

By the end of the day, the biggest story in the Olympics was Ross "Stoner" Rebagliati. Canadian flag stickers were showing up with marijuana leaves instead of maples, and I even saw one bearing a mug shot of Bob Marley. The "performance-enhancing" capabilities of giggle smoke became the hot topic among snowboarders. Ross was immediately booked for talk shows in New York, London, Tokyo, Vancouver, and Los Angeles. Eventually, Ross got his medal back since he had apparently been subjected to second-hand smoke at a party. Meanwhile, the Olympic anti-doping committee was preparing its cups for the real dirtbags of the Olympics, the halfpipe riders.

Rain, Rain, Go Away

I woke up on competition day and heard something weird outside. Rain! Not just a pitter-patter, but full-on sheets of pouring rain. My shoulders sagged, I sighed, and the nightmare began.

At the pipe, there was a crowd about the size of a U.S. Open—big but not Olympic big. The rain kept coming down, and my attitude went downhill too. Oakley was hyping what were supposed to be the best anti-fog goggles on the market. Two minutes on my head, and the goggles were fog machines. The halfpipe walls were hard enough to see with the rain, even though they'd been spray-painted blue for context in the flat light. Visibility was zero.

I'd clean my goggles, but the second I dropped in the rain fogged them up again. As the allotted practice time came to a close, I was wet, cranky, cold, blind, and my run wasn't coming together. The harder I tried, the further away from me it got. Instead of focusing on one run at a time, I began to think about all the opportunities I was going to miss out on when I lost. It was a total mind game. This pissed me off more because I was one of the oldest competitors. I shouldn't have been phased by the pressure.

There were two qualifying rounds, and the best eight riders from each round would advance to the finals. My first run, I ate shit. I thought it was over and accepted it. It wasn't so horrible. It wasn't like I was dead. In fact, it was almost a relief. I went back up for my second run with zero expectations. Everything came together, and, even with a fall, my score was high enough to get me into the finals.

Another perfect run during Nagano practice.

A lot of people, myself included, were pushing to have the finals rescheduled because of the rain. Other, more televised events, like the downhill skiing, had been postponed because of weather, but for the snowboarders, the show must go on. The IOC wanted it over with, and a lot of us began to feel how unimportant we were.

A few hours later that same day, I was in the starting gate for my first run of the Olympic finals. Scores would be based on two runs, combined, so I had to nail both. My head should have been clear. I shouldn't have been able to hear the crowd, but I heard everything—the rain, the cheers, my mind telling me, *If you win this, you could do some pretty big things.* Even talking to my dad didn't help, because I was focused on the outcome, not the procedure. I dropped in, hit a big frontside air, landed way too high on the transition, then pumped too hard on the transition into a McTwist on the next wall, opened up too early after the spin, hit my ass on the lip, and fell to the bottom of the pipe. My voice yelled out, "Shiiiiiiit!" Poof. There went my chance of bringing home a medal.

I was rip-shit angry. I picked myself up, got some speed, and finished my run listening to my own monologue: *You idiot! You just blew it. You blew it. You blew it. You blew it.* On television they showed Lindsy in the bleachers. Her face sank at the same moment I fell. My mom was nearly in tears because she knew how badly I wanted it.

I watched everybody else come down with amazing, near-flawless runs—Ross Powers, Daniel Franck, Gian Simmen, Fabiene Reuter. I'd beaten all of them before, numerous times. It killed me, but it was my own fault. I took myself out of it. I had succeeded in getting rid of the pressure in the worst way possible. It was like my sub-conscious told me, *Fall, and you won't feel it anymore. You may feel something else, but at least you won't feel this pressure in your head.* That was for shit sure.

My second run, I had nothing to lose and only redemption to gain. I did my straight air really big, then a big McTwist, then a frontside 900, another straight air, and two inverted tricks. Someone told me later that it was the highest scored run of the day—a bittersweet revelation that confirmed what I already knew: I did have it in me to win. And that was what made it suck so bad.

Gian Simmen was a kid from Switzerland who had never won a contest in his life. He'd gotten tons of seconds and thirds, but this, the Olympic halfpipe, was his first win. He did what I should have done. He cut through the crap, had fun, and took home the gold medal. Daniel Franck, one of the kids who'd lit a fire under my ass in Norway years earlier, placed second, and my teammate Ross Powers got the bronze. I was happy for Gian, Daniel, and Ross, but I was physically ill with regret. When the

My most dedicated fan—my mom—
at the Olympics.

scores were posted, I saw that I had placed dead last in the finals. That's when a CBS correspondent shoved a microphone in my face and asked me how I felt about being the favorite to win and not making the top three. Frustrated, I held my hand out and blamed it on the rain.

I saw the flowers being brought out to the winner's podium, and I couldn't stomach watching. Some might say that's poor sportsmanship, but I think the riders understood.

Morrow had a shop tour planned for me around Japan, but Chris Owen knew I was ready to crack. He was a bro and said, "Go home."

Lindsy and I packed our bags and flew out of Japan the next day.

Post-Olympic Psychosis

Back home in Breckenridge, I wallowed in misery. I dragged myself as deep as possible into a dark hole and never came up, except to snowboard obsessively and eat an occasional meal. Lindsy put up with my selfish drama and tried to get me to not base my entire self-worth as a human being on the results of my last snowboarding contest. But I felt like shit, and damn it, I was going to continue to feel like shit and treat everybody around me like shit until I won a contest again.

The opportunity for redemption came a week after the Olympics. The ISF Vans World Championships was the same event where I'd taken second place to Terje by a tenth of a point the year before. Everybody who had been at the Olympics would be there. I got to Kirkwood in Tahoe two days early and hiked the pipe so many times I probably sweated out my body weight in water. I was determined to learn the frontside inverted 900, a trick I'd knocked myself senseless trying earlier in the season. The morning before the World Championships, I started nailing them, and my bitterness was transformed into confidence. I dropped the frontside inverted 900 into my bag of tricks with skyrocketing confidence.

I walked up to the pipe on contest day, smiling at all my bros and thinking, *Okay, well good luck to everybody for second place through sixteenth.* I didn't just want to win. I wanted to obliterate the competition by a large margin to show the world what I should have done at the Olympics. When I have this attitude, I can't do wrong.

I stuck the trick and won by four or five points, which wasn't obliteration, but was significant enough to maintain my cocky attitude. I was so self-absorbed I couldn't wait to read in print that I had redeemed myself from the Olympic shit fest. All of a sudden life was good again. I was pissing rainbows.

That's when I first realized the unhealthy trend I'd fallen into for the past year or so. Some subtle, masterfully timed comments from Lindsy helped me see that my happiness was dependent upon contest results. There were these inner demons that ate me alive when I did shitty in a contest, and I had to shred them to pieces with a win.

Some of the things people had been telling me all along started to make sense. You have good days and bad days, and just because you have a bad day in a contest doesn't mean you suck. It sounds so simple, but ever since I'd started winning contests, the pressure had cooked me. My feeling was if I wasn't winning, my career was going downhill. If I put myself in a hole, I'd have to struggle to pull myself back out— a sick, self-degrading strategy I used to stay on top. Worst of all, it didn't just affect me; it affected everybody around me.

More Talent, Less Hype

A lot of people called the 1998 U.S. Open the "real Olympics" and even "bigger than the Olympics" because Terje was there. For me, it was a homecoming. I loved going back to the East Coast in the springtime. I suppose I'd become a little nostalgic in my old age; that or I'd blocked out the memories of the frigid days when my toes almost froze off. Either way, it was good to be home.

You can't just roll up and practice at the U.S. Open the week before because that's when all the aspiring kids are trying to qualify for the legendary event. Photographer Jeff Curtes told me he was going with his brother, Joe, and a couple other pros, Barrett Christy and Mike Michaelchuck, to a good pipe at Killington. Gone were the days of shitty East Coast halfpipes; most mountains now had parks and pipes that were maintained all winter long.

The Killington pipe was fun, and our little group had the right vibe for trying new tricks. I was doing McTwist 720s—a 540-degree rotation with a late backside 180 so I'd come out fakie. I could land the trick, but never pulled it in a contest because it left me in the flat bottom of the halfpipe going fakie and on my heels, which is a tough position to be in when setting up for the next trick.

Someone suggested, "Why don't you go faster for more height and go around 900?" It was a perfect time to try, so I dropped in really fast, snapped it all the way around 900, and stomped it clean the first time. *Holy shit,* I thought. *That was kind of easy.* Jeff shot some photos of it, which became a sequence in *TransWorld*. To this day, I've never pulled a better one than my first try at the Killington halfpipe.

Learning that trick was instrumental because it made a secondary 900 possible on the next wall. And nobody had done back-to-back 900s yet. I kept practicing, and by the end of the day I was flowing it into combination 900s. Now I had that frontside inverted 900 *and* this thing—whatever it was. It was a weird trick: super spinny, upside-down, and scary. I returned to Stratton thinking I was going to win the Open with it, as long as the judges comprehended what it was and scored accordingly.

Back at Stratton, the Curtes brothers started a buzz about this crazy trick I had up my sleeve, calling it the "McNine" or "McSomething." In the days leading up to the U.S. Open, it had been nice and sunny. Contest day: fog. Snow. Rain. The halfpipe looked like a piece of crap, with underlayers peeling away like tree rings. It had melted, frozen, been rained on, and frozen again. Instead of the letter U, it had taken on the shape of a shoe box, minus the lid, with the ends cut off.

The pipe was too sketchy for the McWhatever, but in the finals, I had crazy adrenaline going when I dropped in. I started off with a straight air, and then another straight air, and then another, building up speed for the bottom of the pipe. My friends knew something was coming because I'd usually hit a spin or inverted trick early in my run. At the bottom, I overshot the best place on the wall for the money trick, but I still had to get the job done. I came into the wall with speed, flung my body into this spinning Tasmanian Devil thing, rotated 900, grabbing mute for a millisecond, and somehow got my feet back underneath me before landing off-balance. I barely had enough time to think *Holy shit, I'm still alive,* before I hit the next wall. I pumped up that wall, prayed that I'd be able to get my body around 900. The gods were nice to me. I landed clean, like it was nothing, and heard the crowd going nuts as I slid around at the bottom and looked back up at the pipe with all its mist and doomsday weather. The judges figured it out and gave me the highest scoring run of the day.

Some of my friends and co-competitors, people I really respected like Dave Downing and Billy Anderson, were saying things like, "What in the hell was that?" and "Was that back-to-back nines?" Billy said I looked like a wet cat that got flung in the air, clawing the whole way down and somehow landing on its feet. The perfect description and the perfect name: Wet Cat. By accident, I'd invented a new trick, which for skateboarders and snowboarders means more than any contest win. I was on top of the world. Then I realized, *Oh crap, now I have to do it again.*

While walking back up the pipe for my second run, I looked back down at my friends every few steps and saw them lifting their arms in the sky and shaking their fists. At the top, I got more pats on the back and watched Rob Kingwell have a really good run. Terje was on his game, too. But I dropped in with zero pressure, just ready to have fun. I didn't even care about the result, which was a good thing because I choked on the repeat performance. I landed too low on the first 900, didn't have enough speed for the second nine, and had to gut around a McTwist instead. King-well won, Terje took second, and I got third. For the first time in years, I wasn't pissed at myself for not getting first in the contest. As far as I was concerned, I *had* won, because from that day forward, the Wet Cat was my trick, and nobody could ever take that away from me.

_After the storm, getting my
head screwed on.

JIBBERS AND JUMPERS/
THERE'S NO STYLE
LIKE SLOPESTYLE

By the time the 1998 season ended, only the inhabitants of the most remote Amazon jungles hadn't heard of snowboarding. Thanks to the Olympics, snowboarding was finally a "legitimate" sport (yeah, right). As it turned out, U.S. television coverage of Olympic snowboarding had been decidedly underwhelming—a massive ten-minute segment wedged into five days of live figure skating.

At least I didn't have to relive my personal misery by watching hours of taped footage, but for the riders who had done well and for our families, friends, and all the snowboarders at home, the lack of TV time was nothing less than a bummer.

The Olympics were supposed to ignite a growth explosion for the snowboard industry, but the lack of coverage was more of a fizzle than a bomb. It was a false alarm that made snowboard manufacturers look at their warehouses and say, "Hmmm, what in the hell are we going to do with all these snowboards?" The industry had been rising steadily and demographic studies predicted a gazillion new snowboarders on the slopes each winter. But now the market was flooded with companies, too many companies creating too much equipment for too few snowboarders. For people with MBA degrees, it was totally predictable. For the average pro snowboarder trying to make a living, it meant, "Damn, my royalty check sucks this month." Or worse, "What do you mean, you're restructuring the team? Oh, I get it. I'm fired."

Following the Olympics, the snowboarding industry suffered a brief dark period. It trimmed the fat, and the strong survived. Some companies, like Morrow Snowboards, struggled to hang on, cutting costs everywhere in an effort to weather the repercussions of poor management. I was more than a little worried when I heard rumblings that the company was in trouble, but Morrow's own minister of misinformation (the Jerk) calmed my fears, telling me, "No, everything's fine. You just keep riding like a champ, and we'll take care of the business." My monthly paychecks kept rolling in as planned, so I relaxed.

My old pal who wore tight shirts, Chris McNally, had drawn my newest board graphic: a little kid playing with dinosaurs on a yellow-based board. The bright color reflected my new attitude about life, contests, and snowboarding. I wanted to show the world I was ready to unleash my own personal power. I'd started looking inward for the answers about life and even took some personal growth courses with motivational speaker Tony Robbins. I was now utilizing the strategies he used to influence peak performers in their quest for extraordinary results!

Are you kidding me? Chris and I picked the color because we thought it would sell like crazy and show up well in photos.

Old Tricks, New Style

While dark times threatened the industry, I bought a new car, an Audi wagon, and Lindsy and I moved to Portland, Oregon, for the summer. I'd be close to Morrow's Salem headquarters, there were plenty of good skate parks, and Mount Hood was a short drive away. We rented a cute little house with a white picket fence in a trendy, yuppie neighborhood near Twenty-Third Street, where Lindsy's car was stolen our first week there. The house and the Audi wagon (which I'd bought to haul around snowboards, not baby strollers) were the perfect cover. Nobody ever suspected I was a snowboarder.

There was a jib rebirth in process, due in part to the surge in popularity of street skating. Riders like Scotty Wittlake, Andrew Crawford, and JP Walker and the Forum crew were taking technical rail riding to a whole new level, combining huge jumps with the jib phenom. It was called slopestyle. Seasoned superhero pros like Peter Line and Jamie Lynn had been spinning upside-down vert tricks off big backcountry straight jumps for years, but now they were becoming standouts in the man-made jib/jump movement that a pro named Kevin Jones was mastering and refining with alarming speed. I thought I'd better start venturing out of the halfpipe once in a while.

Ski areas still slobbered over snowboarders in an effort to attract dollars, but halfpipes were no longer the sole attraction to riders. Kids wanted an entire playground, not just a jungle gym, so ski resorts hired snowboarders as consultants while constructing snowboard parks. In the quest to build the best park, mountain managers signed off on huge kickers, roller-coaster rail slides, welded-metal rainbows, gaps to jump over, and buses and Volkswagen beetles to jib—all the things that were previously forbidden for insurance purposes.

Nearby Mount Hood satisfied the demand, too. During summer camps, kids

new tricks on boards by the
same ol' company...

Loyalty

instead of same ol' tricks on boards
by new companies.

>todd richards<
switch-stance 540° indy

morrow snowboards po box 12606 salem, or 97309

This is one of my favorite ads from the Morrow days.

started spreading out on all the playground equipment, and the pipe wasn't nearly as crowded as it used to be.

But summer snowboarding was getting a little old, and one night Lindsy and I started talking about a vacation. Despite all the places I'd visited, I had not been on a vacation since the ski trips I used to take with my parents. I'd never been anywhere without a photographer, cinematographer, or contest to enter. A few weeks later, Lindsy and I were in Hawaii on the island of Maui.

I went nuts at first because I didn't know how to relax. Then we decided it would be fun to learn how to surf. Despite the obvious correlation between the sports, the majority of snowboarders don't know how to surf. I had always been scared of the ocean, but the water in Hawaii is so clear, it takes away some of the fear of the unknown (you can actually see the submarines with teeth under your board, versus imagining them). We bought longboards, and surfing became our daily ritual. Lindsy was way better than me at first, but eventually I got the hang of it. When I finally caught a real wave and went down the line without falling, I was hooked. That cheesy Beach Boys song lyric is true, "Catch a wave and you're sitting on top of the world." It makes you want to do it again and again and again. Two weeks on the Islands was great therapy.

We returned to Portland with ocean fever. This surfing thing was pretty cool, and we wanted to be near the water. Oddly enough, most of the snowboarding companies, including the magazines and some of my sponsors, were located in Southern California. We ended our rental-agreement in Portland, and Chad Dinenna with Nixon Watches helped us find a place in Leucadia, right on the water, which we rented with a snowboard writer named Dave Sypniewski.

One day, Dave brought home a letter that *TransWorld* had received and subsequently run in the September 1998 issue. It read as follows:

"Hey bitch, I mean, Todd Richards: Great interview at the Olympics after your botched run. Nothing like making the United States (the birthplace of the sport, now tremendously overexposed) look like a bunch of whining peter-puffers. Candy-ass kooks like you bug the bejeezus out of me because I know there are tons of kids more capable who would have been ecstatic about a fourth- or even an eighth-place finish. The fact that you, as a favorite, could use rain as an excuse for a sub-par finish is a good one . . ."

Unfortunately, this disillusioned reader didn't hear the part of the interview in which I said that the other competitors dealt with the same shitty conditions; it was edited out. Regardless, I knew what really went down, and I jumped at the chance *TransWorld* gave me to write a response, which ran in the same issue, along with an article by Bill Thomas called "Road to the Olympics: Todd Richards' Journey Down the Highway of Frustration and Glory."

The key word here was "frustration," but other words like "regret" or, "disappointment" were fitting descriptions as well.

Post-Olympic Morrow

The secret to surfing is learning to go where you won't make a complete fool of yourself. Less crowded is better; no crowd is best. In SoCal, both are rare. And unlike mountains and vert ramps, waves are a constantly moving stage. No two are ever alike, and it's nearly impossible for a beginner to stand up for any length of time and figure things out. I was a kook.

It only took me a few weeks to realize that it would be years before I could learn to surf at a level anywhere near snowboarding and skateboarding. The nice thing about surfing, however, is that it isn't nearly as painful. I could fall twenty or thirty times in the water, wake up the next morning, and still be able to walk without a limp. I couldn't move my arms from the shoulders down, but I could walk no problem.

Summer came to a close, and my tenth winter as a professional snowboarder loomed in front of me. I was twenty-eight years old, and I was starting to get questions like, "So, with the Olympics over, are you thinking about retiring?"

Retiring? Some people, mostly out-of-touch journalists who wrote for magazines not related to snowboarding, considered the Olympics the pinnacle of a career. Since I was one of the older freestyle riders still competing in pro freestyle halfpipe contests, these people seemed to think I was ready to throw in the towel. My response to retiring was, "Hell, no." A common follow-up question was, "Then what about the next Olympics? You gonna shoot for 2002?" I always answered, "Yeah, probably. Of course." The next Olympics were still three and a half years away, but I was a competitor with no intention of showing any signs of weakness. The truth was, I was really thinking about surfing and slopestyle competitions. The halfpipe was beginning to feel too much like a job.

I knew that Morrow was in serious trouble when the CEO asked me if I was interested in taking stock instead of paychecks. I said, "No thanks, I'll stick with the cash." My big three-year contract paid me fifteen grand a month, as well as another forty thousand quarterly. When three months came and went without a check, I called Mr. CEO to ask what was up. Again he asked if I'd consider taking stock instead. I said no, and suddenly my monthly paychecks dried up, too. I contemplated suing, but figured that would only cost me more money.

In the summer of 1998, Stephen Astephen started The Familie, a sports marketing company specializing in representing action sports athletes. I'd met Steve while riding in Vail years earlier and heard from other pros that he was a good person to have in your corner. He and a handful of other agents recognized that snowboarders, skateboarders, and the like weren't realizing their full marketing potential, and when they did, they got paid chump change. I trusted Steve immediately and hopped on board with The Familie after one conversation with him. He's a fast-talker who knows his business and can sniff out bullshit like a bloodhound. As my agent, Steve would represent all of my business interests and try to score other, non-industry opportunities. He would also see to it that my contractual obligations were fulfilled.

When I told him about the stock options Morrow was offering me in lieu of cold hard cash, Steve said, "Look, a whole bunch of shares of nothing is still nothing. If they fold, you don't have anything." He knew the company was in serious debt, and he knew that athletes were generally the last people on the list to get paid in situations like this. I was supposed to be smiling and telling the world, "Morrow is the best company in the world," while I was thinking to myself, *Best company in the world, my ass. They haven't paid me in months.*

With a half-million dollars owed to me, I didn't have a lot of motivation to advertise their wares, but I had to keep riding Morrow boards because if I didn't, they would have a reason not to fulfill the agreement they weren't fulfilling anyway. All we could really do was lean on them and allude to legal recourse if things didn't turn around soon.

A Pipe Kid No More

I entered the Vans Triple Crown of Snowboarding at the beginning of the 1998/1999 season. It was December, the pipe was good, as it usually was at Brek, and I took first place. A few weeks later, I entered an FIS event at Mammoth and got second place, but a funny thing happened. The halfpipe wasn't firing me up like it used to. I merely showed up to the contests, went through the motions, and landed my tricks. My motivation was based on anger at Morrow and being able to rub it in their faces, saying, "See? I'm still doing my job. How about a paycheck?" I began to wonder, *Is this what "burnout" feels like?*

Right after the FIS contest I went back to Breckenridge, but instead of going straight to the pipe, I headed to the snowboard park, one of the best in the world, and hit a few jumps along the way. It was actually fun to freeride, so I got on another chairlift and rode all over the mountain. By the end of the day, I'd found all sorts of fun little zones I hadn't known even existed. The jumps were way better in the park, though, and I spent the next day riding there—top to bottom runs in which I'd do different tricks off of every jump and jib. Instead of keeping watch over what everybody was doing in the pipe, I focused on myself, saying I couldn't go home until I landed certain tricks. Old habits are hard to kick.

What little competitive drive I had left in my system was focused on the upcoming X Games slopestyle event. I didn't even enter the halfpipe event, but I did better in slopestyle than the year before by three places—eleventh! Almost top ten. The best thing was that I once again felt the spark of years past. I wanted to win a slopestyle event, and I had a long way to go. The guys who had been riding the park while I was camped out at the halfpipe were good. Really good. To most of them, my presence at slopestyle competitions was more a novelty than a threat, kind of like, "Oh, look. How cute. The pipe guy is hitting jumps."

At the annual SIA tradeshow in Vegas, just before the 1999 U.S. Open, I was fuming because I still hadn't been paid by Morrow. The Morrow booth showcased my pro models front and center, and I had to restrain myself from pulling them off the rack and holding them for ransom. My other sponsors, Oakley, Nixon, Special Blend, and Clive, were great, however, and I'd landed a contract with DC Shoes that replaced Airwalk as my boot sponsor. Still, the company I'd been with the longest wouldn't even return my phone calls. I was on the verge of quitting and suing them, but I kept waiting for a miracle. I was torn: They'd helped me get where I was, but at the same time, I figured that I'd helped them get where they were, too. Nevertheless, Morrow was still considered one of the top five companies, and my pro models were top-selling boards.

It was a weird time for me and other people I knew at Morrow. My good friend Chris Owen was still the Morrow marketing and team guy, and neither of us could look at each other. Rob Morrow was just a figurehead and had nothing to do with the business, but that didn't make things between us any easier.

The SIA tradeshow is one gigantic rumor mill, and Steve Astephen leaked the idea that I was going to quit Morrow and look for a new sponsor. The next day, he walked around and tested the waters for me. In response, he heard a rumor that a company was looking to buy Morrow, but nothing else could be said. Steve told me to grit my teeth and go to the U.S. Open as a Morrow rider.

"Right now," he said, "that's the best thing you can do for your career."

I'm a (Bargaining) Tool

My life was a big question mark when I landed in Burlington, Vermont, for the Open. I was determined to show my dissatisfaction with Morrow while, at the same time, fulfilling my obligation to ride a Morrow board. I wrote "Morrow Sucks" nice and big on the base of my board with a magic marker. Every air I pulled in the pipe was intended not to help me win the contest, but to show the world my feelings about my sponsor.

After a long day of preaching the Morrow un-gospel, I somehow managed a tenth-place finish. Ross Powers took first for Burton.

Right after the Open finals, I got a call from Steve, and he was all business.

"Look there's something going on," he said. "I can't go into details, but are you still interested in riding for Morrow?"

I looked down at my board with its "Morrow Sucks" artwork and said, "Sure, if they pay me."

"All right," he continued. "Well there's a serious deal on the table. My source wasn't bullshitting. Somebody wants to buy Morrow, and you are an integral part of the purchase. Gotta run, I'll call you when I know more. Oh, got another video game deal coming through the pipe. Hang in there." Click.

Much later, I learned that K2 Snowboards made an offer for Morrow, but it was very hush-hush because both K2 and Morrow were public companies and insider trading issues applied. The beauty was that K2's CEO, Rich Rodstein, made it clear to the Morrow CEO who'd been blowing me off for months that K2 wasn't interested in the purchase unless I was part of the deal. Rodstein had talked to my agent and realized that there was a good possibility of a half-million-dollar lawsuit if Morrow didn't fulfill its contractual obligations with me. For obvious reasons, he didn't want to buy a company with a lawsuit pending, and Morrow's CEO was forced to compromise, making me an even bigger thorn in his side than I had been in the previous months.

The compromise was that K2 agreed to pay me if Morrow lowered its purchase price. I wouldn't get the full half a mil owed to me, but a ton of money is still a ton of money, and the satisfaction of knowing that I had been a bargaining tool and got the last laugh made the minor loss worthwhile. Had I sued, there was no guarantee I'd have ever gotten anything. Steve proved himself to be worth his weight in gold throughout this whole scandal, and I knew I had a bulldog in my corner.

Snowboarding Video Games Are Evil

Unlike my love for the halfpipe, my video game obsession was gaining steam. From Coleco to Atari to Nintendo to PlayStation, video games have been an important part of my life. Playing Asteroids at the mall or Atari in my living room helped me weather many an East Coast snowstorm when I was a teenager. But back then, I could only dream of skateboarding games. When I first sat down with PlayStation's *Tony Hawk's Pro Skater* in 1996, I realized just how good kids have it today.

Before the Olympics, Lisa Hudson, former team manager for Airwalk who was now consulting with Sony, called to tell me that snowboarders were needed for a new video game project. I didn't even bother to get the details before I volunteered to be part of PlayStation's first snowboarding game, *Pro Boarders*.

Since then, I've worn countless black leotards covered with ping-pong-ball looking digital sensors. I've strapped into a snowboard and jumped up and down on a trampoline in front of a blue screen for hours, sweating like a pig while programmers yell out harsh directions like crazed aerobic instructors. But the games are therapeutic, realistic, and inspiring. A good snowboarding video game fires you up to go ride the same way a good snowboarding movie does.

If you believe the critics, however, video games are evil. They say video games are just youth-targeted marketing campaigns that encourage kids to sit in front of their televisions and eat junk food. They are the source of everything bad in this world and nothing more than shameless self-promotion. So whatever you do, avoid all snowboarding video games because money is evil, royalty checks are evil, and snowboarding is evil. Of course, if you want to learn how to pull inverted 900s without landing on your head, there's no better way.

Being a character in video games is great. It is to us what getting a major movie deal is to actors, but it still didn't compare to an opportunity that arose later in 1999. Apparently, a toy company wanted to make an extreme sports action figure of me. Are you kidding me? Action figures were my life when I was a kid! To actually become a molded toy that kids would huck into the air and shoot with BB guns was a huge honor. This was way bigger than the Olympics.

The process was pretty basic. I gave Imperial Toys a photo of me wearing my snowboarding gear, and they created a three-inch-high action figure of me and a bunch of other athletes. All the dolls had different color hair and clothes and their individual sponsors were listed on the packages, but their figures and faces were exactly the same. Their arms and legs didn't move, so they were just these stationary standing dudes that didn't really look like me or any of the other "models."

Vashon Island, Here We Come

K2 was located on Vashon Island near Seattle and that became Morrow's new home base as of April 1999. Most of the Morrow team was invited to stay on board, including Billy Anderson, Tyler Lepore, Erik Leines, and Josh Dirksen. I was proud of Josh because I had actually "discovered" him at Mount Hood in 1996. He was a pipe digger at High Cascade Snowboard Camp, but he was better than a lot of the pros who were coaching. I told Morrow to sponsor this kid before anyone else scooped him up.

At the time of its acquisition of Morrow, K2 was widely thought of as the second biggest fish in the sea after Burton, which was still the great white of snowboarding companies. I've been told that bigger-fish companies often buy smaller-fish companies because the smaller fish are eating too much of the bigger fish's food. Once the bigger fish eat the smaller fish, they can control the smaller fishes' food supply and eventually starve the smaller fish altogether. In the end, the bigger fish get all the food and become even bigger.

It's a spooky analogy, and when it came to Morrow and K2, it kept getting spookier. Almost immediately, Morrow was put in its place on K2's totem pole. Morrow was doled out just enough slop (money) to survive. As for the riders, we had a lot of freedom because K2 agreed that Morrow should be a rider-driven company. They wanted Morrow to be the Alien Workshop (a skateboarding company known for involving its team in marketing and design) of snowboarding.

The first thing I did after Morrow jumped on the K2 ship was design a new Morrow company logo. It was a sign of a new beginning. I had agreed to drop my pro-model board and royalty payment system in exchange for a fair guaranteed salary. In order to incorporate my pro model designs into the new Morrow boards, I got together with Josh Dirksen and we created a line called the Truth Series.

With K2's production and Sanders Nye, a board designer who really knew his craft, the Truth boards became the best boards I'd ever ridden. They were lightweight but stiff enough to pop off jumps. While pre-K2 Morrow boards had been known to get soft with time, Truths retained their stiffness. What you picked out in the snowboard shop was what you'd get at the end of the winter.

We marketed the Truths as high-end aggressive freestyle boards you could ride all over the mountain, which paralleled what I was doing with my riding style at the time. I wanted to transfer my freestyle tricks to the parks and other places around the mountain. I could always ride in the pipe, but I was really concentrating on my freeriding and park riding.

But it was tough to shake my halfpipe image. As always, a contingent of photographers converged on Mount Hood during the summer. The magazines put out "hit lists" of their photo needs for the coming winter and, without fail, any time my name was mentioned, the word halfpipe went with it. "T.R.: pipe shots, any new spinny tricks he's pulling," was an item on a hit list I saw that summer. As the photographers worked their way through the lists, they'd ask me, "When are you gonna ride pipe?" I'd say, "Maybe tomorrow," and keep hitting jumps. The halfpipe had become like a bad dinner you're served at somebody else's house. You don't like it, and you try to eat as little as possible to avoid seeming rude, then you go home and chow down on something you really like. The pipe was liver and onions, and jumps were Twizzlers washed down with Coke.

By the end of the summer of 1999, I'd become comfortable with big airs and spins were starting to feel natural, but I still had some fear when it came to inverted tricks off straight jumps. I'd landed on my head a few times, had my wind knocked out, and I'm pretty sure I cracked a few ribs, although I never went to the doctor.

Like most tricks that get unveiled in movies, the frontside 540 corkscrew to fakie (from the *Ticket to Ride* video) was quickly adopted by a bunch of riders, and I started progressing into more tweaked-out versions, more spins, and stalling out the tricks while upside down. Producer Mike "Macdawg" McEntire came up to me at Hood and asked if I wanted to film with him that winter. The slopestyle scene was what all the kids wanted to watch, and he was known for filming only the most progressive technical freestyle riders.

"You want to film me on jumps or in the pipe?" I asked, certain I knew the answer.

"We'll film you in the pipe if you want," he said. "But I'd like to get you on jumps."

Hell yeah.

I headed into the winter of 1999/2000 with a whole new fire. I'd come into my own off the big kickers at Hood. I would turn thirty in December, but I was determined not to become the "old guy." I wanted younger kids to respect me for my gnarly riding. I didn't want them saying, "Check out T.R. He's super-smooth. He used to go so big when he was younger."

Unfortunately, I *was* the old guy. There weren't many, if any, freestyle pros in their thirties who were still competing with the twenty-and-under crowd. But I loved hanging with the younger kids, and I also wanted to kick their butts in competition, which told me I was far from being ready to retire.

Blowing Off Steam in Tokyo

I kept my ears open for word of the first resort openings of the season in Colorado. I was determined to make this the year I won a slopestyle event, and I had to start early. If I had bet the rest of my winter on my performance at the Triple Crown at Breckenridge in December 1999, I would have lost, big time.

The Triple Crown didn't have a slopestyle event, but it did have a big (scary) air that was putting people in ambulances left and right. The halfpipe was eating people up, too. I made the semi-finals in both events, but fell and didn't advance to either final. The highlight of the weekend was watching my protégé Josh Dirksen take home ten thousand dollars for winning first place in the big air.

I did everything humanly possible not to let my poor performance get me down. I still had the 1999 X Games to focus on, which would be held on the East Coast at Mount Snow, Vermont.

There's nothing like a nice shop tour in Tokyo to keep your mind off snowboarding. Now that Morrow was under K2 ownership, upper management wanted to send a good-will message to our Japanese distributors that everything was fine. So Billy Anderson, Tyler Lepore, Josh Dirksen, Erik Leines, and I went to Tokyo for a week that January to meet our distributor, Shigai, who had efficiently planned for us to visit ten shops in one day.

Whenever Billy and Josh got together, trouble wasn't far behind. In Tokyo, they reasoned everything would be much more interesting if we had a beer between every shop visit. There were Asahi vending machines located on every street corner, and we started getting pickled at eight in the morning.

By the seventh shop, we were signing autographs in our own made-up Japanese characters and having extended conversations with the locals in perfect drunkenese. By shop number ten, Shigai was herding us around like lost sheep, desperate to get some food in our systems before things turned ugly. He found us a sushi restaurant in the nick of time, and we ordered emergency pitchers of sake and proceeded to stuff ourselves as though we were advanced- to pro-level sushi eaters. I ate everything from puffer fish to sea urchin.

After the meal, we got together on the street outside for a group photo. Suddenly, Erik Leines ran out to an intersection with his digital camera, flung a car door open, and took a close-up photo of the terrified driver. He ran back to show us the photo, and we were rolling on the sidewalk, laughing our asses off at the driver's expression.

We worked our way down the busy sidewalk with Erik running out into the street at opportune moments to photo-jack cars. We started eyeing the rows and rows of bicycles parked on the sidewalk—hundreds of bicycles, no locks. We'd each picked one out for a little Tokyo joyride, when Shigai thwarted the plan. He begged us not to touch the bikes: "Very very bad. Take bike. Bad, bad trouble." So we agreed to leave the bikes alone.

But we were slap-happy drunk and had to do *something*. That's when Billy got this look on his face, said, "Watch this," and ran full-speed toward a row of six taxicabs parked bumper to bumper. He jumped onto the hood of the first, ran up and over it onto the second, then the third, all the way to the last taxi, denting hoods and roofs as he went. At the end, he jumped down to the street and looked back at us for our approval.

Josh Dirksen was a pipe digger at Hood before I introduced him to a whole new world.

At that exact moment, he was tackled by an irate taxi driver who threw him onto the hood of a car, wrenched his arms behind his back, and handcuffed him. The rest of us looked at one another dumbfounded, *Taxi drivers carry handcuffs?* Within seconds, cops swarmed the place with whistles blowing, and poor Shigai tried to diffuse the situation with, "Sorry, my American friend didn't mean to run over all six of your taxis." The rest of us distanced ourselves from the scene of the crime and watched Billy get thrown into the back of a police car. Shigai ran back to me, handed me his phone and car keys, said, "I'll call you," and jumped into the car with Billy.

There we were, four severely liquored Americans lost in Tokyo with only half a power bar showing on Shigai's cell phone. It took us an hour to locate the van but we sure as hell weren't driving anywhere. So we went into a Karaoke bar and listened to five inebriated sixty-year-old Japanese men sing Elvis's "Ruv me Tender."

After about fifteen seconds of this, Erik said, "Oh god, I don't feel so good." Tyler was looking a little green as well, and we thought it best to return to the van, where Josh and I sat in front and Erik and Tyler sat in back and projectile vomited out of opposite windows. Everybody was moaning, Shigai hadn't called, and I lost it.

"You guys, pull yourselves together!" I yelled. "Billy's in jail!"

"Whoa, man," Josh said. "Mellow out. Take a nap."

So I did. Five hours later, the phone rang. We told Shigai we were still in the van where he'd left it, and he came and got us. He looked totally defeated. The first words out of his mouth were, "Very bad situation. So bad. Billy in big city jail. Tokyo jail."

"When can we get him out?" we asked, and Shigai just hung his head like he was ready to cry.

"Don't know," he said.

Billy spent the night in jail. He'd been three sheets to the wind when he was brought in, but he woke up on the cell floor next to some guy yelling at him in Japanese and holding a bucket and sponge. He thought he was having a nightmare. Later that night, he had to scrub the cell floors and walls in exchange for a soggy bowl of rice with some raw fish on top. The head of Morrow's distribution company in Japan had to cancel his tradeshow schedule so he could go bail Billy out of jail for six thousand dollars.

The rest of the trip, Shigai kept us on a short leash.

Park (Lab) Rat

When I returned from Japan, the February X Games were just around the corner. Every day, I spent five hours in Breckenridge's park, perfecting a handful of tricks. I learned the switch version of the corkscrew 540, which was weird because I had to take off on my heels going backward. But since I landed going forward, I could really hang it out and have all my power and stability for landings. I loved the way that trick felt—just on the verge of being completely inverted.

I'd like to say I was merely focused when I got into park riding, but the truth is, I was obsessive. I wouldn't concentrate on one hit like I'd done when I learned tricks in the pipe; I didn't have time for that. Kids were getting too good too fast. I had to commit to a steeper learning curve, so I'd draw a line—an entire string of jumps and rails—and I wouldn't go home until I'd done it clean. In order for it to be clean, it had to flow. If I landed backward on one jump, I'd hit the next jump going backward. I didn't allow myself to flip the board around in between jumps. Doing that is like nails on a chalkboard for me.

Rails were my nemesis. I wasn't that good and for a while, they really intimidated me. But I forced myself to do them because I knew I needed them in order to do well in slopestyle contests. Eventually, they became fun, but not before I experienced a few good slams that knocked the butterflies out of me.

In February 2000, I showed up at Mount Snow, Vermont, for the fourth annual

My best weekend of riding ever—Winter X Games at Mount Snow, Vermont, 2000.

Winter X Games. I was one of the favorites for the halfpipe, which was funny because I hadn't been practicing in the pipe much. I'd entered a few halfpipe contests in December and January, running the same tricks I'd done at the Olympics two years before, and taken two second places at FIS Grand Prix events. However, nobody considered me a threat as I got ready to take my slopestyle run.

It started off with a half-Cab boardslide on a long rail; to a nose press on a picnic table; then I 50/50ed a mailbox. With the jibs out of the way, my confidence went to autopilot for the rest of the line: a backside 720 off a tiny jump; a McTwist off a crappy quarterpipe (which was more a halfpipe trick that a lot of slopestyle guys couldn't do on a quarterpipe); a frontside corkscrew 540 on a big kicker; a long hill with a big hip where I did an alley-oop backside 360, straight into another hip for a backside 180; then I rode backward down the rest of the run and did a fakie 720 off the last jump. I qualified with the highest score of the day, which surprised everybody, especially me. I repeated the same line for the finals and maintained the highest score until Kevin Jones knocked me out of first, but I didn't care. I'd come a long way since my days of missing the top ten in slopestyle events.

Going into the halfpipe event, I had the low-stress, I-don't-give-a-damn attitude, which is when I do my best. I won the gold and was named the "Athlete of the X Games." I was on top of the world. That was by far my best weekend of competitive snowboarding ever.

In addition, my old friend from the New England Cup, Jason Ford, took third in the Boarder X, ESPN's boardercross race/Chinese downhill. Shaun Palmer, who had been winning world championship downhill mountain biking events lately, continued to show the world that a snowboarder kid from Tahoe could compete on all sorts of stages, this time as a skier in a sort of skiing boardercross. It was good to see other old guys still competing and ruling.

As an added bonus, ESPN awarded me a brand-new orange Volkswagen GTI. Once I got it home, I was informed that I only had a two-year lease on the car, so I put snow tires on it and e-braked it all over town. We called it "The Pumpkin," and it was the designated "rental" that my visiting friends used to get around when they stayed at my house. You could see it from a mile away in a blizzard, usually spinning 360s.

At the Sims World Snowboarding Championships in Whistler over Easter weekend, I took fourth in the halfpipe, fifth in the slopestyle, and seventh in the big air event. I was pissed, but not hyperpissed—quite an improvement from years past. I liked being an overall contender instead of just the pipe kid, er, pipe geezer. Having people like Peter Line (a well-respected slopestyle rider who had been turning heads for several years) compliment my jump and rail riding was worth just as much as a top-three finish. Well, not quite, but that's what I told myself.

The Blindfolded McTwist-Off

If I had to document any one event as my greatest achievement, it would have to be the Todd Richards Blindfolded (blind drunk) McTwist-Off.

Officially, there was only one competitor (me) and one spectator/technical delegate/seeing-eye-dawg (Josh Dirksen). We were at an event sponsored by Jose Cuervo at Squaw Valley, and the margaritas were slipping down like Kool-Aid. We started talking trash, and I boasted that I had McTwists so wired I could do them blindfolded.

Here is my official warning: Kids, I do not condone, nor do I recommend, what I'm about to admit having done. It's very dangerous and *very* stupid. That said, I drank my sixth margarita, rode to the halfpipe, positioned myself on one wall with my board pointed toward what looked like a good spot, blindfolded myself by pulling my beanie over my eyes, and dropped in.

Josh's job was to guide me in on verbal radar: "Three, two, one, tranny, pop!" When I heard tranny, I knew to absorb the transition with my knees, and the pop meant I was at the top of the wall. From there, I would be on autopilot. The first try, Josh (who'd had an equal amount of margaritas) couldn't count right, and I plowed right into the wall. On the second one, I didn't even make it across the flat bottom.

The park wasn't crowded, but when kids saw what was going on, a small group of about six gathered to watch. After a dozen tries, my stomach was killing me from laughing so hard, and Josh could barely stand up. He was rolling around in the snow, having a good time and purposely miscounting so I'd plow into the wall.

Finally, we coordinated everything. He yelled "Pop!" and I threw back, actually McLanded, and rode back across the pipe, arms raised. Josh tackled me, saying, "You did it, man. You did it!" It was an emotional moment.

Josh and the rest of the Morrow team were like the brothers I never had, and stupid moments like these are what really make being a pro snowboarder the best job in the world. The camaraderie goes way beyond friendship. We become family.

_Winning *TWS*'s Rider's Poll award for Best Pipe Rider in 2001 was an honor, since my peers were the ones with the ballots.

THE THREE S's/
SURF, SKATE, SNOW

In September 2000, I bought a second home in Encinitas, California, within walking distance of a surf break called Swami's. Around the same time, my agent dropped off a script for a snowboarding movie being developed by Disney called *Out Cold*. Steve thought I should branch out with my career and try for a part.

So two weeks later, I was on my way to Hollywood. My old friend Palmer "Balls" Brown had moved to Los Angeles and started a skateboard/clothing company called Elwood, and Mark Gebhardt was there for a visit. When I showed up at his house, Balls said, "Oh yeah, all my friends are in town." This translated into, "Let's get sauced and watch Balls run around naked and pee his bed." Like many straight-edgers, Balls had retired his root-beer lifestyle and was making up for lost time.

I didn't get to sleep until four the next morning, five hours before my "reading." Geb was supposed to drive me, but his entire body (except for his middle finger) was suffering from alcohol paralysis. I was in bad shape myself, but a triple grande shocker at Buckies (Starbucks) got me to my audition on time. I'd never done anything like this before and had no idea what to expect.

I made it to the casting room, where I was supposed to read for the part of a character named Barry, which, come to find out, was a significant part. He was a young, wealthy, wheelchair-bound doctor with a beautiful girlfriend. I wouldn't be a snow-boarding extra or a snowboarder, period.

I was really nervous and hungover, which activated my sweating problem. All the poison of the night before poured out of my pores, and I walked around in a cloud of liquor sweat while serious actors practiced their lines. I was called into a brightly lit room where a lady said, "Hi, I'm blah, blah," pointed at a camera, and said, "Okay, go." I looked into the camera, read my lines, and got the hell out of there. It was hor-rible. As I walked through the studio back to my car, I felt like a complete idiot.

I stopped by Balls's place to pick up Geb and then drove the two hours back to

Encinitas. When I was almost home, my cell phone rang. It was Emmett Malloy, the film's co-director.

"You've got the part if you want it," he said. "It's yours. I can work out the details with Steve."

"Uh, great," I replied. "Yeah. Stoked. Thanks."

We hung up and it sunk in. I'd just agreed to play the role of an entirely different person—in a Hollywood movie. I'd never acted in my life, other than trying to act like an adult during interviews and other media situations. I hadn't even been brave enough to do plays in grammar school. The idea of being an actor was great; the scary thing was actually having to act.

My filming schedule for *Out Cold* was supposed to begin early in November and be done by Thanksgiving. The studio sent me a wheelchair and different versions of the constantly changing script. I left the wheelchair in the box and didn't even open a script until mid-October, when I was scheduled to take a few acting lessons so I wouldn't make a complete fool of myself.

After two intense one-on-one lessons with a Hollywood acting guru, I was certain I was wasting my time. Emmett had said, "Just be yourself," but the acting instructor said, "Forget about yourself. You need to be Barry." I'd walk into her studio and try to break the ice by cracking a joke, and she'd say, "Are you in character? That doesn't sound like Barry." Barry and I were over it. We caught a flight to Denver and never finished our lessons.

Lindsy and I met up in Breckenridge to spend some quality mellow time before my hectic winter schedule started up. When I saw her, I could tell immediately that something wasn't right. Lindsy is really in tune with her body and her mind, and she said she hadn't been feeling too well. The vibes she was having told her that she might be pregnant. There was an easy way to find out.

We went and bought a home pregnancy test, came back to the house, and boom! She *was* pregnant. Neither of us believed it, so we went and bought another one and sat down to read the results.

Bingo! Lindsy dropped to her knees in tears. Our fabulous, jet-set lifestyle flashed before our eyes as if we were two deer in headlights. Our self-centered existence was about to be turned upside down. For Lindsy, the thought of several months without snowboarding, surfing, and travel was a bit scary.

We'd been together for a while and had talked about our future together. But the main conclusion we'd reached in conversation had been exactly that—future/together. We hadn't really worked out any of the details yet.

My two cents worth of advice is that if you find somebody you are 100 percent compatible with, even on your shittiest days, hold on to him or her. As reality set in, Lindsy said, "I guess this was inevitable, just a little sooner than I had planned." It reminded her of a relevant saying: "If you want to make God laugh, tell him your plans!"

I called my mom to tell her the news. She loves Lindsy and was completely supportive. Lindsy, on the other hand, was embarrassed to call her parents. We wanted to get married, sure, and had even talked about it, but we didn't want it to seem like a shotgun wedding because of the pressures of society or anything like that. Lindsy was crying when she called her mom, but as she listened I saw her fear melt away into relief. She was smiling when she finally handed me the phone, and said, "It's my dad."

Lindsy's dad said to me in the coolest, most sincere way, "Look, this may never happen again. You two are about to partake on a journey that not everybody gets to experience. You have all the support in the world behind you."

The issue of marriage never even came up.

From the moment Lindsy and I looked into each other's eyes and said, "We're having a baby," I experienced a fairly wide range of emotions, running from *I'm gonna be a dad!* to *Oh god, I'm gonna be a dad?* Self-doubt was my biggest issue. *I can't even balance my checkbook,* I told myself, *or organize my closet or do my taxes. How can I possibly care for a child?*

I was thirty and Lindsy was twenty-five. She'd been working with her sister on a bathing suit company called TNA and had other career plans of her own, but she decided to step back and dive into the pregnancy with exercise, a good diet, holistic living, and everything else to insure a healthy child.

The coffee table snowboarding, skateboarding, and photography magazines were replaced with parenting magazines. I even picked up one of those Idiot Guides to being a father. Probably the weirdest thing was the timing of our new house in Encinitas. We'd bought it only the month before, and had even talked about it being the perfect place to raise kids. The ducks for domestic life were lining up for us.

By mid-November Lindsy was experiencing the classic expectant mother syndrome: She went temporarily insane.

This hormonal tidal wave crested when she skimmed through the *Out Cold* script and discovered that I was supposed to kiss the leading actress. I came back from surfing, found her with the script open to the make-out scene, and thought, *Oh shit.* I shut all the doors and windows just in the nick of time. There was a fair amount of incoherent yelling, screaming, and cursing aimed at me. This was followed by a momentary bout of crying. Then, as quickly as the eruption had begun, it ended. She told me she loved me and said, "Rub my feet."

Diplomatically speaking, women can't be held responsible for their actions while a bun is in the oven. As discreetly as possible, I hid the script and conveniently lost all the sharp knives and garden tools.

Meanwhile, Disney was pushing filming further and further back until my originally scheduled "finish" date became my new "start date." I called Steve at The Familie.

"The Vans Triple Crown is in December," I said. "If this movie interferes with my real career, I'm hitting the panic button."

Moneywise, the movie was worth way more, but I still hadn't taken first at a slopestyle or big air event. The Triple Crown at Brek gave me home-mountain advantage, not to mention the fact that dodging my kissing scene would make my life a whole lot easier at home. Bailing was a win-win situation.

In the nicest way possible, Steve told me, "Do not walk away from this movie deal." He'd done a lot to get me, a first-time actor, the audition to begin with. There aren't a lot of bridges heading into Hollywood, and you don't want to torch them before you cross your first one.

Thanksgiving, Eh?

My schedule began filling up for the 2000/2001 winter, and though Lindsy won't admit it, she must have looked at the number of days, including holidays, that I'd be on the road and realized that raising a child with a pro snowboarder as the father was essentially the same as being a single mom during the winter. Regardless of the challenges she'd face in the future, she was amazingly supportive of my career and competitive aspirations.

The make-out scene, however, was still an issue.

I landed in Vancouver, the "Canadian Hollywood," on Thanksgiving, and spent the day standing in line to get my Canadian work visa. I wasn't in the best mood because I was away from my family and Lindsy. I also hadn't discussed the make-out scene with the director, and I knew I was going to make a fool of myself the following morning. I didn't know anyone, my surroundings were unfamiliar, and I was basically a scared little kid. I sat on my bed, staring out the window, then ordered a room-service hamburger for Thanksgiving dinner.

I was really bummed, so I decided to treat myself to a nice massage, something I discovered a couple years before. I booked something called a "hot rock therapy massage" in the hotel's spa. I lay down on the table and within two minutes, a four-foot-tall Asian woman was standing on the table with her feet against my sides, pressing previously unseen red-hot rocks into my back. My eyes went wide and I gritted my teeth, thinking, *What did I sign up for?* She was an extremely aggressive masseuse, but after five minutes, I adapted to her Crouching Woman/Hidden Hot Rocks routine and it turned out to be one of the best massages of my life. If I could, I'd get one every single day. They are one of the reasons I'm still riding after all these years.

Back in my room, I pulled out the script and, motivated by pure terror, in one sitting memorized my lines—and everybody else's.

To give you an idea of the Oscar-caliber movie I was appearing in, here's the synopsis that Yahoo Movies ran:

> Snowboarding buddies Rick (Jason London), Luke (Zach Galifianakis), Anthony (Flex Anderson), and Pig Pen (Derek Hamilton) are living large on Alaska's Bull Mountain. Partying hard, looking for girls, and doing just about anything to have a good time is what life on Bull Mountain is all about. But when town founder Papa Muntz dies, his son Ted (Willie Garson) decides to sell the mountain to slick Colorado ski mogul John Majors (Lee Majors). Everyone is bummed by his plans to turn the boarding mountain into an espresso-and-tofu ski resort, and it's up to our heroes—along with Majors's beautiful, rebellious daughters Inga and Anna—to keep Bull Mountain yuppie free.

My first "actor's call" was at 5 A.M. at a sound stage, and the first person I saw when I entered the door was Playboy model Victoria Silvstedt, who was playing Inga. She almost knocked me over with her chest cannons. Emmett Malloy came out of nowhere and scooted me off to makeup and wardrobe.

My character, Doctor Barry, was Conservative Handsome Yuppie Guy in a Turtleneck. They gave me clothes straight out of L.L. Bean. I sat down in a chair, and a lady started cutting my hair without even asking what I wanted. Since I'd signed the Screen Actors Guild contract, Disney owned me and my brand-new mullet. I put on my outfit, stared in the mirror, and said, "Rad." It was a zillion times worse than the cowboy outfit at the Olympics.

It was a good thing I was there at five in the morning, seeing how I was done with wardrobe by ten and didn't have a damn thing to do until three but sweat. We'd been shuttled to a house that was rented out for a big party scene so I hung out in my own private "star" trailer that was parked outside on the street. But instead of a star on the door, there was a strip of duct tape with my name scribbled on it.

Everybody assumes making a Hollywood film is really glamorous and cool, but it seemed like a gigantic disorganized mess to me. Nobody appeared to know what they were doing, and neither did their assistants. I don't know how anything ever gets done.

Inside the house, lights and cameras were everywhere. I felt very behind the scenes, so that part was cool. The actors were nice, too—just normal people, eating bagels and drinking coffee. My first scene featured all the "snowboarders" sitting around the fireplace. Pig Pen was supposed to come in, throw his jacket into the fire, and say, "What are we gonna do now?" My first big Hollywood line was, "I can fly you guys to Anchorage if you want," or something like that.

After an hour of lagging, the director's seven assistants began chanting: "Quiet on the set." "Quiet on the set." "Quiet on the set." "Quiet on the set." "Very quiet on the set." "Very, very quiet on the set." "Very, very, very quiet on the set." And finally the director said, "Action!"

The camera rolled and within five minutes, I realized I was the only one who knew his fricking lines. They were seasoned actors, but I guess they figured they would learn their lines as they went along. They constantly asked the script supervisor, "What's my line again?" or, "Line!? I need my line here!" This stalled everything, so the assistant to the director asked the assistant to the assistant to the director for a bottled water with a lemon slice, and I realized that Hollywood is all about asking the assistant if it's okay to hurry up and wait.

As for me, my lines weren't a problem but my legs were. I was really nervous, and I kept forgetting I was paralyzed from the waist down. We'd be deep into the scene, and the director would yell, "Cut! Todd, your legs," and then I'd notice I was tapping my foot on the wheelchair. Caroline Dhavernas, who was playing Barry's fiancée Anna, was sitting on my lap during the scene, which was shot from like two hundred different angles, three hundred different times. Everything had to be exactly the same each time it's shot so it can be edited together.

Everybody was patient with me, but they also had fun giving me, the rookie, a hard time. They knew I was a pro snowboarder, not an actor, but still referred to me as the mullet guy in the wheelchair. "You're out of character, mullet boy."

My first day ended at 10 P.M. and people were saying to me, "See you on Monday." I was like, *Monday? We gotta get this thing done. I have a contest in less than two weeks. I have to practice!*

Actors, however, don't work on weekends. We were told to report promptly at 5 A.M. on Monday morning. I told the lady in charge of the lady in charge of actors that I was going to fly to California to go snowboarding at Mammoth Mountain. I told her I'd be back Monday morning.

"Uuuuuh, maybe not," she said. "Wait just one minute." Her assistant checked with the assistant to the assistant director, who checked with the assistant to the assistant's assistant. By 11 P.M., I got the okay to leave, which was a good thing because I'd already booked a flight.

I rode stress-free on Saturday and Sunday and flew back to Vancouver late Sunday night in time for the 5 A.M. actor's call on Monday, which amounted to sitting around, drinking coffee, and eating food all day long. Basically, I did nothing, which pissed me off because I could have been snowboarding. It was, however, a good time to tell the director that I wouldn't be able to kiss Caroline/Anna, which I was contractually obligated to do. Emmett was really approachable, and I took him aside and explained the situation:

"I was wondering if . . . Do you think there's any way that . . . Honestly . . . Well . . .

You know, my wife and I are having a baby. She's pregnant right now, and I don't think I can kiss Caroline for that scene."

Getting it out was difficult enough. Waiting for the response was torture. Emmett looked at me, added a nice, long dramatic pause, and finally said, "We can work around that. Don't worry about it."

Thank. God.

On Tuesday, a little plane flew us to a tiny airfield somewhere in the interior of British Columbia. My big scenes were coming up, and anticipation was killing me. I don't like to have too much time to think about stuff. I want it to be over with, but the plan for that day was to check into our hotel in a small town called Salmo. The town's claim to fame was that the Steve Martin movie *Roxanne* was filmed there. There was a Wal-Mart and a main street for entertainment, but I spent most of the day in the hotel room feeling bitter about the time I was wasting. The panic button was looming large.

I was invited downstairs to the hotel restaurant for dinner, where the actors were hanging out at a big table. I met Willie Garson, whom I recognized as the gay guy from *Sex and the City,* and A. J. Cook, who played one of the lead roles in The *Virgin Suicides.* I ordered a drink and was scanning the table when I saw him:

Holy shit, I thought. *It's the Six Million Dollar Man!*

I'd watched his show religiously and played with his action figure when I was a kid—the bionic arm with its removable computer chip, the bionic eye with a real magnifying lens. I wasn't starstruck by the other actors, but the *Six Million Dollar Man*? I was having dinner with Lee Majors? This was Hollywood. This was what I signed up for, right here.

The waitress took our orders, served second and third rounds, and everybody focused on Lee Majors as he told amazing stories from his heyday as *The Fall Guy,* being with Farrah Fawcett, the days when blow was really popular, and how so and so used to fire the devil's dandruff back like a "goddamn Hoover." He admitted that he loved fame and his fans. He said that whenever he went to Vegas, he'd have himself paged in the casino. "Lee Majors, please come to the VIP desk," and then he'd walk over and sign autographs.

Lee hadn't paid any attention to me to that point, but suddenly he looked over and said, "Who are you? You playing Barry? Aren't you some kind of skier? What are you?"

"Todd Richards," I replied. "I'm a snowboarder."

He nodded like it made sense and politely lied, "I've heard of you." He started giving all of us shit, and I tried giving it back.

"Is everything in Texas as big as they say it is?" I asked him.

"Well, sweetheart," he said, looking at one of the waitresses. "Why don't you tell him?"

We were amazed, not only by his candid stories, but also by the amount of booze he was consuming. He was the hit of the party without a doubt. As we staggered into the restaurant's adjacent bar and billiards room after dinner, I attempted a slow-motion bionic run, just like I used to do when I was a kid pretending to be the six-million-dollar runt. I don't know if Lee even noticed my tribute, but I was having a blast anyway.

We kept drinking while Lee played pool with some of the locals. The music from the jukebox was loud, and when I turned around from talking with Jason London, there Lee was, playing air guitar with his cue stick and belting out, "Who let the dogs out. Woof! Woof! Woof! Woof! Who let the dogs out! Woof. Woof. Woof. Woof." The Six Million Dollar Man had become "the bionic drunk."

That night made the entire movie-making experience for me. I woke up early the next morning, practiced my lines, and rolled around in my wheelchair. I tried to learn how to do wheelies and 180s, both of which proved too difficult and frustrating. My big scene was when Barry showed up in town to meet Anna. You'll have to see the movie to understand, but basically, the "snowboarders" were ready to kick Barry's ass until they saw he was in a wheelchair, and that made them feel bad. I had to drive up in a van and roll down a ramp onto the street, where Caroline was to run up and kiss me (but it only *looks* like we kiss). I was at the top of the ramp looking down, and it was snowy, icy, and scary steep, but the cameras were rolling and I had to drop in. So I did, and I immediately went into a wheelie, flipped the wheelchair over, and slid down on my back. After a few tries, I got the balance right and pulled it clean. Other scenes, including the ones with my big lines, like, "You're the Jacuzzi Cassanova," took hours and hours to film.

My last scene took place at the airport, where I had to take off in my plane (I was a surgeon *and* a pilot) and flip off Lee Majors as I flew over the town. In the movie, the plane is rocking back and forth in a snowstorm, but if you look closely, the snowflakes are falling straight down, not whipping past the windows. The plane never left the ground. It was rocked by some of the crew while the director yelled, "Look like you're flying! Hit some switches! Look out the window! Throw us the bird!"

When I was done, I checked with the assistant to the assistant who signs out actors, and she said, "Thank you, Mr. Richards. You've been released from the movie. All your scenes are completed." I flew to Calgary, from there caught a flight to Denver, and as the plane took off, I had the most peaceful, serene feeling—like I'd just taken the biggest dump of my life. Acting in that movie was one of the most stressful things ever, and it was a gigantic release to be done with it. Much later, I auditioned for *Charlie's Angels II,* but didn't get the part. They gave it to a professional surfer named Christian Fletcher because he's way more extreme. They wanted an action-sports-secret-agent bad guy, and I didn't fit the profile.

Various people asked me later, "Why didn't you ride in the movie?" And I had to remind them that I was in a wheelchair.

Hucking for Dollars

The Vans Triple Crown at Breckenridge in December 2000 didn't have a slopestyle event. Instead, there was a big air competition—basically a single huge jump judged on height, difficulty of trick, and smoothness of execution—and a halfpipe event.

Josh Dirksen stayed at my place before the event and blew me away. He was riding so smooth and going so big, he reminded me of that slow-motion Chris Roach style I'd wanted to emulate in the early nineties. It always helps to ride with people who are better than you. That weekend, I was just drafting behind Josh.

At the Vans big air event, Josh busted out a perfect strobe-light-slow backside 900 and stomped the landing like he was doing it in his sleep. Fifteen riders were in the finals with him, including myself, and I knew that jump would be hard to beat, but I tried anyway with a Cab 900. I stuck the landing and ended up taking second place, nine-tenths of a point behind Josh. Getting top two with a friend I respected was an honor. Getting beat by a kid I'd helped discover was an even bigger honor. Josh had become one of the most well-rounded and respected freestyle riders, and I was proud as hell.

After taking second in the big air, I got competitive and decided to enter the halfpipe event the following day. People were saying that the snowboarders who showed up for this event represented the best collection of pipe riders to compete against one another in years.

There was a changing of the guard going on in the halfpipe, and riders who had been considered the up-and-coming kids—Shaun White, J. J. Thomas, Danny Kass, and Xavier Hoffman—were schooling the old-timers, like Daniel Franck and me. The younger guard was ripping the pipe to shreds during practice.

I went into the competition secretly hoping I'd kick some ass, but I didn't have any expectations. Faking myself out to lower the pressure worked—I took first place. Lee Crane was there, reporting for *TransWorld SNOWboarding*'s web site, and that night he posted a story that read as follows:

> Once most snowboarders hit thirty, they start looking around for something else to do. Todd Richards just keeps getting better. He's won this event before, but this time the win seemed even sweeter. All weekend he kept trying to fake himself out of feeling the pressure that is always with him when he competes at his home mountain. First he said he was only going to do the big air to keep his mind off the pipe. Then he ended up taking second place. When it came time for his final run he connected with back-to-back 900s, first a backside and then a frontside, and kicked down the best halfpipe run in Breckenridge history.

Lee had been reporting and announcing contests longer than almost anybody else in the snowboarding media; on top of that he's a brutal critic. Reading these words from him elevated my spirits more than any other article I've ever read about my riding.

_Big inverted airs over gaps in perfectly shaped parks became my obsession once the slopestyle era kicked in.

OVERALL GUY/
PIPES, PARKS, AND RAILS

On February 1, 2001, I rolled into the X Games at Mount Snow, Vermont, saying, *No more of this second-place bullshit. I'm going to win the slopestyle.* The X Games had a great format—the best of three runs—and you could really hang it out there and push yourself. This low-pressure format was perfect for me, and after the first round I had the highest scoring run. After my second run I was still in first place, but in the final round Kevin Jones pulled out the 450, a really sketchy spin onto a boardslide landing on a rail. At the very top of his last run, Kevin nailed it, and just when I thought I was going to edge him out, he won, and I placed second.

When I saw the scores posted, my first thought was, *Redemption!* The halfpipe contest was the next day, and I knew I could take it, even though I hadn't been in a halfpipe since a Grand Prix event on January 8, where I took second behind Danny Kass. I was a little too cocky and thought I'd just roll up without practicing and take home another gold. I'd whooped most of these guys a month earlier and hadn't seen anything that could beat my back-to-back 900s.

I got spanked into thirteenth place. You'd think I'd have mastered my mind by this point, but I still let myself get out of hand emotionally. I was thinking, *Should I get pissed and see if that helps me kick ass in tomorrow's big air event, or should I be bummed and have to win in order to dig myself out of the hole?* I didn't really have a choice, because I was too pissed to be bummed. The anger worked out for me, and in the big air event, a fakie 900 put me on top with an 89.33 score that nobody could beat until the last rider came down. A kid named Jussi Oksanen edged me out with a 90.00.

I was cursed all over again.

I Want My Two Dollars

The month after the X Games, tremors started up at Morrow again. Greg Hughes, who had been with the company forever, was the brand and sales manager, and Rebecca Herath was the marketing manager. Together, they were pretty much the go-to people, so I expressed my concerns to them when one of my paychecks was a couple weeks late.

Rebecca told me she wasn't aware of anything drastic going on, but that she knew Morrow's sales weren't where K2 wanted them to be. That sounded like a hint if I ever heard one. In early April, K2 asked Greg and Rebecca to negotiate a new three- to four-year contract with me, which sounded like good job security—until I heard the amount. Their offer was roughly two-thirds lower than my current deal. I saw the writing on the wall and quit.

Three days later, Rebecca called me and said, "Morrow just folded. The entire team got cut. We have a half hour to empty our desks and vacate the offices." I was pissed at Morrow when Rebecca told me the news. I figured they must have known what was going on and kept it from the team. Now I suspect that Greg and Rebecca made me that crappy lowball offer as a warning to "get the hell out." Looking back, I have a feeling that K2 wanted to wrap me up in a long-term contract representing some crappy price-point (i.e., lower quality, lower price) brand, which could have been the kiss of death for my career.

In reality, Morrow didn't fold completely. K2 proceeded to sell the excess boards and turned Morrow into a price-point brand. The Truth boards Sanders Nye had designed with Josh and me started being produced in China and are now sold for around two hundred dollars retail, at least three hundred less than the original models. I won't comment on the current quality of the boards, but you can do the math and make your own judgment.

The biggest blow was that when I quit and everybody else was laid off, nobody at K2 seemed to give a damn. I didn't get a single phone call. Ten years of loyalty to Morrow, including two years of hard work for K2, didn't matter. I was just a piece of paper in an archived legal box. Hell, I even came up with the logo they use to this day!

This Space for Rent

Ending a ten-year relationship with a sponsor is like parting ways with a good friend. It doesn't matter what the reason is, you still can't help but reflect on your time together.

I was bitter for a while. Then bitterness faded ever so slightly to sadness, not for leaving Morrow behind, but for having to say good-bye to all my teammates with whom I'd shared so many memories. Even though teams weren't as tight as they'd been in the eighties and early nineties, we still spent a lot of time together. We traveled together, destroyed rental cars together, slept in shitty hotel rooms, smelled one another's gas, celebrated when one of us won, and shared the disappointment when one of us lost. It was a support group with bonds I hoped would last forever, but just like with high school friends, you eventually drift apart.

On top of the sentimental bullshit, I was going to be a dad, and I had lost my major source of income. I'd planned well, so it wasn't like we were hurting, but the well would eventually go dry if I didn't get my butt in gear and find a sponsor while I was still a marketable commodity.

I hadn't ridden any other boards in a decade. I called different companies—Burton, Lib Tech, Gnu, even my old sponsor Sims—and got everybody to send me their boards. Being able to ride those boards was a huge eye opener. It was amazing how differently they reacted on snow. Without any contractual responsibilities, I accepted an offer from *Stuff* magazine to do a board test, which made me really think about construction and board designs while riding everything from groomers and powder to bumps, kickers, and halfpipes.

Here's a Glam shot of Lindsy and me on the way to our wedding reception.

LOVE, AMERICAN STYLE/
DON'T CHOKE THE CHICKEN

Things started stacking up in spring and early summer of 2001. Still no sponsor; the ESPN Action Sports and Music Awards were set for April 7; Lindsy and I were getting married on April 12; April 25 was the Sims World Championships in Whistler; and the baby was due in June.

The ESPN Action Sports and Music Awards show was basically the Oscars and Grammys for action sports: Five men and five women were nominated by their peers. The talent level of the nominees was amazing, and many were athletes representing sports that for years had been overlooked: surfers Kelly Slater and Andy and Bruce Irons; skaters Tony Hawk and Bob Burnquist; snowboarders Tara Dakides and Shannon Dunn; BMX freestylers Matt Hoffman and Dave Mirra; motocrossers Jeremy McGrath and Ricky Carmichael; skiers Seth Morrison and Shane McConkey. Nominees for Male Snowboarder of the Year included Terje Haakonsen, Kevin Jones, Bjorn Leines, Peter Line, and me.

The athletes also got to vote for their favorite musical artists who had performed or been affiliated with the different sports over the years, including Black Sabbath, Metallica, Linkin Park, Jack Johnson, Eminem, and a boatload of other superstars.

I was in awe of the entire spectacle, and it gave Lindsy and I a chance to get dressed up and make believe we were celebrities. Kevin Jones, the slopestyle super-hero, took home Male Snowboarder of the Year, and I got the People's Choice Award.

At the ESPN gala that night when people came up to me for autographs, I remembered the girl who'd ripped me to shreds at the Vision Pro In The Snow after-party for introducing myself by my full name. People I didn't know or didn't recognize were standing there kind of staring at me, and I freaked out because I wasn't sure if I should say, "Hi, I'm Todd," or "Hi, I'm Todd Richards." I worried that if I just said "Todd," they'd think, *Oh, you think you're so famous, you can just say your first name and I'm supposed to know who you are?* Or if I said "Todd Richards," it would be the Vision Pro girl all over again. More than a decade later, I'm still haunted by that experience.

I wear goggles on the mountain and therefore 99.9999 percent of the world doesn't recognize me on the street the way they would somebody like Tony Hawk. But if you do recognize me and want to come over and say "What's up," don't take it the wrong way if I don't introduce myself by name. One on one, my social skills sometimes short-circuit.

The morning after the awards, Lindsy and I flew to Maui and got married in a private ceremony with only a pastor and photographer. Lindsy was seven months pregnant, so it was impossible for her to lie down on a surfboard and paddle out in Honalua Bay, where we had decided to say our vows. Instead, she sat on the twelve-foot-long board, and I walked her out. Once we were in deeper water, I got on the board and sat facing her with the photographer and the pastor wading alongside us. She was wearing a white bikini, I had on black board shorts from Quiksilver (my newest sponsor), and we both had fresh flower leis around our necks. I was so nervous I thought I was going to capsize the massive board, which under normal circumstances would have been as stable as a dock.

As the sun began to set, we stared into each other's eyes and both lost it as we said the vows that had made the journey to sea in a Ziploc bag. It was the most magical moment I'd ever experienced, despite the two severely sunburned snorkelers who surfaced to watch the ceremony.

Back on shore, we walked through the sand and kept saying, "We're married." Now, if you're still reading and haven't stuck your finger down your throat at all this cheesy, romantic stuff, you will when I tell you what happened next.

We were looking out across the bay and, I swear to god, two huge whales breached side-by-side and crashed back into the ocean. I have to admit, it was pretty powerful, not to mention a good omen for the rest of our lives.

After our wedding and a weeklong honeymoon in Maui, I kissed my wife goodbye and flew to Vancouver for the 2001 Sims World Snowboarding Championships at Whistler. There isn't really a classified section in the newspaper for pro snowboarders, but word had gotten around that I still didn't have a board sponsor. In order to make things perfectly clear, I wrote "This Space For Rent" on the white base of a Gnu prototype I planned to ride in the contest.

I felt great going into this event. I was happy to be married, excited—albeit a little nervous—about becoming a dad, and now, more than ever, I really appreciated my job. Of course, I was also thinking, *It sure would be fricking great if I could win this slopestyle event.*

The planets must have been aligned just right because although the weather started out pretty crappy, in the afternoon, the sun came out and recharged my batteries. And I knew I'd need every bit of juice to pull this one out. Jussi Oksanen was in first place going into the finals, Travis Parker was spinning fierce nines, and Kevin Jones was on fire with the rails, but I edged them out and finally won my first slopestyle event. It was about time.

I couldn't pull a repeat in the pipe, but I did take third, which, when combined with the slopestyle win, amounted to a thirty-five thousand dollar paycheck that more than covered our wedding, honeymoon, and the assorted baby paraphernalia piling up around our house in Encinitas.

What Are You, Psychic?

Back home in the land of palm trees and unassembled baby strollers, I contemplated my options for board sponsors. Sims remained a strong brand, but word on the street was that it faced more organizational problems. My friend Chris Owen had parted ways with Morrow before the K2 occupation, and since he had become the team manager for Quiksilver and Mervin Manufacturing. There was no bad blood between us regarding the half-million-dollar Morrow rip-off, and I was busy greasing him up with point-blank requests like, "Dude, get me on Mervin. Work your magic. Help a brother out." I was relentless, but it was the wrong time of year to be hunting for sponsors, unless, of course, your name is Steve Astephen, agent extraordinaire.

"Todd," he said, "I've got a couple of people on line, tell me what you think." He ran down a list that included Bert LaMar's new start-up company called Elevation, Sims, and Rossignol.

"Rossignol?" I responded. "No way. No way in a million years."

I had always clowned Rossignol as a ski company, but in reality they'd been in the snowboarding game longer than most of the other companies. It wasn't that the company wasn't respectable, it was just . . . Rossignol.

That night, I tossed and turned, stared at the ceiling, and tried to dream about what to do, which was something Lindsy recommended I try. But I didn't dream about anything and only stressed myself out. Lindsy was super-pregnant, and I wanted to get this sorted out so we could relax for a few months after the baby was born. Despite all the jokes I'd made about Rossignol in the past, I couldn't think of a legitimate reason why I shouldn't ride for the company. Andrew Crawford, the epitome of snowboarding and eighties rock culture, rode for Rossi as did Dionne Delesalle and Jeremy Jones, a sick big-mountain freerider. But all my friends said, "Dude, don't ride for Rossi." I was too conflicted and needed help.

Enter Lindsy's astrologer, David Pond, whom I'd always clowned as well. Lately, though, my skepticism was fading a little because he'd called out gnarly stuff. The guy was so on point he scared me, but not in a bad way. So, why not? I let him do my charts, and he zeroed right in on my sponsorship conflict, the reasons behind it, and the reasons behind the reasons. After we were through, I signed on with Rossignol without even riding its boards. I'd never felt more confident about a business decision in my life, and the deal, which included a pro model and royalties, was good.

Rossignol wanted shots of me for the following year's advertisements and press releases. So in May I headed to Mount Hood Meadows to film a part for a Forum video called *True Life*. I asked Dane Hjort and Christine McConnel, Rossignol's brand and marketing dynamic duo, to send the entire quiver of freestyle and freeride boards to my hotel, and when I arrived a dozen boards were scattered around the room. I flexed a few, set them up against the wall to check their sidecuts, and finally drew straws to pick a winner. I mounted some bindings and went up on the mountain hoping I'd like the board since I had to perform for the camera, not to mention the fact that I'd signed a multiyear contract with the company. On top of that, I'd picked a wood-core board, a type I hadn't ridden consistently since the days on my Kidwell board from Sims.

Within two minutes on the board, I knew I'd made the right decision. It was snappy, fun, and alive—the best board I'd ever ridden. I'm not getting paid to say that; it's the truth. I thought, *Holy shit, this is what I've been missing?* From that day forward I was pumped on Rossi.

I had to rush to get graphics for my pro model, so *Snowboarder Magazine* ran a contest on their website. Some guy named Jeremy Lanningham apparently knew my history and submitted a picture of a cat in a kiddy pool (a "Wet Cat" reference), and I loved it. (Jeremy won and eventually became an art director at *TransWorld*.) Rossi combined the graphics with some of my board specs and a few months later, I had a pro model on the shelves.

I had plenty of other ideas about customizing Rossi boards. Rossignol's logo is a rooster, and I thought it would be funny to show the Rossi rooster getting strangled, kind of a choke-your-chicken reference. But I didn't know how that would go over with the Rossi people, so I kept it to myself. Rossi's employees are super-loyal to their company, which makes sense considering that it is one of the most successful companies in the history of skiing. In fact, when I signed on, I received a call from a guy at the parent company in France, a sort of welcome-to-the-team pep talk. The guy had a heavy accent, and at the end of our conversation, he said, "Todd, you understand what a Rossignol is now, what it is to be a Rossignol? Rossignol is to sing when you have a great voice. It is opera."

Great, good to know, thanks, I thought. The guy was funny, but I respected his

My Rossignol "Bat Board" graphics.

passion, which was something that had been missing at Morrow the last couple of years. I just hoped my irreverent attitude wouldn't get me fired. I don't think the guys at corporate headquarters would have been too pleased if they knew that I was going around telling my friends, "I'm riding the cock."

The Womb Raider

After endless hours of research and influence from pro skater Danny Way's wife, Kari, Lindsy decided she wanted to have a home birth. The idea terrified me; I thought she'd totally lost her marbles this time. She made me do my homework on the subject and I soon learned that this was the only way to go. Plus, if anyone could pull off something so gnarly, Lindsy could. As her due date approached, I got more and more nervous, and my surf sessions got shorter and shorter because I didn't want to be

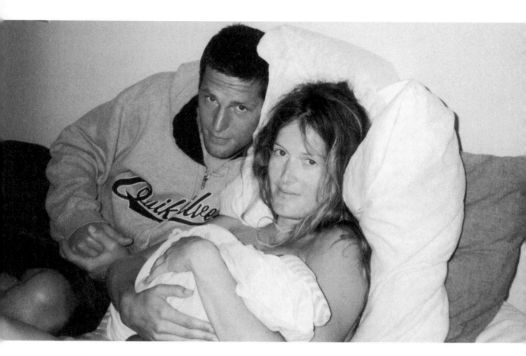

At home in Encinitas with Super-Mom, moments after Cam's birth.

away from my cell phone for more than a few minutes. But her June twelfth due date came and went, and the baby was very happy just where he/she was.

On June 16, Lindsy and I went to see *Tomb Raider*. It was so horribly bad, it induced birth. Unbeknownst to me, Lindsy began having contractions on the way home from the movie, which we will forever call "Womb Raider." She didn't tell me about the contractions because they weren't urgent yet, and she knew I wouldn't sleep if I was aware of what was going on. She wanted me rested up for the big day. At five the next morning, she woke me up and told me to call Catherine, the midwife.

"You serious?" I said. She was, and Catherine rushed over as I called our parents to tell them, "Game on!"

Lindsy had been prepared to take the no-drugs, nothing-but-breathing-and-warm-water approach. The baby was hung up in a weird position, though, and after six hours of intense labor, we were on the verge of going to the hospital. Catherine was playing catcher, and I was behind Lindsy. The adrenaline was flowing. I'd tense up whenever Lindsy pushed hard—I thought her head would explode. It was humanity in the raw. Finally, the baby moved, and then there was a split second between "I'm an expecting father" and—kapow!—"I'm a dad."

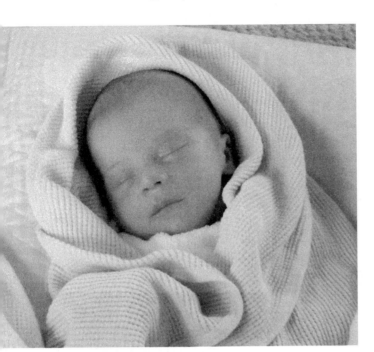

Cam, one day after he entered the world.

Everything changed right there. Up until then, I lived like it was part of my job description to not grow up. But the moment our son, Camden Thorne Richards, was born, I transformed from a thirty-two-year-old kid into an adult.

The rest of the summer was about diapers and sleep deprivation, for Lindsy especially. Cam wasn't a very good sleeper, and it wasn't the easiest time in our lives. It wasn't like we could just put Cam in the closet when we were done playing with him. A massive tectonic shift in priorities had occurred, and as a result there were a few earthquakes in the Richards household. I could see why my mom and dad had decided to stop after one child.

One day, when I was changing a particularly odiferous diaper, I got a phone call. A reporter from a men's lifestyle magazine had tracked down my home number and wanted to know if I had a few minutes to answer some questions. I was holding the phone to my ear with a shoulder, dirty diaper in one hand and diaper rash cream in the other, but the guy went ahead without waiting for my response.

"So, you're a favorite for the 2002 Olympic team," he said. "What are your chances for a gold medal this time around?"

The nightmare had begun—again.

_A powder slash is timeless, and helps
remind me why I'm a snowboarder.

BOARD OF THE RINGS/
THE SEQUEL

As if being an action figure wasn't rad enough, *Out Cold* premiered on November 21, 2001. We walked the red carpet, wading through crowds, Lindsy wearing leopard-skin pants, me with blue-tinted Euro shades and a little stubble on my face for that rough Hollywood look. We'd geared Cam up in Quiksilver and dyed his hair purple. The paparazzi were all over us. The movie grossed $400 million the first weekend, killing *ET* and *Jurassic Park*'s opening night ticket sales, and I bought an Audi dealership with my backend royalty payments. Then I woke up.

The reviews were okay, the ticket sales were okay, and the premiere was fun. I went on Thanksgiving night with my wife and her sisters and kept my head down. Most of the critics were nice and realized it was just a fun movie for teenage boys; others ripped it to shreds. The coolest part was seeing a movie in a whole new light and realizing how much hard work goes into the most mundane scenes. I'll never watch a movie the same way again, and if I ever do another movie, I want to be running around shooting a gun and spouting off Arnold one-liners like, "Stick around" or, "He had to split." Now that's Hollywood.

Under Pressure

If it isn't already obvious, I'll spell it out: I hadn't concentrated on the halfpipe since the 1998 Olympics. I could still roll into a halfpipe contest and win because I had my two 900s and various other money moves that were still beating most riders. For a while I felt like I could reclaim the top-three range with minimal practice. But that was before I watched Danny Kass win the 2001 X Games—Danny going ballistic in the pipe, and me seeing the results of laziness: I wasn't top-three material anymore.

Just after Thanksgiving 2001, I said good-bye to Lindsy and five-month-old Cam so I could temporarily move to Mammoth and regain my focus. J. J Thomas came with me to start practicing for the first two of five Grand Prix Olympic qualifiers.

The Mammoth park was really fun, and that's what I rode. I figured I'd hop into the halfpipe a few days before the event and qualify, no problem. But I had another thing coming. I could probably place some blame on the prototype Rossi board I was riding, but that would just be an excuse. If I'd ridden the pipe and not the park for the two weeks leading up to the event, I would have figured out in time that the board was too soft and had another one shipped to me.

J. J. and I rode together a lot, so it was somewhat comforting to see him sucking balls too. After we both got beat at the Grand Prix, we said, "Man, we better get on our shit." While everybody else was going to party after the event, J. J. and I hiked the pipe. Mammoth employees were pulling banners off the sides, so we dodged them and rode until it was pitch-dark out. We put our noses to the grindstone like Ross Powers, Tommy Czeschin, and all the other riders taking the Olympics seriously had been doing. Danny Kass was just plain scary: He was so relaxed, he looked like he was asleep at the wheel the entire way to his first-place finishes.

After riding the Mammoth pipe for another day, we took off to Breckenridge for the Vans Triple Crown, which had become sort of a tradition for me. I needed to get the slopestyle event out of my system so I could concentrate on the halfpipe for the Olympics.

Our practice in the Mammoth park paid off: I placed first and J. J. scooped up a third behind Travis Rice in the Triple Crown's first-ever slopestyle event. I felt like I had my feet back underneath me for the next Grand Prix.

Immediately following the awards ceremony, J. J., Erik Leines, and I went to practice on the frozen tundra–style Brek pipe. I didn't even feel like entering the Triple Crown halfpipe, which should have told me something right there. I just went through the motions of doing my tricks over and over again and thought about all the cool things that would happen at the Olympics this time around.

I wanted to go for the wrong reason. I only saw the gold medal at the end of the tunnel, but I skipped all the work it would take to land it. I had a nice long talk with my dad and, in my own way, prayed that I'd find the fire I needed to compete. I called Lindsy every night to keep tabs on all the things Cam was doing while I was away, and I did my best to focus. I knew I could beat these people. I just had to focus.

Rossi sent me a stiffer board, and I slowly got my halfpipe tricks back. All of a sudden it was Christmas, our first as a family. Back home in Encinitas, Lindsy had been run ragged by our little insomniac. My mood didn't help matters much, although we both knew it was all worthwhile. When it was time to leave, I could see the fatigue and stress in Lindsy's eyes. It killed me to get on a plane and go snowboarding.

My happy little family.

I returned to Brek for more practice, and then went on to Mount Bachelor, Oregon, two days before the third Grand Prix, scheduled for January 6. Waiting for me was the best fricking halfpipe I'd ever ridden. It was hazy and foggy out, but the snow was ego-soft and I could do whatever I wanted.

The day of the qualifier rolled around, and I won it. I'd gotten my shit back and was ready for the finals. First run was the gnarliest I'd ever done in my life, the most difficult, technically sophisticated string of combo tricks I'd ever pulled, and they were all clean: a big backside air, big frontside air, backside 900, frontside corkscrew 720, Cab 720, frontside 900, and finally a McTwist. The crowd went nuts.

Unfortunately, the FIS judging criteria doesn't reward you for spinning that much. I'd only done two (simple) straight airs, and I was supposed to do at least three. The scores came up horribly low, and the crowd moaned with me. I was steaming. *I just had one of the best runs of my life, and it's not good enough?*

A contest announcer ran up to me and shoved a wireless microphone in my face. "Todd, you were spinning all over the place," he said. "The score they just gave you, what do you have to say about it?"

"Look," I responded, "if the FIS wants to promote nonprogression with this type of judging, great. They are just stunting our sport." I was as bitter as I'd ever been. My run was way better than my winning qualifying run. If I had been smart, I could have done a basic method instead of a McTwist on my last hit, and won.

On my second run, I decided to play the game. I dropped in and did a big backside air and a frontside air. Then, on the backside nine, I pulled out too much and landed flat, thus canceling my chances of qualifying for the Olympic team at that event.

I was so pissed, I hiked straight back up and some spectators helped me up the pipe wall. I stood there on the deck, stared at the judges, and thought, *Fuck this! They don't reward me for my progression? I'm going to show these people I am on it.* So I tucked the rest of the pipe and—boom!—pulled a huge backside 1080 near the bottom. It meant nothing for my run, but it felt good.

I got fourth place behind Ross Powers, Andy Finch, and Tommy Czeschin, in that order. The Bachelor employees began taking down banners and trying to close the pipe, but I wanted to ride. I had to get rid of the negative energy eating me up inside, and I kept telling the employees, "Leave it open!" A crowd was hanging around, as were some of the riders, and I was determined to pull off a backside 1260. Fueled by anger, I hiked the pipe three times and on the third try, stuck the 1260. This confirmed what I already knew: I was on it. My run had been as good as, or better than, any of the riders there that day. The Fédération Internationale de Suck didn't see it that way. If it had been the Triple Crown or the U.S. Open, I would have won.

In order to make the Olympic team, I had to win one of the next two Grand Prix events, both in Breckenridge. First though, I had to cool off. I had time to fly back to San Diego, drive home to Encinitas for an afternoon, play with Cam, and sort of have dinner with Lindsy before catching a plane to Denver.

During practice before the January 10 event, the Olympic team coach, Peter Foley, came up to me, put his hand on my shoulder, and said, "Todd, that was an insane run at Mount Bachelor. You know it. I know it. Everybody knows it. But you've got to play by their rules."

I thanked Pete, but unfortunately, my fundamental theory about Olympic sports was in direct conflict with the FIS rules. I'd always been taught that the Olympics were all about putting everything on the line, pushing your limits, and showing the world the best your sport has to offer. I thought the Olympics would be a venue where the best athletes did their best tricks in the best run they could possibly put together. FIS judging makes that impossible by setting up parameters that, in the end, hold the competitors back. These parameters yield "contest runs" that don't promote creativity or experimentation; they merely compel the athletes to do the same runs over and over again.

Well, at Mount Bachelor I'd done the best run of my life and it wasn't good enough for the FIS. That made it hard both to concentrate and believe in myself. I didn't *want* to play by their unimaginative rules. I was tempted to do the same run again just to spite the judges, but I knew that would only be argumentative and bitter. I had to get my head screwed on straight because the Olympic hype machine was once again building up steam. My sponsors were checking in after practice days, asking how I'd ridden and promising that I would get giant bonuses if I medaled at the Olympics. And magazines were once again calling me out as a favorite to medal. The carrots were dangling.

On the day of the fourth Grand Prix, a cold wind was blowing up the mountain and it was gray and snowy. Not a good day for me to get stoked on. The pipe was really big, really icy, and really scary. I wanted to do a 1080 but on my first run, I decked out on a backside 900—the same trick I'd blown in Bachelor—and gave myself a painful hipper. The same thing happened on my second run because I chicken-shitted it. I had convinced myself I couldn't do my money trick, the backside 900 I'd been doing in my sleep for years.

I had one last chance to make the Olympic team, and my mind was repeating the phrase, *I need to win the next one. I have to win the next one, because if I win it, I'm going to the Olympics.*

Ross Powers and Tommy Czeschin had locked up their spots on the Olympic team, and the final 2002 Grand Prix would determine who would take the remaining two places. The maybes included Danny Kass, J. J. Thomas, Shaun White, Keir Dillon, Luke Wynen, Andy Finch, and myself.

January 13 was quite possibly the worst weather day in Colorado history. That morning, it was snowing sideways, the wind was howling, and the pipe was in horrible shape. It looked like somebody had cut it with a jackhammer. Driven by Nagano flashbacks, I tried to rally everybody to boycott the event until the pipe was fixed.

"There's a lot on the line," I told them. "We should have a great pipe." The top riders agreed, but then people got paranoid. Everybody started thinking, *What if so and so rides anyway and dicks us? Then we're screwed.* The alliance crumbled under that doubt, and I psyched myself out before I dropped in. I hesitated on my 900 and smashed my black-and-blue hip for a second time.

And that was that.

I played it off like, "No big deal, the X Games are next week," but I was lying. J. J. won the event, and he and Danny Kass made the team.

Cam's First X Games

The X Games were the following weekend in Aspen, and Lindsy and I brought Camden along. It was his first plane flight, his first time in Colorado, and the first time he'd

Cam is completely comfortable in front of the camera.
We call this one: "Cam in Chair with Teeth."

seen snow. Luckily, he slept through the part when Daddy almost killed himself in the fricking halfpipe.

In practice, I once again succumbed to the 900 mind game. I went a little too big, decked out, bounced to the bottom, hit my head, caught my weight on my hand, and broke my wrist. But since nobody in a white coat was standing by to tell me my wrist was broken, in my mind it wasn't. This was a game I'd played for years. I called it "Don't Go to the Doctor, Because He Won't Let You Go Snowboarding."

I really wanted to compete in the slopestyle the next day, so I pulled out of the halfpipe competition and popped a thousand milligrams of ibuprofen. I took third place in slopestyle, which wasn't so bad considering my wrist was the size of my forearm. J. J. won the halfpipe event the day before and had some momentum. He and I knew each other well and had ridden a lot together in the past, plus he was my teammate at Oakley. So I thought this was a good time for me to step in and help him keep the ball rolling. We went back to Breckenridge after the X Games, and I rode with him as much as possible. I tried to keep him relaxed and downplayed the whole Olympics thing so he wouldn't psych himself out.

The Show Must Go On

The second Vans Triple Crown event was held at Snow Summit in Southern California on February 10, 2002—the same day as the women's Olympic halfpipe finals in Salt Lake City, Utah. I was trying to keep my mind off of the Olympics, but at the same time I kept calling Gus Buckner at Oakley to see how J. J. was holding up the day before the men's event. I took first place in the Vans slopestyle event, but it didn't feel the same without J. J. and the rest of those guys. Even though I'd just won a big event, I felt pretty isolated and kind of like a loser. All I had to do was just sign up at the next Triple Crown, and I'd have enough points to drive away with a new Chevy truck.

I drove the two-plus hours home to Encinitas that night and found out on the way that Kelly Clark had won the gold medal in the women's halfpipe. I was stoked for her and was glad there was an American on the winner's podium. As I was on the way to Snow Summit to do some filming the next morning, Gus gave me play-by-plays on the men's halfpipe qualifier runs. Through my cell phone, I could hear the crowd in the background, and it sounded huge. My heart was pounding.

The entire men's American halfpipe team made the Olympic finals.

During the finals, I was supposed to be hitting jumps for a cinematographer, but every ten feet, I was either answering Gus's frequent calls or calling him myself. I should have known that trying to stay away from it all wouldn't work; the whole thing was too big a part of me.

I was sitting there on the side of a Snow Summit run, the cell phone glued to my ear, when Gus yelled out, "Holy shit, they swept it! Ross, Danny, and J. J. swept it! All Americans, gold, silver, bronze! Holy shit!" The roar of the crowd was like a waterfall in the background—and then it hit me. Instant depression. I wanted to be there alongside them so badly; I wanted to be there on that podium. I felt like I'd swallowed a brick.

I called J. J.'s cell phone, thinking I'd leave him a congratulatory message, but to my surprise, he picked up. His voice was electric with excitement.

"I'm getting ready to walk into the medal ceremony," he said. "I can't believe it! I just pulled that run out of my ass!"

"Well, go get it," I said. "Congratulations."

I couldn't even fake being punk-rock and acting like I didn't care. I did care, more than I had realized until that moment. It was a sad and lonely drive to Encinitas. The world felt silent and black, and I relived that run at Bachelor, torturing myself by saying, "It's a simple process, Todd. You just needed to do one more straight air."

The next day, I tried to put on a happy face, play with Cam, and do all the things you're supposed to do if you're a good father and a good husband. After a while, I couldn't take it. I put in the video of the Olympics Lindsy had made for me and watched the entire event. I didn't say a word, but Lindsy knew I was in pain. I was stoked for the guys (they were the first Americans to sweep an event since men's figure skating in 1965) and I was pissed, too. The pipe was perfect, the snow soft, the day sunny, the crowd huge—the kind of conditions I win in. I knew I could have taken it.

I was worthless and feeling sorry for myself. I added four years to my age and realized I'd be ancient at the next Olympics. At thirty-two, I was already ten years older than the oldest guy on the Olympic snowboarding team. Then I thought, *Well, there won't be any pressure, that's for sure. Four more years . . .*

And I left the book open.

Back on the home front, for months Lindsy had been shouldering all the responsibilities of our household, our son, and our happiness, and all I wanted to do was go surf, skate, and snowboard. *What a selfish bastard I am,* I thought. *I've been on the road for months, and I want to go snowboarding?* I had no right to do anything but stay home and be with my family, but Lindsy sat me down and told me, "You have to go snowboarding." I promised to make it up to her in the summer.

Time Heals All Wounds

Riding alone is always good therapy, and being back in Breckenridge was good for me. Lindsy and I talked on the phone constantly, and I began riding really well. I learned some new tricks in the park and realized the whole world didn't think I sucked. Snowboarding became fun again, and my competitive drive came back from the dead.

I decided that a good capper to the season would be the twentieth U.S. Open. The event was always fun, and it would give me a chance to see my mom on the Cape. But deep down, I had another reason: redemption. I didn't want to go into the summer without proving myself in the pipe, and—what the hell?—I might as well win the slopestyle, too.

A few days later, I headed to Stratton to check out the conditions for the U.S. Open, which was scheduled for mid-March. The East Coast had experienced some weird temperature fluctuations around that time, which meant there was plenty of glacial ice on the mountain. With this in mind, I took a break from practicing for the slopestyle event to ride over to the pipe and have a look. I stopped on the deck, then rolled in the backside wall to feel the tranny. I'd planned to pop out on the frontside wall, but the deck was solid ice and my edge slipped out from under me. I fell backward fifteen feet to the bottom of the pipe, landed right on my hip, and blew it out. I rolled around in pain, which popped it back into place but at the same time gave me a gigantic hematoma, a Jell-O pocket of blood and fluids under the skin. I didn't need anybody in a white coat to tell me what this meant: "No U.S. Open this year."

I flew out of Burlington on Wednesday, exactly one day after my arrival.

Revival of the Jaded

Back home, I took turns playing with Cam and my jiggly hematoma. Without my usual physical outlets, life wasn't a bowl full of cherries, and I was pretty depressed. At the end of March, however, Bob McKnight of Quiksilver called to tell me they were in need of my services.

Our mission was to go and ride powder for four days in British Columbia. It wasn't a photo shoot, nor was it a research and development meeting. It was simply one big "Thank You" from Quik to its riders. Luckily, my injury wouldn't prevent me from riding soft powder.

I took a bus from Vancouver to Whistler, where I got picked up and flown by helicopter across the amazing Coast Mountains to a private lodge on a lake in the middle of snowboarding heaven. The weather was perfect and the snowpack was solid, which meant an avalanche was unlikely. Nevertheless, our guides insisted on giving us a quick refresher course on the use of avalanche beacons and helicopter safety, after which we piled into the helicopter and suddenly found ourselves on the top of a mountain with a huge, untracked bowl below us.

The guide did a few slope tests for snow stability, then pointed down the mountain a couple miles away and said, "I'll see you down there." I dropped in and couldn't stop hooting as I made huge turns in deep powder the whole way down. When we got to the bottom, we found another helicopter waiting to take us to another mountain. The first one, tracked up by all of six runs, was considered "done."

I had forgotten what it was like to not ride in a park or pipe. I'd done several powder runs for photographers and filmmakers, but they weren't much fun because I was either hiking a kicker all day or milking a run and stopping every thirty or forty yards. At resorts, I went straight to the park, which was an improvement from going straight to the pipe, but I was still a snob. If the jumps weren't groomed perfectly, I couldn't be bothered. My goal was usually to get my damn board off the ground. Carving? Powder? Whatever. I had seriously lost touch with riding the mountain.

At the end of each run in British Columbia, I'd look back up at our tracks and say, "Oh. My. God." That day rejuvenated my stoke, especially the last run on one of those edge-of-the-world slopes, so steep you can't even see over the edge until you're two or three turns into it. As we prepared to drop in, the guide told us about a crevasse at the bottom, described what we'd see once we got going, and explained where to go to avoid slough (the snow that slides down with you on a steep slope). I stood at the top shitting my pants while listening to all this. Then he dropped in first to cut the slope and gave us the signal to go. After my third turn on the steepest run of my life, it was all shits, giggles, and bottomless powder.

In fact, it was probably the most fun I'd ever had on a snowboard, and my board never even left the ground.

It revved me up to complete my first instructional video, *Todd Richards' Trick Tips, Vol. I,* a project that was being produced by 900 Entertainment and was scheduled to be filmed at Squaw Valley in April 2002. I recruited Billy Anderson to help me out, and we got in front of the cameras to teach park and pipe basics, such as picking lines and pulling some basic tricks, as well as slope etiquette and safety, including "how to fall." We had to show what not to do, which included scary things like leaning back on a railslide or catching a toe edge in the flat bottom of a pipe. Basically, we were stunt men who sacrificed our bodies to show kids how not to kill themselves on a snowboard. Since it was my video, I made Billy do most of the painful stunts while I announced the play-by-play on a microphone.

It ended up being a lot of fun (for me, anyway), and it got me excited about doing a more advanced version the following season.

Diapers and a Dope Summer

The summer of 2002 flew by thanks to a blissful routine that went like this: wake up early with Cam, watch the news and eat breakfast, put him in his three-wheel, all-terrain stroller, and walk down toward the Cardiff reefs to check the waves. Sometimes, when he took his afternoon nap, I'd even get to sneak in a surf.

Lindsy got to sleep for the first time in about a year, and for a few months we were a real family. My snowboarding obligations consisted of minor things, like photo shoots or having a mold made for another action figure.

The second action figure was way better than the first, but getting it done was a lot harder. I showed up to X-Toys in Los Angeles thinking they'd take a picture of me, maybe measure my nose, and I'd be off. Nope. They sat me in a barber's chair and asked me if I was claustrophobic. When I said no, they shoved two plastic straws up my nostrils and painted my entire head in plaster. The plaster tightened, and the straws seemed to get thinner and thinner until I couldn't breathe very well, but I couldn't complain because my lips were encased in concrete. I was amazed at how disconcerting it was not to be able to wiggle my nose or open my mouth. I stared at the clock for half an hour, telling myself over and over again, *Don't freak out. Don't freak out. Don't freak out.*

Finally, they popped the mold off, and I could breathe again. The first action figure had really bad hair, but when I asked how they'd be doing it this time around, I was informed that it wasn't an issue because my figure would have a removable beanie. How cool is that? The arms and legs would also move, and it would come with removable goggles, watch, and snowboard, which had removable bindings and matched the pro model available in stores.

A few weeks later, my head showed up in the mail for my approval. I opened the box and sure enough, there I was.

_On the long highway, 2003.

FULL CIRCLE/
LIFE, DEATH, AND REBIRTH

As always, I began the 2002/2003 season early in December with the Triple Crown competition at Breckenridge. I was riding well in the slopestyle event, and after one run, a young rider for Rossignol named Benji Ritchie told me that he thought I was on fire, and that he wanted to ride like me one day.

I don't know if it had to do with being a dad or reflecting back on the days when I looked up to Kidwell or what, but for the first time, I thought I might be making a difference. I'd always wanted to give something back to the sport, and hearing that compliment from an up-and-comer meant the world to me. I left the event without making the top ten, but I still felt like a million bucks. More importantly, I didn't feel like I had to redeem myself at the next contest. Thanks, Benji.

After the Triple Crown, I went to Salt Lake City to attend a Rossignol sales meeting. I was excited to ride with some friends at Park City before the meeting, which was scheduled for December eighteenth. I met up with Jason "J2" Rasmus and Hanna Beauman at the mountain, and we rode powder for a while then hit the park. It was sunny and the mountain had just gotten about eight inches of snow—one of those weird, surreal days where snowflakes drift around in the sunshine.

Although it was hard getting speed in the fresh snow, we were still hitting jumps and having a good time. On our fourth run of the day, Twos (J2) was playing follow the leader, right on my tail. I hit a jump and another one and landed backward, gearing up for a fakie 540, but I didn't have enough speed. I gutted it around anyway, came up short, and bounced on the landing. I went down and J2 rode around me. As I slid down on my back, I laughed at my stupid bounce and put my hands down behind me to slow myself down, but it threw me into a starfish. Suddenly, something made me say "Ouch." It felt like somebody had Charlie-horsed my arm really bad. *Hmmm, that was weird,* I thought. Then I looked down at my right arm and realized I couldn't feel it. I couldn't feel my hand, I couldn't move my elbow, and everything started spinning. I yelled out to J2, "Shit! I broke my arm!"

I remembered seeing a kid compound-fracture his arm while skateboarding in Golden, Colorado, back in 1993. He hit a jump on a street course, landed on his arm, and immediately started screaming, moaning, and rolling around on the ground. When I went over to him, there was a pool of dark, tarlike blood pooling around his forearm, which had a bone sticking out of it. Blood was squirting out, and I almost puked it was so gnarly. People were already helping him, which was a good thing because I had to look away. I thought he was going to bleed out right there, but he survived. The vision of that kid's arm had been in my mind ever since, and the thought of it now put me into shock.

J2 yelled for someone to get the ski patrol, and I lay back, scared to take off my glove or jacket because I thought they would be full of blood. I kept saying, "My season's over. My freaking season's over."

I tried to ignore the pain in my arm and thought about my career. I stared up at the falling snowflakes circling around the sun and shook my head in disbelief at what I'd just done to myself. The sport was so cutthroat. Ripping kids were coming up like weeds, and a rider's success always depended on what he or she did that season. Results and coverage governed a rider's place in the hierarchy for the following year. I had been more concerned about trying to stay ahead of these kids and learning all the new tricks when I should have been focused on what I was good at. But to relax meant to surrender, because everybody wanted my piece of the pie.

The bling-bling was important to me. I wanted to make more money, stay ahead of the other guys, drive the nicest car, and have the nicest house. If I saw a kid doing a new trick, I'd think, *Oh shit, I have to learn that because if I don't I'm going to get squeezed out.* Sometimes my head would get really wrapped around that stuff, but I never let myself think about how long I'd been snowboarding for a living. The one thing I'd taken for granted was that I hadn't been seriously injured. A lot of riders who had been under the knife multiple times would say, "T. R., you never get hurt," or, "You've had a good run, but you're due."

One reason I've been able to do this for twelve years is that when I came into the sport, the jumps weren't ninety feet. A good portion of my snowboarding career was based on the fact that I could put my hand on the board. It wasn't about rotations; it was more, "Whoo-hoo, fruit salad air! Yippee." I grew as the jumps did. Kids today roll into a park and get to choose between the thirty-footer and the sixty-footer. It's hard to learn like that. It's hard to build your way up in do-or-die situations.

Just recently, ski areas started building "beginner" parks, but for the most part, it's been, "Here you go. Have fun." I see kids who can't turn or stop, but they're pointing their boards at huge jumps or kinked rails and hurting themselves. Take it from me: Start out small. If you're scared, there's a reason.

J2 was doing everything he could to keep me from going into shock. Every time I moaned, he'd say, "Ahhhh, shut up. Quit being a wimp. They'll be here in a minute." Then he'd offer me some chewing tobacco, knowing I wouldn't accept.

"You're gonna be out for a while," he said as he put a huge glob in his lip. "So you may as well start chewing now. You're gonna need something to do."

The patrol finally got there, and I guess my face was scraped up and bleeding pretty bad because she immediately said, "Oh, your face!"

"It's not my face," I growled. "It's my arm. Believe me, it's my arm."

A patrol member thought I might have a dislocated elbow. After we figured out it wasn't a compound fracture—thank god—he gently tried to manipulate my arm. I screamed and he said, "Okay, we won't touch it." I got my first sled ride, and every bump was so painful, I wanted to barf.

They x-rayed my arm at the first aid station, and within ten minutes I was told, "You have to go to the hospital right now. You need surgery."

I remember the ambulance ride, being in a hospital bed, and being told that I was having surgery at nine-thirty that night. For some reason, I thought it was Christmas Eve (even thought it was only the seventeenth) and said, "What about Christmas?" Then I lay there and waited for the surgery that apparently had to be done right then, that second, i.e. nine hours later.

I was really nervous but wanted to get it over with. I didn't want to be in pain anymore. I also didn't want to hear how bad the injury was, so I didn't really ask. When I went into the operating room, a guy with a blue surgical mask said, "I'm your anesthesiologist, and we're gonna take good care of you. Count backward from ten."

"Ten, nine . . ." I never finished. When I opened my eyes, a nurse leaned over me and said, "You're all done." I'd never lost time like that, and it made me feel out of control. Like nothing was real.

The following morning, I opened my eyes and thought for a moment that I'd never gone to Utah, that it was a bad dream. A surgeon came in and shattered that fantasy. I had undergone seven hours of surgery by a neurologist, an orthopedic surgeon, and some other pedic or ologist. It turns out that my humorous bone was shattered so badly, the surgeons had to piece it back together like a jigsaw puzzle that had to be wired and screwed. In addition, a bone shard had poked a nerve and had to be repositioned. He told me my hand might not work again, and I probably would never be able to straighten my arm all the way.

I was scared shitless and looking for the panic button. The next best thing was the morphine button connected to the IV in my arm.

I woke up that afternoon and another doctor was reading my charts.

"Will I be able to do what I used to do?" I said, and he asked what I used to do.

"I snowboard."

"Well, you might want to find something else to do for a living," he said. I couldn't tell if he was being funny or serious, but didn't ask because I didn't really want to know.

Before the surgery, Rossignol had contacted Lindsy, and I'd spoken to her in some morphine-induced fog, but I didn't really remember it. In the time since, she'd talked to my mom, and they'd arrived at the conclusion that my injury had happened for a reason. My mom thought it was some higher force telling me to take it easy for a while.

Pissing Glass

I never really associated a hospital with healing. Just the smell of it brought me back to that night in the emergency room, where I waited to hear if my dad had survived. My grandparents also died in the hospital.

After the doctors told me what was up, I was like, "Okay, so let me go home." But they told me they wanted to keep me for four days. It seemed reasonable for all of an hour, after which I was saying, "Four days? Screw that!"

Sometime later, I hit my buzzer and an ogre in a nurse's outfit came in, closed the curtain around my bed, and said, "Let's get you cleaned up." She pulled back the covers and started to scrub me down with a sponge. At first I was so shocked that I didn't know what to do. Then I pulled the covers up and said, "No, thanks." So she brought out a comb, saying, "Well, let's at least comb your hair." I shook my head and gave her the mental finger.

What the nurse was trying to tell me was, "Look, kid, you smell bad, and you look awful. Let me help you out here." She handed me the sponge, said, "You might want to clean yourself up a little," and left me alone.

Every time I woke up from a morphine cocktail, I called Lindsy. She was worried about me and wanted to know when I'd be home. She was helpless, I was helpless, and nobody would budge on the four-day minimum hospital stay. "We really need to observe you," they told me. *Observe me? Observe me doing what? Lying in bed?*

Finally, a younger, cool-looking doctor came in, and I told him, "Hey man, is there any way you can help me out? I gotta get out of here." He looked at my chart and started to say, "Well, it looks like they want you to . . ." but I cut him off, saying, "No, you don't understand. Today. I gotta get out of here today."

I guess I looked sufficiently panicked, because a half hour later, ogre number two arrived wearing rainbow-colored scrubs and carrying a plastic pitcher.

"If you want to leave," she said, "you've got to do three things: pee, eat, and walk." She handed me the pitcher and said, "Call me when you're done so I can look at it. And by the way, you were catheterized overnight, so you might experience a little burning."

I'd no idea there was a tube up my wiener all night and thanked god they'd yanked it out before I woke up. I positioned the pitcher under the covers and couldn't squeeze out a drop. After an hour of trying, I told the nurse I wanted to stand up and try. I sat on the edge of the bed, which gave me a massive head rush that made the room spin, but I weathered the tornado and ten minutes later, the room stopped moving. I headed for the bathroom with ogre number two following me, but I waved her off with the pitcher in the air and promised I'd show her my results.

Standing made all the difference, but the second I got it going, my mouth dropped. I was pissing shards of glass. It was the most tortuous experience of my life—even worse, I couldn't shut off the tap.

Next I had to eat Salisbury steak, mashed potatoes, and green peas with a side of lime Jell-O. Everything on the compartmentalized plate was pretty soft, so I swallowed the meal whole then took a lap around the room, dragging my IV bag behind me.

Brian Craighill from Quiksilver picked me up, fed me real food, and got J2 to take me to the airport. I found a baggage handler to help me with my gear. I looked like I'd been through a train wreck. My face was scraped up and bandaged and I had an eighty-pound cast on my arm, which apparently made me a prime suspect for terrorism, because I was hauled into secondary-checkpoints for bag and body searches at every possible location. Normally, I have no problem getting checked. I fly enough to appreciate the precautions and even have my own superstitious ritual that involves reaching over and knocking on the plane's door as I board, kind of like knocking on wood. But this day, the painkillers were making me nauseous, and I just wanted to get on the fricking plane and go home.

I flew to San Francisco to spend Christmas holidays with Cam, Lindsy, and her family. The pain diminished, the drugs worked their way out of my system, and on the day before Christmas Eve, we went shopping downtown. It was total urban chaos, but it was good to be alive.

We were in a shop picking out something for Cam when I started having trouble breathing.

"Is there enough air in here?" I asked Lindsy.

"What's wrong?" she asked.

I got so dizzy I had to sit down. I didn't feel like I could get enough air into my

Cam and me at my second home—the airport.

lungs. I had my doctor's card from the hospital in Utah, and I immediately called him to explain what was going on. He made me feel so much better when he said, "Go to the emergency room right away. You might have a blood clot."

Lindsy and I rushed to the nearest hospital and waited and waited and waited. I asked one of the docs what they'd do if they found out I had a blood clot as a result of my recent anesthesia or injury.

"Well, generally we'll put you on blood thinners and your body will absorb the clots," he said. When I asked when I'd be able to snowboard if that was the case, he said, "Oh, I don't know. Six to nine months."

Eight hours later, all the tests came back clear, and no one had an explanation for what had happened.

When It Rains, It Pours

On Monday, January 6, I was back home in California when I got a phone call from Rossignol. Bad news. One of Rossi's youngest rising stars on the snowboard team, Tristan Picot from France, had been killed in an avalanche at Jackson Hole, Wyoming, over the weekend. He was nineteen. I hadn't met Tristan, but I'd heard he was an amazing rider who'd been featured in both *TransWorld SNOWboarding* and *Snowboarder* magazines and was well on his way to the top. It was heavy and sad and made me reflect back to when I was nineteen and getting started.

Tristan's death was the beginning of a shockwave of grief that rocked the snowboarding community during the winter of 2003.

Around 3 A.M. on January 19, the phone woke me up. Phone calls that late at night always mean wrong numbers, partying friends, or bad news, and I was almost afraid to listen to the answering machine. It was my friend Brian Nelson, who was staying at my house in Breckenridge, and his message sounded really shaky:

"Todd, you've got to call me back as soon as possible. There's been a fire at your house. It's bad."

I called him and found out everybody was thankfully okay. The people who rent a room from me were away, and Brian had gotten out when he discovered the fire. When I talked to Brian the place was in flames, and I remembered my trophies and the *Star Wars* and Godzilla toy collection that I kept on display there. I didn't keep a lot of other personal stuff in Breckenridge, but I thought for sure I'd lost my snowboard bag with all my gear, including snowboard boot liners I'd been breaking in for years. Comfortable boot liners are the second most important piece of equipment next to my snowboard, and that pair was irreplaceable.

I called the Breckenridge fire department the next day and they told me that the fire had started in a kitchen wall (an electrical wiring problem) and two stories were basically destroyed. I flew to Colorado immediately and couldn't believe I was looking at my house. The windows were broken, the walls were black, and the inside smelled like burnt plastic and charcoal. The television set was a puddle of melted goo, and the heat had melted some, but not all, of my trophies. My toys were covered in black, the living room had been torched, but the couch had somehow protected my snowboard bag.

It was unbelievably lucky: No one had been hurt, and fortunately I had fire insurance. For a five-thousand-dollar deductible, the house would be completely repaired. Basically, I got a new house with new wiring, walls, carpets, paint, roof—everything.

Back in SoCal a couple days later, on January 21, I woke up and turned on MSNBC before Cam and I went to check the surf (a ritual I maintained, even though I was injured). There was a media frenzy in the town of Revelstoke, British Columbia, which is known as a backcountry ski and snowboarding mecca. Apparently, seven skiers had been killed in an avalanche.

Almost everyone I knew in snowboarding had been to Revelstoke at some time or other in their careers—on photo shoots, hiking trips, or to tool around on the snowmobiles, snow-cats, and helicopters that the backcountry lodges offered. The story, however, said the avalanche victims were skiers: No less tragic, but chances were slim that anyone close to me had been killed. Later that day, my friend Dave Sypniewski called.

"Have you heard the rumor?" he said.

"What rumor?" I asked.

"I heard that Craig Kelly died," he said.

My mouth dropped, and I had to sit down, thinking, *No way. There's no way.* But I turned the news back on, and at the bottom of the screen it read, "World champion snowboarder Craig Kelly, 36, dies in avalanche."

Craig was a hero of mine. He was a hero to pretty much anyone who has ever strapped a snowboard onto his or her feet—a four-time world champion, three-time U.S. Open Champion, all-time inspiration. He was the ultimate competitor in snowboarding, but he got burnt out on contests and started riding for fun. He fell in love with the back-country, and although I hadn't ridden with him in years, everybody who had done so said they felt safe with him because he'd done his homework and didn't take chances.

I still hadn't forgotten the moment at the A-Basin lodge when Craig walked in, lifted his chin the way he always did, and called me T.R. for the first time. Way back then, he'd given me the nickname that had stuck over all these years. That memory, the image of his smooth style in the pipe, and the fact that he left behind a two-year-old daughter drove the tragedy home for me.

Craig had been one of the Mount Baker Hard Cores, and I knew Mike Ranquet and some of his other friends would be having a gathering at Mount Baker in his honor. My arm was still tweaked and there was no way I could ride, so I took some time and memorialized Craig in my own way. Images of him are forever imprinted on my brain: magazine photos and video footage, but mostly his old halfpipe runs of the late eighties and early nineties. People said he had the "smooth groove," which became the title of the first snowboard movie to focus on essentially one rider. *The Smooth Groove* was classic Craig. He was the sport's greatest legend, and now he was its biggest loss.

You couldn't talk to anyone in or around the snowboarding community without feeling the weight of the tragedy. And it really bothered Lindsy, too, knowing he'd left behind a young daughter. She was also uneasy about the future.

"First Tristan, then Craig," she said. "It happens in threes. I feel like it's going to hit even closer to home soon."

Stir Crazy

By mid-February, I was going nuts. After fifteen years of competitive snowboarding, this was the longest I'd ever been off the snow. I couldn't believe I'd actually been burnt out on halfpipe riding two months earlier, because at that moment, I would have paid a thousand dollars for a one-way lift ticket to the top of the shittiest pipe in the world.

Living in Southern California helped a little. At least I didn't have to stare out my window in Encinitas and watch it snow. Regardless, every winter storm on the news or phone call from a friend who was sitting on a chairlift, heckling me with, "Dude, it's soooo good today," put me into a funk.

I couldn't go surfing either, but I had gotten heavily into physical therapy. My orthopedic doctor in San Diego said my wrist and elbow were healing amazingly fast, and that my range of motion was nearly 100 percent. He said that motion like this after my type of injury was unheard of.

I liked the doctor. He understood what snowboarding meant to me.

"When do you think I can fall from fifteen or twenty feet and land on my arm with all of my body weight?" I asked him.

"Well, you really want to make sure it's healed, first. You don't want to bend any of that hardware in there." Then he tapped his finger on his desk and said, "Don't quote me on this, but maybe, if you heal well, you'll be back up and riding *carefully* by the springtime. For sure by next winter." Most of the other doctors I'd visited said, "Never."

The following week, I went surfing. I hadn't asked the doctor if it was okay, but he never told me not to. And I really had to do something, even if it was just paddling out and sitting there on my board.

During this time, I began to understand how important my family was in a whole new way. I was starting to see the light at the end of the tunnel of this injury, and Cam and Lindsy were the reason I hadn't gone completely wacko. Watching Cam discover the world around him was a snapshot back to my childhood. And that made me want to fight to continue my own discoveries. I wasn't through yet.

I was invited to go to Japan with Quiksilver on February 20 for a shop tour and to hang out at a contest. Just packing for the trip was good therapy. I went down my mental checklist (boots, bindings, goggles, jacket, pants), and I bought a child-sized knee brace from the store to protect my arm (I could have gotten a real one from my doctor if I had told him I was going snowboarding, but I knew he'd say no).

Getting off the plane in Tokyo was like arriving in Disneyland. Even though I wasn't in Japan to compete, I was so happy just to feel like I was doing something productive and to see friends I hadn't seen all winter. I was also excited to buy toys for Cam.

From Tokyo we went to Nagano, where five of us were crammed into a hotel room the size of a shoebox. We'd bought these toy pellet guns in Tokyo, and our room became a war zone. Anyone who entered was ambushed; if you overslept in the morning, you were awoken by a shot to the big toe, usually a well-aimed shot by Brian Craighill.

On the mountain, I carved around on groomers and was super-duper careful with my knee-braced arm. It was the best feeling in the world to be riding again. One afternoon, after running into the Anderson brothers while riding, I got together with Billy for lunch. We talked about the Morrow days, how his little brother Jeff was ripping, and how unbelievable it was that Craig Kelly was no longer with us.

Marc Frank Montoya won the contest on February 24, and after the awards ceremony everyone was partying and having a good time. I hung out with a lot of old friends, made plans for breakfast the next morning, and called it a night. Downstairs in the lobby the next morning, I saw J. P. Tomich leaving the hotel.

"What's up? No breakfast?" I called out to him. When he looked at me, I saw that his eyes were red and puffy. In fact, everyone around me looked like crap. "What's the matter?" I asked.

"We lost Jeff last night," he said.

My first response was, "What? Where'd he go? You can't find him?" Then it hit me that Jeff Anderson had died. Stunned, I asked what had happened.

"He fell down some stairs," J. P. replied. I thought Jeff must have been sliding a rail or jibbing something on his snowboard. But when I asked, J. P. shook his head "No."

Sometime after midnight, Jeff had been doing what all of us have done at some time in our lives: sliding down the hotel's exterior stair banister on his butt. But he lost his balance and fell over backward four stories to the ground below. The first people to get to him were Marc Frank Montoya, Blue Montgomery, Dean "Blotto" Gray, and Ethan Fortier. Ethan rushed for help, and Marc and Blue did CPR until the ambulance arrived. Jeff had survived the initial fall, but the trauma was so severe, he had no chance for survival.

Billy was asleep in his hotel room at the time, and I don't know who told him about Jeff, but it must have been a terribly difficult thing to do. Billy and Jeff were best friends. Then I found out that Billy had to sign the order to turn off his brother's life support.

Upon hearing that, I lost it. Billy is like a brother to me. We'd been on the Morrow team together, I hid from reporters at his house in Mammoth during the first Olympic qualifiers, and he was one of the first people to see my son. I did everything possible to track Billy down, but I couldn't, so I called Lindsy. She'd already heard about Jeff. That's how fast news travels through the snowboarding grapevine.

I had to get some air, so I went outside and stared at the snowy funeral skies. The grief was so close and so overwhelming. I'd just seen Jeff a few hours before. He was laughing and having a good time. He was only twenty-two years old.

What ate me up the most was that his death was the result of a pointless accident. He was out with his buddies, drinking, having a great time. Somehow, it seemed like it would have been easier to accept had he been snowboarding.

I thought about the things I'd done when I was just screwing around. Now that I have a family and a responsibility to other people, I definitely think twice about things. If I'm not sure about a jump or something else, I'll walk away from it. Of course, this sense of self-preservation also comes with age. When I was twenty-two, forget about it. I got away with crazy things, but I was lucky.

Jeff's death made me understand how my dad felt after my friend Darryl had been killed. I didn't understand then why my dad had gotten so emotional and had hugged me and told me that he loved me. But on February 25, 2003, all I wanted to do was fly home from Japan, hug my family, and tell them how much I loved them.

This One's for Jeff

The following Sunday, a group of people gathered together at Mammoth Mountain to pay tribute to Jeff Anderson.

It was an emotional roller coaster. When I saw Josh Dirksen, we both smiled, and then we hugged each other and started crying. Tyler Lepore and Erik Leines were there, too: We all had memories associated with Jeff, and we were all hurting.

Billy Anderson raises his board at his brother's memorial on top of Mammoth Mountain—
a time to mourn a death, celebrate a life, and rethink the future.

The day before the memorial, I padded up my arm with the knee brace again and rode with Billy. Every run I took with Billy was a run he'd taken a hundred times with Jeff. I don't know how he did it, but some inner force gave him strength. He was a rock. He told me, "This is what Jeff would want me to do, so I'm just going to ride and have fun."

I was there to be strong for him, but he ended up consoling me by reminding me how Jeff had seen more in his twenty-two years than an average person saw in a lifetime. He said that Jeff got his education hands-on, out in the world, as opposed to reading it in a textbook.

"Snowboarding is a gift," he said. "And right now, Jeff is just reminding us how special it is."

The next day, when the last gondola dropped off the last person at the top of Mammoth for the memorial, there were probably 500 of us standing together in the snow. I don't know of any other sport that would bring 500 people, ranging from little kids to senior citizens, to the top of a mountain in a blizzard. Some were carrying balloons to release, some had pictures of Jeff taped to their boards, and all of us listened when Billy stood up and said something along the lines of, "Jeff is my brother, and we're all brothers. This gathering is just an extension of his spirit. This run is for Jeff."

We cheered and cried and walked to the edge of a powdery bowl. Just as the first group of riders dropped in, the sun broke through the clouds, and the atmosphere that had been gray and dull became clear and bright. You could feel the electricity in the air; it was magic.

Watching the waves of snowboarders ripping down the mountain in this massive gathering was an intense experience. And when the mountain ran out, I got off my board and walked away. It was closure.

The road back to Encinitas from Mammoth is a long one, running between the Sierra Mountains and the Inyo Mountains. The drive home with my family on that long, straight strip of blacktop was a time to reflect.

Jeff's memorial reminded me that before snowboarding became my job, it was fun. Simple as that. The fun aspect became easy to brush aside as I became more and more successful—measured by contest results, paychecks, and magazine covers.

Back in Paxton, I hadn't gotten into skateboarding because I wanted to make money or get famous. I got into it because I wanted to be a part of something, and then I stuck with it because I loved it more than anything else in the world. Snowboarding became an extension of that, and as I got older, I realized that I wanted to make a living doing something I loved. And I set lofty goals, including one that I put on a résumé way back when: "To become the world's most recognized freestyle rider." Did I make it? Who knows? I still see Terry Kidwell, Craig Kelly, and Chris Roach as the best freestyle guys ever, and Terje still rules the planet without ever having dropped into an Olympic pipe.

But snowboarding is bigger than even the biggest individual rider. For snowboarders, it's everywhere. It flows through our veins. We dream about it. We long for it. We smell it. We feel it.

Like surfing and skateboarding, snowboarding is something you have to figure out. You have to earn it. You have to make it over different hurdles before it reveals its soul. And when that happens, its soul becomes part of you.

Being on top of that mountain with all of those people with a common bond was a reminder that snowboarding means so much more than a contest or a paycheck. The loss of Jeff Anderson made me realize this and brought me back to where I needed to be.

It's a rebirth of sorts. I'm coming back from this injury, and at the time of this writing, the 2003/2004 season is around the corner. It doesn't matter if my new hurdles will be in the pipes, the parks, or the powder. All three inspire me. Above all they're fun. And at the end of the day, that's what really matters.

EPILOGUE/
LIFE GOES ON

Before the snow melted in the spring of 2003, I took a flight from San Diego to Denver, and then a shuttle to Breckenridge, where I geared up to ride the park one last time before summer set in. The ritual of tightening my binding screws, making sure my board's sticker job was looking good, and sliding onto the chairlift at my home mountain was the best feeling in the world.

I hadn't caught air on my snowboard since my injury at the beginning of the season and I was nervous, even though the doctor had given me the green light to "test it out." I rode the park top to bottom without hitting any jumps or rails.

Some young locals I recognized were going off, spinning slow-motion 540s, 720s, and the occasional retro mute air, grabbing the board tip just like I did in the late eighties. I was witnessing the snowboarding equivalent of the classic rock phenomena: Everything that was once cool is destined to be cool again.

My next run through, I hit a few tabletops with basic straight airs, just to get my wings back. Then I graduated to 180s with a little more speed. Within a few hours, my confidence was back, and I started spinning and hitting bigger and bigger kickers with more and more speed. I was on autopilot. For me, snowboarding is as natural as walking.

Of course, everybody trips once in a while.

The minute I hit the top of the jump, I knew I was off: mid-spin, sideways, and still gaining altitude. The doctor who "didn't get it" flashed before my eyes, his recommendation booming in my ears:

You might want to find something else to do for a living.

I landed on my side from fifteen feet in the air with my right arm, *the* arm, smashed between my ribs and the hard snow. The impact was hard enough to knock the wind out of me. Rolling over, I slid off to the side of the run and ever so carefully moved my arm at the shoulder, and then at the elbow, and finally at the wrist. Taking off my glove, I wiggled my fingers.

It was one of the hardest slams I'd ever experienced, and I was fine. Now I was ready to get on with my life.

ACKNOWLEDGMENTS

Lindsy,

My beautiful wife, you are my best friend in the whole world. You have taught me so much about myself these past six years. You understand the word "passion" more than anyone I have ever met. Your devotion to family and your constant support and understanding make it possible for me to be me. As far as I'm concerned you have set the standard for motherhood. You are an inspiration to me, both in heart and soul. My backbone. My rock. My hero. I love you.

Cam,

Thank you for helping me rise to the greatest occasion of all: being a parent. You have given your father the gifts of patience and selflessness, two things I needed badly. Seeing the world through your eyes has given me a second chance at childhood. The greatest joys I've had in my life have been watching you reach your milestones. Seems like just yesterday I was cleaning up poopy diapers and keeping you away from sharp objects. Oh wait, I was? I love you.

Mom,

Where do I start? You have made me the person I am today. I am certain my strong work ethic and drive for perfection came straight from you. Your strength and perseverance is something I aspire to. You have been an amazing mom and now an amazing nani. I love you.

Dad,

I miss you, and I'm bummed that you couldn't be here to share all this. Thanks for instilling in me my work ethic and remaining a driving force, if only in spirit, throughout my life. I hope I've made you proud.

The Lozanos (Linda, Mamo, Lisa, Leslie, Cindie),

I feel honored that you have welcomed me into your family with such open arms. Since Lindsy and I have been together you have been my biggest support team. I can't put into words how much that means to me. Having people like you in my corner helps me "get out of the gate" with confidence. You have helped me through ups and downs, thick and thin, and everything in between. I can't begin to thank you enough.

Jake Burton and Tom Sims,

I don't care who came up with modern snowboarding first, but thanks for giving me something to do in the winter.

Eric Blehm,

How you pulled all this info out of my head is beyond me. Thanks for putting up with my crazy schedule and making my boring life seem glamorous.

Trevor Graves,

You took the first picture and launched my career. Thank you.

Geb,

You are a great friend and the reason I have this jacked sense of humor. Thanks, I think.

Palmer "Balls" Brown,

You have shown me how to be serious about not taking myself too seriously. Thanks. G.F.R.

Thank You:

Quiksilver, Bob McKnight, Brian Craighill, Mark Oblow, Taylor Wisenand, Rossignol, Christine McConnell, Dane Hjort, Pat Bernie, DC, Ken Block, Damon Way, Brian Botts, Nixon, Chad Dinnena, Andy Latts, Clive, Spy, Chris Saydah, RDS, Colin McKay and Syd, Pro-Tec, Premier, The Familie, Steve Astephen, Chris Whittker and the gang, Tim Swart, Dave Sypniewski, Todd Finney, Embry Rucker, Chris and Amber Owen, Matt Goodman, Dave Seaone, Mike McEntire, Morgan Stone, Whitey, Brad Kremer, Fall Line Films, *TransWorld, Snowboarder,* Joel Muzzey, Pat Bridges, Jon Foster, Jeremy Lanningham, Shem Roose, Jen Sherowski, Cody Dresser, Morrow team O.G., Robbie Morrow, Josh Dirksen, Billy Anderson, Tyler Lepore, Erik Leines, Rebecca Herath Roose,

Nate Bozung, Joe Dorazio, Jay Twitty, Gus Buckner, J2 Rasmus, Dionne Delesalle, J. P. Walker, Jeremy Jones, Kevin Jones, Steve Ruff, Raul Ries, Kris Swierz, Jason Ford, Jeff Brushie, Tara Dakidas, Tonino Copene, Miki Keller, Mark Welsh, Brian Besold, Chris McNally, Nemo Design, Sabrina Salotti, Annie Versteeg, Katharine Miller, Tamar Burris, Bouler Dicks, Tara Sullivan, Jeff Borgault, BC Surf and Sport, Tony Hawk, Kelly Slater, Sal Masakela, Ron Semio, Chris Gunnarson, Breckenridge, Emmitt Maloy, At the Drive In, Danny Kass, Grenade, Frank Wells, Rob Wells, Lisa Hudson, High Cascade Snowboard Camp, Homer Simpson, Kris Jamieson, B. J. Leines, J. J. Thomas, Ross Powers, Neal Hendrix, Alexei Garrick, Mike Frasier, the guy who invented the PlayStation, all the photographers who were nice enough to take photos of me, and all the other people who are reading this sentence totally pissed off that they weren't mentioned in the above paragraph. And lastly, I'd like to thank all the redneck dumbasses at Wachusett Regional High School class of 1987, who made me not want to be anything like them and get the hell out of Massachusetts.

Eric's Acknowledgments:

Thank you, T.R., for trusting me with your life (story) and for putting up with my five-minute-long voicemails every day for the past six months. Thank you, Lindsy, for tracking Todd down for me on a weekly basis. Thanks to all the snowboarding journalists who actually put dates in their articles over the past eighteen years—it made fact checking more bearable. Thank you, Google.

Other people who made the behind-the-scenes coordination of this story a possibility: First and foremost, Renée Iwaszkiewicz at ReganBooks for approaching us to write this book and Judith Regan for publishing it. Thank you, Brian Saliba, for seeing the manuscript through with your fine editing skills and Lorien Warner (my wife and P.I.C.) for your patience and editing from conception to finished product. Also: Christy Fletcher, Liza Bolitzer, Trevor Graves, Shem Roose, Jon Foster, Billy Miller, Pete McAfee, Matt Goodman, Lee Crane, Fran Richards, Kevin Kinnear, Joel Muzzey, Amber Warner, Terry Snyder, Jamie Meiselman, Sherman Poppen, Dad, Macintosh, Microsoft, Hewlett Packard, Sharon Harrison, Andy Blumberg, John Stouffer, Time Swart, Ali Berkley, Kurt Hoy, Jason Ford, Scooter Leonard, Jon Foster, Michael Lucas, Marissa Shalfi, and Tom Hsieh, founder of *ISM*, who first showed me that you can indeed make a living writing about snowboarding and snowboarders.

PHOTOGRAPHY CREDITS

All photos courtesy of the Richards family except the following:

Trevor Graves: v, vi–vii, 28, 44, 55, 56 *(both)*, 58, 60, 62, 63, 69, 74, 77, 81 *(bottom)*, 82, 85 *(left)*, 90, 92, 96, 101, 105, 112, 116, 120, 123 *(both)*, 125, 142, 146, 161, 166, 173, 183, 203 *(top)*, 207, 209, 211, 216, 229, 256; Rob Gracie: viii; Trevor Graves/*ISM*: 71; John Sposeto/*ISM*: 81 *(top)*; Bud Fawcett: 85 *(middle)*; Ken Achenbach: 85 *(right)*; *Snowboarder*: 102; Jon Foster/*TWS*: 106, 168; Jon Foster: 114, 134, 138, 141; Chris Owen: 131, 177, 180, 200, 203 *(bottom)*; Greg Adams/*TWS*: 153; Shem Roose: 176, 231, 234, 253; Lozano family: 189; Trevor Graves/Rob Gracie: 219; Embry Rucker: 244, 268, 279.

Insert:

Trevor Graves: 1, 3, 4–5, 6, 14, 15, 16; Embry Rucker: 2; Shem Roose: 7, 12–13.